SOCIAL ASSISTANCE
DYNAMICS IN EUROPE

National and local poverty regimes

Edited by Chiara Saraceno

The POLICY
PRESS

First published in Great Britain in January 2002 by

The Policy Press
34 Tyndall's Park Road
Bristol BS8 1PY
UK

Tel +44 (0)117 954 6800
Fax +44 (0)117 973 7308
e-mail tpp@bristol.ac.uk
www.policypress.org.uk

British Library Cataloguing in Publication Data
A catalogue record for this book is available from the British Library

ISBN 1 86134 314 0 paperback
A hardcover version of this book is also available

Chiara Saraceno is Professor of Sociology at the University of Torino, Italy.

Cover design by Qube Design Associates, Bristol.
Front cover: photograph supplied by kind permission of Mark Simmons
Photography, Bristol.

Printed and bound in Great Britain by Hobbs the Printers Ltd, Southampton.

Contents

List of figures and tables

Figures

Tables

Acknowledgements

This study was made possible by European Union funding under the Targeted Socioeconomic Research Programme (TSER: Contract ERB-SOE2-CT-95-3001, project ESOPO), which we gratefully acknowledge. It is the result of the work of many people, in addition to the individual authors of the chapters. First of all we would like to acknowledge the PhD students and research members of the national teams who collected the data, prepared some preliminary analyses and participated in all the different phases of the project: in France, Jean-Yves Dartiguenave, Vincent Guillaudeux, Laurence Loison, Typhaine Mahé, Emmanuel Peignard, Nadia Rachedi, Maïté Savina; in Germany, Katja Schulte and Holger Stoek; in Italy, David Benassi, Fabio Quassoli and Antonino Campennì; in Portugal, Ana Santos, Ricardo Mamede and Marta Varanda; in Spain, Maite Montagut, Rosa Mur, Ana Morcillo and Imanol Zubero; in Sweden, Eva Franzen and Anders Giertz.

We also wish to thank the social workers and people responsible for the various services in the cities included in the project, who not only provided us with data, but with precious insights, information and feedback. Without their collaboration, this study would have been impossible. Finally, we would like to thank the local administrators and politicians who facilitated our access to local social assistance data and generally supported our research. Their understanding of the value of this project, both from the scientific and social policy point of view, has been an invaluable resource for all national teams.

Ms Angela Spencer edited the language of all the contributions, working through the different expertise and linguistic usage of the various authors. The fact that none of the authors have English as their mother tongue has certainly been one of the challenges of this study. However, it has also been one of its resources. Having to place country-specific institutional definitions and practices into a language that does not readily represent any of them compelled us to detail what we were talking about much more extensively and carefully, rendering us sensitive to possible misunderstandings, as well as to different intellectual, policy and administrative traditions.

Notes on contributors

Yves Bonny is Associate Professor of Sociology at the University of Rennes, France. His research topics include general theory, political sociology, historical sociology, identity construction processes, modernity and postmodernity. He is currently coediting a book on Norbert Elias and preparing a book on modernity and postmodernity.

Nicoletta Bosco is Assistant Professor of Sociology of Culture and Communications at the University of Turin. Her recent publications include 'Percorsi nell'assistenza delle madri sole in Europa: la rilevanza della contestualizzazione per la comprensione dei diversi modelli di sostegno', *Inchiesta*, April-June 2000; *Il welfare in diretta: Welfare, consenso e comunicazione*, (forthcoming) Guerini e Associati, Milan.

Marisol Soledad Garcia is Associate Professor of Sociology in the Department of Sociological Theory and Sub-director of the Research Centre on Citizenship and Civil Society at the University of Barcelona, Spain. She is a member of the Editorial Board of the *International Journal of Urban and Regional Research*; President of the Research Committee on Urban and Regional Research within the ISA; Visiting Fellow at St. Antony's College, Oxford; Research Fellow at the Royal Institute of International Affairs, London; Visiting Researcher at the European University Institute, Florence; and at the University of Amsterdam. She has published 'Cities and citizenship' for the *International Journal of Urban and Regional Research* (1996) and *Ciudadanía: Justicia Social, Identidad y Participación*, with Steven Lukes (1999).

Björn A. Gustafsson is Professor at the Department of Social Work, Göteborg University. He has been commissioned by several public authorities to write special reports. His research covers empirical studies on social assistance, poverty, the distribution of economic well-being and the welfare state and immigrants. Another of his research interests is the distribution of income and poverty in the People's Republic of China. His publications include, 'In search of smoking guns: what makes income inequality vary over time in different countries', *American Sociological Review*, vol 64, 1999, with J. Mats and *Poverty and low income in the Nordic countries*, edited with P. Pedersen, (2000) Ashgate.

Yuri Kazepov has a PhD in sociology and is Associate Professor at the University of Urbino where he teaches urban sociology and welfare systems. Since 1999 he has been a member of the scientific board of the Observatory on Urban Poverty at the University of Milan-Bicocca. He is an expert of the EU Commission (DG Research and DG Employment) and has published extensively on poverty, social policies and citizenship from a comparative perspective. His publications include *La cittadinanza Spezzata: Il dibattito teorico e metodologico su esclusione sociale e povertà*, edited with Enzo Mingione (1994), Armando Editore, Messina; *Le politiche locali contro l'esclusione sociale*, (1996) Presidenza del Consiglio dei Ministri, Rome; *Armut in Europa*, edited with Wolfgang Voges, (1998) Chmielorz Verlag, Wiesbaden; *How generous social assistance schemes are: A comparative analysis of benefit levels in Europe*, with Stefania Sabatinelli, (2001) Stakes, Helsinki.

Enzo Mingione is Professor of Sociology at the University of Milano-Bicocca. His fields of interest are welfare systems, poverty and social exclusion, and the informal sector, as well as more general theoretical and comparative issues in economic and urban sociology. He was on of the founders of the *International Journal of Urban and Regional Research* and is a member of the European group of experts on the Future of Work. His publications in English include *Fragmented societies*, (1991) Blackwell; and *Urban poverty and the underclass*, (1996) Blackwell.

Rolf Müller has studied sociology at the university of Bremen. For the last few years he has been working as an assistant in the 'Household dynamics and social inequality – an international comparison' project at Special Research Center 186 at the University of Bremen, Germany.

Nicola Negri is Professor of Economic Sociology at the University of Turin and Director of the advanced studies program in social policy and social services. His recent publications include 'Out of welfare: functioning of income support in Torino', in *Quality and Quantity* (1999) with N. Bosco and D. Contini; 'Povertà, disoccupazione ed esclusione sociale', in *Stato e Mercato*, no 59, 2000, with C. Saraceno; 'Poveri e non poveri: i confini incerti dell'utenza di edilizia pubblica a Torino', with M. Olagnero, in M.L. Bianco (ed) *L'Italia delle diseguaglianze*, (2001) Carocci, Milano.

Marco Oberti is Associate Professor in Sociology at Sciences Po, Paris. His areas of interest are social and territorial differentiation, social exclusion, urban segregation and local regulation. He particularly looks at these themes comparatively between French and Italian societies. His recent publications include 'Social comparative structure of middle cities', in A. Bagnasco and P. Le Galès (eds) *Cities in Europe*, (1999) Routledge; 'Ségrégation spatiale, évitement et choix des établissements scolaires' with C. Barthon, in van Zanten (ed) *L'école: L'état des savoirs*, la Découverte, Paris; *Le sociologue et son terrain*, with H. Mendras, (2000) Armand Colin, Paris.

José António Pereirinha is Associate Professor of Economics and Social Policy at the ISEG (Institute of Economics and Business Administration), Technical University of Lisbon. He gained a PhD in development studies at the ISS, the Hague, in 1988, with a dissertation on income inequality and economic development in Portugal. He has coordinated a master course in social policy analysis. His main research interests are welfare economics, income distribution, inequality, poverty and social policy analysis. He has published reports, articles and books on poverty, social exclusion and social policy in Portugal.

Chiara Saraceno is Professor of Sociology of Family and of Comparative Social Systems at the University of Torino, Italy. She has published extensively in Italian, English and French on gender and the family, social policies, poverty and social exclusion. She is a former member of the European Observatory on Policies to Combat Social Exclusion and is Chair of the Italian Commission on social exclusion. Her publications include *Sociologia della famiglia*, with M. Naldini, (2001) il Mulino; *Politiche contro la povertà in Italia*, with Nicola Negri, (1996) il Mulino; *Separarsi in Italia*, with Marzio Barbagli, (1998) il Mulino; 'Family change, family policies and the restructuring of welfare', in *Family, Market and Community*, Social Policy Studies No 21, (1997) OECD, Paris; 'Gendered policies: family and social policies in Europe', in T.P. Boje and A. Leira, *Gender, welfare state and the market*, (2001) Routledge.

Wolfgang Voges is Professor at the Institute for Sociology and the Centre for Social Policy Research at the University of Bremen, Germany. His major research interests are social structure analysis and social policy, health and social inequality, methods and techniques of international comparative empirical research. He has directed the German part of several projects within the EC-Program TSER and co-directed the 'Social Assistance Dynamics' project of the Special Research Center 186 of the German National Science Foundation. Currently he is directing a project on 'Foundations and Methods for the Way of Living Approach' for the German government. He is the co-editor of a book series on social policy research. Voges's recent publications include a volume, *Pflege alter Menschen als Beruf. Soziologie eines Tätigkeitsfeldes (Sociology of occupation and skills exemplified at the Labour market area taking care for the elderly)*, and an edited methodological volume, *Dynamic approaches to comparative social research*. Recent articles and book chapters include *Social policy towards poverty, material hardships and social justice, Social inclusion or exclusion by Minimum Income Support Programmes in Europe*.

ONE

Introduction: exploring social assistance dynamics

Chiara Saraceno

The social construction of the poor and of social assistance 'careers'

In the German and Swedish cities of Bremen, Halle, Gothenburg and Helsingborg over 50% of social assistance recipients are young people under the age of 21. However, the same is true for only about one quarter of social assistance recipients in the French cities of Rennes and Saint Etienne, the Italian cities of Milan, Turin and Cosenza, the Spanish cities of Vitoria and Barcelona, and Lisbon and Porto in Portugal. In Barcelona and Lisbon, nearly half of social assistance recipients are aged over 40. At the same time, in the Swedish, German and French cities and also in Barcelona, the absolute or relative majority of recipients live in one person households, while in Lisbon, Vitoria, Milan, and to a lesser degree in Turin, the majority of recipients live in households that comprise three or more members. Childless households represent over two thirds of all households receiving social assistance in Bremen, Gothenburg, Helsingborg and Rennes, over half in Barcelona, Halle, Vitoria and Saint Etienne, but less than half in Lisbon, Milan and Turin. Whereas job loss is the main reason for entering social assistance in the German cities, and to a lesser degree in Barcelona, other causes (from marital disruption to sickness, disability, some kind of addiction, and the insufficiency of other sorts of welfare) are the main route into social assistance in Milan, Turin, Vitoria and Lisbon. As for the duration of social assistance recipiency, Helsingborg and Milan – the two cities with the fastest exit rate – show striking similarities, although the two programmes have contrasting features in terms of coverage, generosity and recipients' obligations.

These cross-country and within-country differences, as well as unexpected similarities, are the empirical findings of our study and are the object of our investigation. What is their cause? How can they be explained on the basis of what we know concerning the incidence of poverty, the unemployment rates by age and gender, and the generosity and variety of social assistance systems in the various countries and cities? We cannot easily argue that the young and childless in Germany and Sweden are more vulnerable to unemployment and poverty than in Portugal, Italy and Spain, and more in Bremen than in Halle. Or that the economic and labour market context is so different in Milan and Turin as to account for such large differences in the time people remain on social assistance in these two cities. Is joblessness really more serious in Germany than in Portugal? Is it possible that the meagre Milan programme, offering only limited short-term benefits, is as efficient in promoting self-sufficiency among beneficiaries as the generous Swedish income support scheme, which is coupled with a wide range of social and employment services?

The answers to these questions can only be found by looking at how national and local systems 'construct' and select social assistance recipients. This obviously involves looking at the incidence of poverty and at the demographic and social characteristics of the poor in the various countries and cities. It also involves looking at patterns and criteria for entitlement to support in the various national welfare systems. Finally, it means analysing the nation-specific patterns, that is the varying combinations and divisions of the spheres of social security and social assistance, and the manner in which they impact, react to and shape the life course of individuals. In fact, in a broad sense, social policies including education policies, family policies, social security and social assistance policies, may be interpreted as the means of institutionalising and normalising an individual's life course (for example, Kohli, 1986, 1988; Mayer and Müller, 1986; Mayer and Schöpflin, 1989; Mayer and Blossfeld, 1990; Saraceno, 1991). Yet as Leisering and Leibfried (1999, p 7) recently pointed out, "national welfare traditions differ with regard to life course policy: they pursue different normative models of the life course, they intervene to different degrees in people's lives and they emphasise different fields of life course policy". One of the fields in which there exists great variation in policy is that dealing with the management of social risks and unforeseen discontinuities in the life cycle: unemployment, illness, marriage breakdown, poverty. From this perspective there is no 'European model'[1], rather there seems to be a number of very distinct patterns.

Our thesis is that social assistance policies and the construction of the poor or socially excluded as social categories are as much a part of the process by which individuals and groups *become* poor or socially excluded, and/or exit from poverty and social exclusion, as labour market processes or family processes. They offer in fact – to different degrees and with different outcomes depending on the institutional framework, local cultures and circumstances – social definitions as well as resources, opportunities as well as constraints (see also, for example, Becker, 1997; Leisering and Leibfried, 1999). Following Simmel's almost century old insight (Simmel, 1908a), Paugam argues that,

> It is from the moment they are assisted, maybe from the moment their conditions might entitle them to social assistance, even if they still do not actually receive it, that they become part of a group which is characterised by poverty. This group is not unified through the interaction between its members, but through the collective attitude society as a whole adopts towards it. (1997a, pp 23-4)

Thus, social assistance recipients are not only, as Leisering and Leibfried maintain (1999, p 5), a good social indicator of the reliability and effectiveness of a given welfare state as a whole, but of the degree to which labour market, employment policies and other social security and family policy schemes fail to offer adequate provision. They are also an indicator of what kind of 'failures' are acknowledged as being entitled to receive support and under what conditions. These in turn become elements in shaping recipients' options and self-perceptions. Together with national policies, local institutional frameworks and practices are crucial elements in the process of the social construction of the poor, both in terms of defining who and what the poor are, and in existing social assistance, shaping social assistance 'careers': the timing of entering and exiting social assistance, the patterns of experiencing it and so forth.

The process of social construction of poverty and of 'the poor' begins even before specific measures addressed to 'the poor' or 'the socially excluded' are put in place. This occurs in three ways. Firstly, it is closely linked to how other systems of social protection work in a given country or given locality: including the level, coverage and duration of unemployment benefit, the presence of a universal old age pension, the degree to which the cost of children is acknowledged and supported through some kind of child benefit, the extent to which unpaid family work is recognised, and so on. In fact, where such systems exist, they may prevent individuals and families from falling into poverty, and therefore from appearing in the rolls of the poor, despite temporary joblessness, insufficient family income, old age or (gendered) family obligations. Child benefits are a case in point, in so far as it is often cases of imbalance between the number of family consumers and family income that lie behind the phenomenon of the 'working poor'[2].

More generally, the way in which a national social protection system protects and streams individuals and households through the various safety nets is an important factor in shaping the kind of population that finds itself needing income support. In this perspective, given the recent phenomenon of mass migration and refugees from war and/or persecution, the way 'non-citizen' residents – mainly immigrants, refugees and asylum seekers – are dealt with is likely to be an increasingly significant factor in the construction of the poor. Moreover, as pointed out by Leisering and Leibfried (1999) on the basis of their study of German data, in addition to the overall institutional framework of social protection, the administration too may be responsible for increasing the number of the poor. Delays in granting an allowance, in paying a pension and so forth can fill the poverty roll and push people who are fully entitled to other benefits into social assistance. Their study suggests that such people make up a large percentage of those receiving *Sozialhilfe* (social help). In this case, entry into social assistance is triggered, not by unfortunate events in the beneficiaries' lives, but by malfunctioning in other parts of the social protection system. Similarly, when these beneficiaries exit social assistance, this simply means that they have at last started to receive what they were entitled to in the first place[3]. Another example is the German law, which prohibited asylum seekers from getting a job until their request was settled. This compelled them to depend on social assistance (and/or to work in the unprotected informal economy), with added stigmatising consequences. It is significant that this law was repealed in spring 2000 due to the growing awareness of its adverse effects.

Secondly, social assistance policies define de facto the 'deserving' and 'undeserving' poor, or at least different degrees and shades of deservedness. This may occur explicitly, as in the case of policies targeted only at specific categories of the poor, as in most Italian cities and in Portugal (before the introduction of the RMG [*Rendimento Mínimo Garentido*]), or implicitly, through the application of age limits (in France those aged under 25 are not entitled to the RMI [*Revenue Minimum d'Insertion*]), or by the lifting of specific requirements usually demanded of beneficiaries, for example that of being available for work. Some particular categories of social assistance recipients – such as lone mothers with young children – are exempt from this requirement in most, but not all, countries. Certainly, the definition of 'deservedness' can be double-edged: depending on the time and place, it may have the effect of stigmatising these 'privileged' categories as being either incapable of self-sufficiency or scroungers, or both. This now appears to be the case of lone mothers in the UK and the US and, to a lesser degree, in the Netherlands. While previously considered the most deserving group of the able-bodied due to their role as child carers, they are now becoming a negative symbol of welfare dependency. Whereas before they were defined first and foremost in their role as mothers, they are now defined in terms of their joblessness. This view is more similar to that found in the Scandinavian countries and in the former East Germany, but may sometimes be in contrast to the women's own self-perception and to still prevelent cultural and gender models.

Thirdly, the process of social construction depends on the way in which poverty is assessed or measured. This involves the relationship between the criteria used for estimating the incidence of poverty ('counting the poor'), and those used to define the income threshold below which one is entitled to income support, and the maximum amount payable to given kinds of recipient. It is well known that estimates of poverty in any given country will vary according to an 'absolute' rather than a relative concept, whether one refers to half the *median* income or half the *mean* income and the kind of equivalence scale that is used; that is what patterns of needs, consumption, household sharing and so forth are expected in poor households (Atkinson, 1998a).

These are not only research choices but also features of public discourse on poverty, which in turn may constitute a reference point for policy. Aubert (1997/98) has shown that different policy institutes in France define (income) poverty at different thresholds, with two poles – the 'minimum living level' and the 'decent minimum', with the RMI being the most basic or minimum level. In Aubert's words, "this [the RMI's] threshold is the means by which the poor whom the state is willing to help are individuated, according to the rules and conditions fixed by the state itself" (p 21). The same might be said of any country. The consequences of decisions on thresholds, however, affect not only the level of consumption acknowledged as necessary and the number of people covered, but also the kind of people covered by social assistance and the resources they possess for coming off welfare. In fact, the lower the threshold, the greater the likelihood that only the severest cases are covered. These are the people least likely to have the capacity to become self-sufficient – or at least to do so in a short time. In addition, before even receiving support they must have already exhausted their existing resources.

Countries therefore differ in terms of at least four dimensions: the existence or not of an explicit set of policies addressing poverty; the degree of categorisation (or universality) of assistance; whether income support is near pure subsistence level or at a decent minimum; and the kinds of obligations and controls attached to the status of beneficiary. The object of this study is to examine these dimensions in detail. We shall attempt to discover how they shape social assistance policies, and how they help to construct the populations of beneficiaries and their social assistance careers, by looking at the interplay between the national and local context and the social assistance regulations. We therefore do not consider the poor 'in general' nor the 'socially excluded', but all those receiving social assistance; that is those who have an officially acknowledged or even enforced status as poor. Among these, we examine in particular the case of the so-called 'able-bodied' poor. Depending on the degree of universality of a given measure and on the generosity of its income threshold, the population of beneficiaries may approximate to a greater or smaller degree that of the poor as defined by research estimates[4].

We believe that a comparative analysis of the social construction of the poor and social assistance 'careers' is crucial for a comparative understanding and evaluation of the efficacy of the various measures in this field. This is particularly relevant for policy making, in so far as evaluations of policies at the national and comparative level too often focus exclusively on the performance of the measure itself, paying little or no attention to its location within the overall package of measures and the way in which the measure selects its beneficiaries, either in principle or in practice. However, looking only at national policies is not enough, if we are to understand both the characteristics and 'careers' of those receiving social assistance benefits. It is also necessary to look at how nation-specific forms of acknowledgement of poverty and vulnerability are transferred to the local level in the actual implementation of policies. This will depend on the local welfare culture, and also the local economic, social and human capital resources. In other words, it depends on the specific demographic, economic, cultural and political features of the local society.

The concept of local society owes a great deal to that of 'social formation'. One can speak of a local society when one can identify specific, long-standing constellations of economic conditions, social actors and processes, social and political cultures, including patterns of family and kinship, their organisation and participation in civil society, and so forth. This core concept of sociological analysis has proven particularly fruitful in the analysis of specific regional areas within Europe (for example, the 'third Italy' or the concept of the 'industrial district', see Baguesco, 1997, and more generally Giddens, 1983). It has been revitalised as a tool in political analysis by the highly debated work of Putnam (1993) on social capital and civic cultures. From a different perspective, we can retrace it in the most recent conceptualisations of different kinds of cities (for example, Sassen, 1994)[6]. Individual cities are distinct and diverse social formations, both spatially and socially, with specific economic and cultural histories, which give rise not only to different forms of vulnerability and poverty, but also to different ways of perceiving and addressing them. Cities are also places where poverty is more likely to be concentrated (see for example, Madanipour et al, 1998).

Specifically, within national and even regional welfare systems there exist local versions, which can be distinguished by the development and implementation of welfare policies and packages 'on the ground'. This is particularly so for anti-poverty and means-tested income support policies. Not only is their implementation often assigned to local municipal governments, but they may also constitute a complex package of measures, including locally organised social services and forms of (implicit or explicit) cooperation with relevant local actors. Therefore, in order to understand the actual working of these policies, it is essential to examine both the local level and the national level. In fact, the whole idea of a 'welfare mix' points to a range of situations and actors, which are mostly locally based. Of course, the degree to which the local context makes a difference depends on the type of national framework (Alber, 1995). A comparative study therefore needs to include an assessment of this variation.

Although not always rendered explicit, the relevance of local patterns of implementation is recognised in many cross-country studies of social assistance and family policy, which aim to compare *national* policies. In cases where national data or averages (for example, public housing rents, fees for childcare services, or waiting time before receiving benefit) are not available, it is necessary for national informants to report on the situation and practices in a given city. However, it is not always made clear why the particular city has been chosen or to what extent it is representative[7]. On the contrary, in our study the local context is analysed specifically and treated as an independent variable.

In addition to its local focus, a perspective that is both historical and longitudinal is essential to our comparative approach. The former helps us to understand how specific policies have developed in relation to specific national welfare state models, also in relation to local political and economic contexts, and therefore the context-specific kinds of social vulnerability. The latter allows us to reconstruct and compare – across categories as well as across cities – the individual histories and experience of social assistance receipt not only at a given point in time, but over time. This means being able to reconstruct the dynamics of individual and family biographies, of the local labour market (for example, recession or expansion), of patterns of social assistance implementation, and of opportunities and constraints deriving from the income support measures themselves. Income support is therefore not viewed and assessed as the only, or even the main, element in the set of resources (and/or constraints) available to beneficiaries, nor as the main determinant of the strategies they are likely to adopt. Rather, it is viewed as one item within a complex package, which has material as well as relational and symbolic dimensions.

More specifically, in the ESOPO project we have analysed and compared the performance of social assistance means-tested income support policies for the so-called 'able-bodied poor' at the level of individual cities in six EU countries. We have selected the able-bodied poor because this is the fastest expanding group of recipients of income support (and in some cases a relatively recent type of recipient). At the same time, from the point of view of policy definitions, it is also the most problematic group. Most of the debate at the national and European level concerning the efficacy, and even legitimacy, of income support specifically concerns the able-bodied.

In order to understand how poverty is acknowledged in the different systems and how the different policies shape 'social assistance careers', we have reconstructed the institutional framework both at the national (when relevant) and local level, as well as the local patterns of implementation in each city. This has included an examination of explicit and implicit criteria, forms of negotiation between the different actors, patterns of cooperation and so forth. We have also created a joint data set on the basis of local records on social assistance recipients, which has allowed us to trace and compare social assistance careers over a four year period. Although this time span is clearly limited, it has proven more than adequate for identifying specific local patterns. And although the need to standardise the local data for comparative purposes has compelled us to reduce the richness of some of the municipal data sets to match the minimum common information level, the resulting data set is still the largest currently available in Europe on social assistance. It covers eight cities in five different countries.

In Lisbon, Vitoria and Barcelona records were manually reconstructed and electronic archives developed for this project from existing paper archives. We could not, however, integrate all the cities in our study into this data set. Only after the study was well underway did we discover that in France, due to legislation on privacy, social assistance archives were not accessible. Longitudinal data of a different kind have been collected through a retrospective survey of RMI recipients in the two cities in the study, but for obvious methodological reasons could not be integrated into the data set. In the Italian city of Cosenza on the other hand, records of recipients were not available since social assistance is not a standardised process. The same applied to Porto. Data for Halle were not made available due to unsolved problems of ownership and an academic rift, which the German researcher on the project was not able to solve in time for this study. Thus a full set of data, particularly longitudinal data, is not available for all the cities in the ESOPO study. Nevertheless, we believe that the data presented here, though not complete, has considerably enriched our understanding of the way local social assistance regimes work.

In a study of the dynamics of poverty, it could be claimed that a reliance on social assistance archives is misleading, in so far as it is based on the – unfounded – assumption that all the poor receive social assistance. On the contrary, we feel that in a study of the workings of social assistance it is particularly fitting, since it allows an assessment of the impact of welfare policy on beneficiaries' life chances. In order to obtain the point of view of individual actors, we integrated the data from social assistance records with in-depth interviews with a small sample of both current and past social assistance recipients. These were conducted with a common framework in each city, and allowed an assessment of the direct personal experience of the interviewees in relation to the specific pattern of social assistance they were exposed to, as well as the local context in which they lived.

The relevance of time in the analysis of social exclusion and social assistance

The relevance of a time perspective in the analysis of poverty has been acknowledged at least since Rowntree's (1901) pioneering studies over a century ago. Rowntree, in fact, was well aware that the poor are not always poor over their whole life. For London's manual workers and their families, the chance of being poor was linked to specific stages of their life and circumstances: being a child, or having children in need of support, being old (in pre-welfare state times) and, from a gender sensitive perspective, we might add being fatherless, or being a widow, increased their vulnerability. Thus, any headcount in a given year tells little about the life experience of the poor: how long they have been thus, and how long they are likely to remain in a condition of poverty. A headcount also tends to under-represent the number of people who experience poverty during their life course. Both of these aspects of poverty – the fact that it is a dynamic rather than a static phenomenon, and that it may affect more people than estimated by static poverty rates – can be taken into account only by a life course approach, on the basis of longitudinal data.

This insight has been present, if unsystematically, in poverty research since at least the 1960s (see for example, Commissione di Indagine sulla Povertà, 1985; Glatzer and Krupp, 1975). However, until recently, longitudinal data have been lacking and Europe has lagged behind the United States in providing them. Thus, de facto, the discourse on poverty has continued to be based on headcount data, however sophisticated the techniques for 'counting the poor'.

Moreover, as pointed out by Leisering and Leibfried in the introduction to their book (1999, pp 19-20), even studies of poverty that use a dynamic perspective have shared, until recently, the assumption that time was always an aggravating factor in the dynamics of poverty and social exclusion. Poverty was seen as a cumulative process in which life experiences, including that of receiving social assistance, negatively reinforced each other. Concern for the multidimensionality of poverty risked creating a negative 'labelling' effect for those affected by poverty (and unemployment), and also social assistance, by presenting them as mere victims of society, launched on a hopeless downward path, with no agency of their own. This same assumption lies, more or less explicitly, behind contemporary concern over 'welfare state dependency', supported by research strategies that have privileged the study of a specific subgroup of the socially assisted: those defined as being the most marginal, whether because of specific biographical vulnerabilities ('deviant' lifestyles, physical or mental disabilities, immigration) and/or the long period for which they have been receiving social assistance.

Since the important Panel Study on Income Dynamics (Duncan, 1984), US research has now undermined the idea of poverty as a necessarily long-term and cumulative experience. In this study, it emerged that the number of people susceptible to poverty was much greater and more heterogeneous than estimated by static measures, and that it comprised very different circumstances: individuals and families who experienced poverty once in their life time, those who experienced it many times for varying periods, and those who experienced it for lengthy periods, possibly throughout their entire life. The hypothesis of negative, cumulative and mutually reinforcing processes certainly holds for the last group and is possibly a risk for the second, but does not hold at all for the first. The second group is possibly the most interesting. It illustrates all the expected causes of vulnerability – gender, inadequate education and professional skills, family composition, lack of adequate means of social protection –

as well as the various ways in which one can enter or exit poverty: illness, marriage breakdown, unemployment, the birth of another child, which may be causes of poverty, and employment, marriage, a child leaving the household, finding a job, etc, which may offer a way out. This stress on the dynamics of poverty was further developed both empirically and theoretically by Bane and Ellwood (1986, 1994). A further important contribution, although one that is not always fully acknowledged in mainstream life course poverty research, has come from US and European studies on gender-specific vulnerability to poverty. These include studies on the consequences of marital instability and divorce (for example, Weitzman, 1985), and particularly on women's vulnerability to poverty in old age due to the combined effects of family careers and social security regulations (for example, Allmendinger et al, 1993; Joshi, 1989, 1993).

In addition to life course research in general, and life course studies on poverty in particular, there has been a growing interest in European research in the structuring role of social policy (see Leisering and Walker, 1998; Leisering and Leibfried, 1999). On the whole, however, life course research on poverty is still lacking in many European countries. The only countries where the dynamic approach to poverty is particularly developed are Germany, the UK and the Scandinavian countries, where there is adequate longitudinal data at the national level. The scope for comparative studies has thus been limited. A basis for a European-wide perspective could be provided by the European Community Household Panel data, which has been used to this purpose in the Gallie and Paugam (2000) study, as well as in the EUROSTAT study on social exclusion (2000), but the sample is rather small and the time span still rather short. More importantly, it was not designed for the study of poverty and social exclusion, either from the point of view of the sampling method or the items in the interview schedule. Therefore it needs to be used with great caution when analysing the dynamics of poverty and social assistance.

In parallel to these developments in poverty research, there has been a focus on country-specific[8] or comparative (Duncan and Voges, 1993; Duncan et al, 1995) social assistance dynamics, using social assistance records. Unlike previous research on social assistance recipients, this more recent work is based on representative samples of social assistance recipients (usually at the municipal level, but sometimes also at the regional or national level), and therefore yields a more diversified view of this population, largely matching that found in research on the dynamics of poverty. The distinction between these two pictures (of the poor and of social assistance recipients) depends mainly on the degree of universality and generosity of the systems of social assistance, that is on the extent of coverage they offer.

All these studies indicate great variability in the duration of social assistance. Nevertheless, they show that only a minority of recipients remain on social assistance for a long time. Seen against what we know of poverty dynamics, this may be explained by the fact that spells of poverty may affect a substantial part of the population, becoming part of the risk of a 'normal' life course. This generates a demand for social assistance, where it exists, but in these instances the spells of dependence may be short, since social assistance acts simply as a stopgap for coping with such an event, without creating any risk of welfare dependency. Focusing exclusively on long-term social assistance may thus yield a limited, stereotyped view both of poverty and social assistance recipients. It can also hide the wider area of vulnerability. A restrictive focus such as this can inspire policies – such as 'welfare to work' or workfare measures – which are over-coercive or misplaced, and in some cases even counterproductive[9]. Furthermore, this stereotypical view of welfare dependency may prevent an understanding of the reasons why beneficiaries become long-term recipients.

In their analysis of social assistance careers in Great Britain, Walker and Shaw (1998) point to two important findings. First, there was no evidence of a large number of people adopting social assistance as a permanent way of life. On the contrary, the vast majority "are engaged in a determined, continuing struggle to find work" (p 241). Second, "it seems that people do not become long term recipients through a process of learning or corruption, but because of characteristics that they have, or the circumstances that they face, when first they claim benefit". And they mostly keep trying to find work, even though their chances of exiting social assistance diminish with time: as they become older, tend to lose their skills, or their skills become obsolete and they find themselves competing for jobs with younger people with a more recent working experience or better, more updated skills. We will see that the number of beneficiaries in this situation at any given time and place depends to a large degree on the patterns of implementation of the policies themselves. The more selective and less generous they are, the more beneficiaries are likely to be launched on a long-term path of dependence, if there is no rule concerning duration of entitlement.

We should perhaps add that the current concern over mass unemployment seems to be obfuscating all other reasons for social and economic vulnerability: as if the weakening of the position of the male breadwinner – in the form of adult male unemployment – is rendering poverty more unacceptable and a risk for social cohesion. This is despite the fact that those most at risk of poverty and social exclusion are children, housewives and older people: that is individuals who do not even appear on the rolls of the unemployed. Recent studies on poverty and on social assistance recipients indicate that there exists a much broader range of social risks, many of which have always been present, although their specific causes and circumstances may have changed. For instance, as in the past, the end of a marriage exposes women and children to the risk of poverty and the need for social support, though now the cause is more likely to be separation rather than death of the spouse. Old age too still represents a risk, particularly for older women, and when age is associated with frailty. On the other hand, there are some new and growing causes of poverty such as 'flexible employment', immigration and non-standard lifestyles (Duncan, 1984; Glotz, 1984; Beck and Seewald, 1994; Paugam, 1997a, 1997b; Leisering and Leibfried, 1999; EUROSTAT, 2000).

Leisering and Leibfried (pp 245-9), on the basis of their study of social assistance careers in two German cities over a six year period, identify four main groups of recipients, plus two special categories cutting across these. They claim that the range of these groups "exposes the diversity of conditions between exclusion in a strict sense and full inclusion" (p 246). It also helps to distinguish between poverty as material or even immaterial deprivation, and social exclusion as a severe constraint on social participation. The aim is not to write-off the former as not severe enough. On the contrary, the intention is to give serious attention to both. The main groups are:

- *Relatively secure members of the middle class* (often labelled as the 'new poor') who are now more exposed to social insecurity than in the past, either for family reasons (marriage breakdown) or because of labour market vagaries. They see benefit claiming as both temporary and instrumental to actively combating their situation.
- *People with permanently low income, living just above the poverty line*, but always at risk of falling below it since they lack a cushion of protective resources, either because of their structural position or stage in life. Although they are integrated in society, their integration is always under threat and they constantly run the risk of falling into the next category.
- *The long-term deprived*, who suffer significant material or non-material deprivations, but are not necessarily and comprehensively excluded from participating in social life: not through work, but through consumption and embeddedness in family, kin and community

networks (see also Paugam, 1997b on a similar group among French RMI beneficiaries).

• *The long-term socially excluded*, who are not only deprived of material resources, but are also excluded from social participation due to active social discrimination or to their inability to cope, which render it difficult for them to be active members of meaningful social networks. The homeless, the mentally ill and those whose biographies have for some reason been seriously disrupted belong to this group, which has long dominated public imagination concerning the socially excluded or the 'fourth world'.

In addition to these four types, they identify two further groups:

• *People with an unsettled mode of existence*, whose lifestyle on the edge of society is in part an expression of deliberate choice. But they might also be seen as hazardous 'commuters' between a normal life course and social decline. They often use social assistance deliberately in a 'strategic' though often intermittent way. However, it is not, as in the case of the first group, in order to bridge an occasional spell of misfortune and reorient their lives (as in the case of a marriage breakdown), but a systematic way of supporting their chosen lifestyle. While the long-term socially excluded are the main reference point for much debate on poverty, the 'unsettled' are more or less explicitly the reference group for pointing to the combined risk of welfare dependency and social assistance scrounging.

• *New immigrants*, who are by definition in a transitional situation. Depending on circumstances, they may end up in one of the other types, or exit poverty and social assistance altogether.

In any given place, the likelihood of these various groups being found among social assistance recipients, their specific social and demographic characteristics, as well as the permeability of the boundaries between them, depends as much on the mechanisms of the social protection and social assistance systems as on the social, demographic and economic characteristics of the population[10]. This holds nationally, but even more so between countries. Thus, it is highly unlikely to find members of the first group in the Italian cities, not because the middle class is fully shielded from temporary poverty in Italy, but because, in the absence of a national scheme, local definitions of the deserving poor – in terms of income threshold and social characteristics – tend to exclude this group from forms of social assistance based income support[11]. The same applies in

Portugal due to the very low threshold of the new minimum income scheme, in the Spanish autonomous regions, and to a lesser degree in France. In France, lone mothers with very young children will not be found among RMI recipients either, since they are entitled to other specific and more generous benefits. On the other hand, in the UK lone mothers make up the bulk of long-term recipients, mainly because they are not required to look for work until their children cease to be dependent (Walker and Shaw, 1998)[12]. While in most countries lone mothers are strongly represented among those who take the longest to exit poverty, this is not so in the Swedish cities due to the infrastructure and cultural support given to working mothers.

Thus, the social and economic situation in a given time and place, as well as the workings of the social assistance system – its definition of the deserving poor (in terms of income and category), the time limits it imposes and constraints attached to social assistance recipiency – have a strong influence on social assistance dynamics and also on the type of person who becomes a social assistance beneficiary. The outcome, in terms of the social assistance career and successful exit, is strictly linked to the regulations governing entry and duration. This is why any comparative effort must first look closely at the institutional framework and implementation patterns of the policies involved.

Minimum income policies within national welfare systems: a comparative challenge

A recommendation adopted by the EEC Council in June 1992 encouraged all countries in the Community to include a means-tested minimum income scheme in their social protection system[13]. Thus, we might say that the guarantee of minimum resources has become part of a developing 'European social model'[14]. Within the EU, at present only Italy and Greece do not adhere to such a scheme as a part of institutionally acknowledged social rights. In other countries, such as the UK, Denmark, Sweden and Germany, such schemes have a long-standing tradition, although they may have been reformed several times over the decades and play quite different, nation-specific roles within the overall social protection package. In yet other countries, such as France, Spain, and more recently Portugal, it is a very recent addition to the system of social protection.

The recent, relatively fast development of minimum income schemes in the countries that previously did not have one is occurring in a social and economic context that is quite different from that of the early schemes set up in the postwar years. At that time, there was a generally shared expectation that the two pillars of the welfare state – stable and full employment, at least for men, and stable marriage – would remain solidly in place. Minimum income schemes were therefore perceived as residual measures designed to address only emergency and normally short-term situations. In recent years, pressure for the development of such schemes has increased in response to growing poverty due to the collapse of those two pillars, and to the emergence of new needs and problems experienced by new, or newly visible, social groups (for example, Third World immigrants, asylum seekers and so forth). According to the authors of a report on minimum income schemes in the EU, the spread of guaranteed income throughout the countries of Europe, and the importance it has acquired on the international political agenda, can be regarded as a response by the social protection systems of developed countries to the challenges posed both by a perceived crisis in the welfare states and by unacceptably high levels of poverty (Guibentif and Bouget, 1997, p 2).

These schemes are now increasingly having to deal with the spread of poverty among the able-bodied: those who 'ought' to be able to support themselves and their dependent family members, but cannot. This is happening either because they do not earn enough, or because they are out of work altogether. In coping with this situation, these schemes represent yet another instance in European history in which the boundaries between deserving and undeserving poor have been moved and the mutual obligations between a society and its citizens redefined[15]. In the welfare state systems, the able-bodied have traditionally been the best protected group, at least when, as men, they were in the social security covered labour market, and as women, were married to a social security covered worker. But they were also the least protected when they did not meet these conditions.

One might even suggest that while minimum income schemes are now acknowledging unemployed able-bodied men as deserving poor, the inverse process is occurring for women. Many countries previously had a special income guarantee for lone mothers – whether due to widowhood, separation or divorce, or non-marriage – both on account of being women, and hence less able than men to achieve economic independence, and their status as mothers. In recent years, however, these benefits have been reduced, and women and mothers redefined as prospective workers: thus, to some degree, considered less 'deserving' than before[16]. These shifting definitions and boundaries indicate the complexity of the values and definitions involved.

Income support measures for the poor are only one part of social assistance, and social assistance itself is only one part or sector within the welfare state package. Therefore, it can only be fully understood by looking at the whole package, including the internal boundaries between social security and social assistance, and between means-tested benefits and contributory and/or universal ones (see also Kvist, 1998). First, not all means-tested measures are per se measures targeted at the poor. Gough (1994) for example, distinguishes between general means testing and poverty testing. Only the latter provides resources for people who are defined and acknowledged to be poor, whereas the former may simply be used as a means to define service fees, or to restrict access by the well off, as in the case of public housing. Second, social assistance may include measures that are categorical, but not means-tested, such as special assistance for immigrants, frail older people, or orphans. Third, even restricting one's attention, as we do in this research, to 'poverty-tested' measures and those involving direct income support, the target population can vary, not only on the basis of entitlement criteria, but also depending on the working of other schemes.

Thus, for example, if a country has a financially adequate non-means-tested basic old age pension for all, there may be no need for a means-tested social assistance old age pension for those whose contributory record is too short or non-existent for granting an employment-related pension. Although the former system certainly protects older people from poverty, lack of entitlement to an old age pension would not be framed as an issue in policies to combat poverty, and older people receiving only a basic pension would not be included among social assistance income support beneficiaries. On the contrary, in countries such as Italy, Spain, Portugal and France, where means-tested social pensions for poor older people who are not entitled to a contributory pension do exist, this measure would be included among social assistance measures, but distinct and separate from income support specifically for the non-elderly (and non-disabled) poor. Similarly, the administration of unemployment benefit (in terms of linkage to contributions and previous work history, duration, degree of coverage of lost wages and so forth) is a crucial boundary-setting device between social security and social assistance. Possibly even more important is whether a legally regulated minimum wage is in place, in so far as it constitutes a kind of minimum income reference threshold. In a different sector, child benefit measures (depending on their generosity and the entitlement conditions) may affect the proportion of families with children who remain above the institutionally defined poverty threshold in a given country, but not be defined as measures against poverty.

Further, income support measures targeted at the poor are in themselves a complex package. They may link to other benefits (housing, free social services, and so on), the value of which should be taken into account not only in comparing policies, but also in assessing the strategies recipients develop to make use of income support measures.

It is not surprising, given the complexities of income support systems and the constraints they impose on the availability of adequate data, that although there have been a number of studies on the performance of such schemes, the few comparative studies in this field have investigated not so much the actual implementation or performance of minimum income schemes or the characteristics of recipients, but the legal/institutional framework and the formal entitlements of beneficiaries. Thus, as Gough et al (1997) observe with reference to means-tested social assistance in general, the growing importance of means-tested schemes in practice is not matched in academic studies, particularly from a comparative perspective. In their words,

> ... we have little comparative knowledge of the nature of different schemes, how benefits are calculated, whether they are rights-based or discretionary, the conditions attached to benefits, the levels of government responsible for financing and operating them, their effectiveness in reducing poverty or their efficiency in targeting those in need. (1997, p 18)

Four studies are worth mentioning here. The first is the well known report *Social Assistance in OECD Countries*[17]; the second is a study prepared for the European Seminar on Minimum Income, held in Lisbon on 27-28 September 1997 with the joint support of the European Commission and the Portuguese Ministry of Social Solidarity and Social Security, on the occasion of the launching of the new Portuguese scheme[18]. The third study was undertaken by the OECD and investigates selected member countries (see OECD, 1998b). The fourth is a collection of country studies edited by Paugam (1999).

From these studies we have information on the formal characteristics and differences between existing minimum income schemes from the point of view of eligibility conditions, forms of administration, linkage with other benefits and relationships with other social minima (for example, minimum wage or benefits for special categories). Much less comparative data is available at the EU level on the actual amounts paid[19], the duration of social assistance or the demographic characteristics of beneficiaries[20]. There is very little information available on the demographic characteristics of beneficiaries since few countries are able or willing to provide it, often due to the decentralised administration of schemes. Moreover, the data are highly dependent on eligibility rules, which can skew them towards the more mature age brackets (where young people are excluded) or towards women (since women are more likely to be included, even when young, if they have children). Where there are no age limits, it seems that the gender ratio among the beneficiaries is very similar to that in the population as a whole. Differences in the incidence of single childless adults or families with children tend to be dependent on the generosity of child allowances, while differences in the incidence of lone mothers depend not only on the policies, but on the patterns of women's participation in the labour force in the various countries.

With regard to eligibility rules, the main differences concern age, residence, nationality, and the ways in which the resources are evaluated. The minimum age for receiving a minimum income is de facto or in principle 18 years old (except when there are children). But in France, Spain and Luxembourg, it is 24 years old (if there are no dependent children) and in Germany parents are responsible for their adult children as long as they are in school (university included), even if they do not live with them. In Italy, there is, in theory, no age limit beyond which a parent is no longer financially responsible for a child if the latter happens to be in financial need. In Sweden, on the other hand, 18 year olds are entitled to income benefit even if they still live with their parents. All schemes have a legal residence requirement, and in decentralised systems it may be necessary to be resident in the region paying the benefit. Moreover, several countries restrict access to minimum income benefits to those who comply with a minimum period of residence, which may be as long as 10 years, as in some Spanish regions for non-natives to the region, or in Luxembourg for non-nationals. In fact, nationality, together with residence, is another requirement, either in the form of exclusion of non-national and/or non-EU citizens, or in the form of stricter residence and other requirements for non-nationals (for example, having a longer residence, certified legal residence, belonging to specific groups, such as refugees or asylum seekers).

In addition to these requirements, there are sometimes others. Thus in Ireland, people working more than 30 hours a week cannot receive any income support, irrespective of their disposable income. A 16 hour week working time threshold applies in the UK. Here, however, since October 1999, families with children where a parent works 16 hours or more are entitled to another more generous benefit: the Working Families' Tax

Credit. In Denmark, applicants must have suffered traumatic changes in their life, in addition to being in financial distress. This indicates that the Danish minimum income scheme is conceived as a temporary stopgap measure for crisis situations, not for people suffering permanent poverty or social exclusion because of the inability to work. Able-bodied unemployed people are expected to be on unemployment benefit or some kind of retraining programme.

With regard to the evaluation of resources, there are several ways in which the process of means-testing itself can vary, depending on the boundaries of the household and the degree of inter-family solidarity which is expected, the criteria according to which household incomes are equalised (equivalence scales), whether any part of earned income is disregarded, and lastly, the evaluation of assets, including own housing.

As far as household definition is concerned, this may range from a minimum unit consisting of the couple and their under-age children (in some Scandinavian countries), to a maximum unit, which also includes non-cohabitant kin to whom there are legal support obligations (or who have legal support obligations towards the applicant), as in Portugal and some local Italian schemes. The whole disposable household income may be taken into account, or part of it discounted (for example, child allowances or part of earned income). The same applies to assets, particularly owner occupied housing, which in some countries is totally exempted from calculation. In others, it is exempt up to a given value, and in others fully included in calculations.

In relation to the forms of administration, social assistance in general and minimum income schemes in particular are the most decentralised items of the welfare state. This is partly because they derive from the old tradition of assistance to the poor, but now increasingly because of the role assigned to local governments and social partners both in assessing eligibility and integrating income support with other measures. Most frequently, social assistance in general, and especially minimum income schemes for the able-bodied, are administered at the local level, but within a nationally defined framework of rules and criteria. The situation is, however, strongly diversified on the basis of the institutional framework itself. This ranges from the highly centralised systems of France and the UK, to the extreme autonomy of Portugal, before the RMG was introduced in 1999, and Italy (where, in the absence of national regulations in this sphere, regional and municipal authorities may legislate and make special provisions for the poor, but are not obliged to)[21]. This differentiation overlaps with the federal/centralist state. Thus, the Swedish or Norwegian centralist states have more local autonomy in setting thresholds, amounts and so forth than the German *Länder* (although since January 1998 this has changed in Sweden and a more homogeneous system is now in place). In fact, in the most decentralised systems (excluding the Italian case, which is not only decentralised, but discretionary), the amounts, equivalence scales, range of additional benefits (for example, housing), integrative social services and also insertion measures offered, may vary from one locality to another.

Finally, in all countries, great importance is attached to work as a means of countering economic dependence and the risk of social exclusion, as well as of checking possible abuse by beneficiaries. Thus in all systems there are obligations for adult recipients, with a few exceptions (mothers of under-age children and people nearing retirement age), to be available for work. Yet, there seem to be two somewhat distinct models (see also Milano, 1995). On the one hand, the majority of systems (Sweden, Germany, some of the Spanish regions, and the UK among them) establish a direct link between lack of income and the fact of being unemployed. As a consequence, they strictly enforce (in almost all cases) the requirement of availability for work, and expect beneficiaries to seek work using all available means, including those provided by the welfare offices themselves. Recipients of minimum income benefits, unlike those receiving unemployment indemnity, may be expected to accept jobs even outside their area of training. Additional services provided mostly concern support in the job search: training, counselling and sometimes disregard of a portion of earned income. There may also be negative incentives in the form of suspension or suppression of benefit if the requirement of availability to work is not complied with. The UK is possibly the country that in the past few years has made the most innovations, both on the incentive and the disincentive side.

On the other hand, some systems are based on a broader concept of social exclusion, where lack of income is considered a symptom of problems requiring solutions other than just obtaining a job. In these systems availability for work is integrated, and sometimes substituted, with other requirements concerning health, education or housing. Moreover, they often stress more explicitly the recipients' agency through recourse to formal negotiation processes, the signing of agreements, contracts and so forth. These systems are still a minority (France, Belgium, now Portugal, and some of the Spanish regions), but it is interesting to observe that the newly introduced schemes all tend to follow this second model, whereas the longest established ones are more similar to the first. Also in the UK, the concept of a contract (the word used is 'deal') is increasingly being employed in welfare reform and action, but the focus remains strictly on paid work as the route to social integration. Other means of integration are not envisaged, at least in public discourse, although if one looks at the range of measures actually taken to encourage beneficiaries, including lone mothers, to enter paid work – counselling, training, provision of childcare, housing and so forth – the approach seems much more integrated and complex.

Given the lack of importance assigned to means-tested social assistance schemes in academic analysis, only a few comparative welfare state studies have considered schemes addressing poverty a crucial item in constructing typologies. The most important is the study by Leibfried (1993), who argues with great insight that the way a welfare state addresses poverty is a testing ground for evaluating the contents and limits of social citizenship. On this basis, he adds a fourth 'regime' – the 'Latin rim' – to the three proposed by Esping-Andersen (1990). Building on this approach, and on the results of an important study on all means-tested social assistance programmes operating in the OECD countries (Eardley et al, 1996), Gough et al (1997) develop a more complex map of social assistance regimes. They identify eight distinct social assistance regimes, within which we may locate minimum income schemes for the poor. This typology is based on three dimensions: extent and salience (expenditure on social assistance and number of beneficiaries); programme structure (centralisation versus local variation, rights versus discretion, individual entitlement versus wider family obligations, liberal versus tough means-testing and work-testing); and generosity (level of benefit and replacement rates). The eight regimes are defined as follows:

- **Selective welfare systems**, in which all benefits are means-tested and programmes are categorical and rights-based. Australia and New Zealand belong to this type.
- **Public assistance state**, mainly a US experience, although qualifications should be made for certain states having a higher level of benefit than the US average. This type features a wide range of means-tested benefits, hierarchically organised in terms of stigma and acceptability. Benefits are variable and tend to be low; there are strong work incentives and procedural rights are well entrenched.
- **Welfare states with integrated safety nets** include Britain, Ireland and partly Canada. In these countries, income support for the poor is a national, general programme. It is relatively generous (around social insurance levels), and is rights-based with some work incentive, particularly for families with children.

- **Dual social assistance states** include Germany, France, Belgium and Luxembourg. These provide assistance schemes for specific categories, such as older people and people with disabilities, or lone mothers with very young children, and offer a general rights-based safety net, although there may be a degree of local discretion.

- **Citizenship-based but residual assistance** includes the Scandinavian countries, except Norway, and the Netherlands. Here there is a single general scheme with relatively high benefits. There are national regulatory frameworks, but the role of local authorities is substantial. Strict means-testing combines with an individual view of entitlements and a citizenship-based appeal system. The tradition of full employment and/or universal welfare provisions relegated the role of social assistance to the margins of the welfare state until the late 1980s.

- **Rudimentary assistance** includes Southern Europe and Turkey. National social assistance programmes cover only selected groups, mainly older and disabled people. Otherwise, there is discretional relief provided by municipalities and religious charitable bodies. With the exception of Turkey, obligations tend to include a range of relationships wider than the nuclear family. Benefits are low and for certain groups of able-bodied poor, while in other areas are non-existent, even if means-testing is not particularly stringent.

- **Decentralised, discretionary relief** includes Norway, Austria and Switzerland and is somewhere in between the Scandinavian and Southern European models. Assistance consists of localised discretionary relief, linked to social work and wider kin obligations. Benefit levels are relatively generous, but few people claim social assistance, not only due to the relatively high levels of employment, but also to the stigma attached to welfare and the powers accorded to social workers.

- **Centralised, discretionary assistance** includes Japan, and incorporates features of both the British and the Austrian model. It consists of a long-standing nationally regulated social assistance programme with very little local variation, but shares with the decentralised discretionary relief model a wide concept of family obligations and a high degree of stigmatisation.

The virtue of this typology lies in its avoidance of the suggestion of hierarchy or continuum, and the fact that it shows the complexity of elements and dimensions involved. It is certainly more useful than prevalent typologies for comparative welfare state research and especially for analysing the role and features of income support measures for the able-bodied poor. We might possibly argue against lumping all the Southern European countries together in the rudimentary assistance regime. Taking the same indicators used by Gough et al (1997), it could be claimed that Spain, and to some degree Portugal since 1998, are nearer the dual social assistance regime, in so far as these two countries now have a general safety net that supplements the categorical assistance schemes. Moreover, whereas Gough et al point out the crucial role of charities in the residual model, they totally ignore it in the dual social assistance and integrated safety net models, where a crucial, even institutionalised role is played by volunteer non-profit and often religious agencies, particularly in the accompanying services which are increasingly being attached to income support schemes. Finally, other important differences that might add further detail to the typology are somewhat underplayed: the role of the requirement to be available for work, the application of the concept of social integration, and so on. Both the role of actors in the so-called third sector (non-governmental, non-profit bodies, cooperatives, charities and so forth), and the way beneficiaries' obligations are defined, are crucial features of the way social assistance works in practice. They are also important elements of within-country, as well as cross-country differentiation.

These are dimensions that we explore in this study. Our aim is not to propose yet another typology, but to show how the various systems work in practice, and to what effect for their beneficiaries. In fact, although there appears to be a strong consensus in comparative welfare state studies that welfare states 'come in types' and can therefore be grouped into clusters, the continuing effort to develop new typologies and to find new ways of clustering them indicates the limitations of a typology-oriented approach: the risk of superficiality, of overlooking important dimensions for lack of comparative data, and ignoring important within-type variation (see also Daly and Lewis, 1998). The most recent comparative analyses of welfare systems – whether examining anti-poverty measures or gender equality – seem increasingly aware that typologies vary depending on the criteria included (see for example, O'Connor et al, 1999). For instance, it has been argued that the inclusion of social service provision is the most important critique of mainstream welfare state typologies (for example, Taylor Gooby, 1991; Alber, 1995; Daly and Lewis, 1998).

The need for in-depth national case studies, not necessarily as an alternative but certainly as an integration of quantitative comparative studies with an institutional orientation, is being requested not only by outspoken critics of standard typologies, such as Daly and Lewis, but also by scholars more sympathetic to the efforts at defining typologies, such as Kvist and Torfing (1996). Even one of the creators of typologies themselves, Esping-Andersen, in his latest book (1999) points self-critically to the risks and costs of creating typologies on the basis of aggregate data.

The choice of countries and cities

Given that our aim is to detect variation rather than homogeneity, we have chosen to over-represent in our sample the two regimes in Gough et al's typology that should, according to our hypothesis, have a greater degree of inter-country and intra-country variation: the dual social assistance regime (as in Germany and France) and the rudimentary assistance regime (Italy, Portugal at the time of the study, and Spain, which falls between this regime and the dual social assistance one). We have only one country – Sweden – to represent the citizenship-based residual assistance type. Furthermore, we have both centralist states (Sweden, France, Italy and Portugal) and federalist states (Germany and Spain).

All of these countries, except Italy and until 1998 Portugal, have a minimum income scheme targeted at the poor, which is either centrally, federally or regionally regulated. This scheme may be the latest addition to a series of social minima, as in France, Spain and present day Portugal, and therefore address only or mainly those who are not beneficiaries of other income support schemes. Or it may be more comprehensive, as in Sweden and Germany[22]. The cities examined are: Gothenburg and Helsingborg in Sweden; Bremen and Halle in Germany; Rennes and Saint Etienne in France; Milan, Turin and Cosenza in Italy; Barcelona and Vitoria in Spain; Lisbon and Porto in Portugal.

The programmes we have analysed are the *Socialbidrag* in Sweden, *Sozialhilfe* in Germany, *Revenue Minimum d'Insertion* in France, the Basque *Ingreso Minimo de Inserción* and the Catalan *Renta Minima de Insercion* in Spain. In Italy the *Minimo Vitale* and *Minimo Alimentare* in Turin and Milan, and *Assistenza Economica* in Cosenza, the *Subsidio Mensal* and the *Prestações Pecuniárias de Acção Social* respectively in Lisbon and Porto in Portugal[23].

In retrospect, we might well agree that the missing case is the UK, given its unique mixture of universalism and high (and growing) incidence of social assistance measures compared to social security ones (Walker and Ashworth, 1998). However, we do not completely agree with Gough et al about the generosity of the UK system. The fact that income support is near the social security level is due to the fact that unemployment indemnity in the UK is a flat rate benefit: it is not linked to previous earnings, and thus protects less from lost wages than in other countries. This made it easier in 1996 to conflate the two benefits for the able-bodied into the benefit now called the Jobseeker's Allowance. The basic difference between the two is that those becoming unemployed may claim Jobseeker's Allowance for the first few months without being means-tested. No such conflation would have been easy in any other European country as unemployment indemnity elsewhere is linked to previous wages; those receiving it would never perceive themselves as similar to those receiving income support.

There are two reasons for not having included the UK, both of them practical. First, at the time of writing the proposal for this project, none of the group of contributors that was forming had close connections with a UK scholar interested in longitudinal research on social assistance. Although the UK was one of the first European countries to set up a longitudinal study of the population (British Household Panel, initiated in 1990), no study on the dynamics of poverty and/or social assistance based on longitudinal data had been published to our knowledge, nor did we know anyone working on local archives. Admittedly, this is not a very scientific explanation for our choice. Yet, anyone who is familiar with the time limits on setting up teams and writing projects to meet TSER requirements will understand, particularly as this project was presented in one of the very first waves of EU funded social research, when cross-national EU teams were just starting to develop. The second reason is the complexity of the British system. As it has for some time been undergoing numerous modifications, we were cautious about including a national case that would be difficult to monitor properly. A similar problem occurred with Portugal, in so far as the RMG was introduced during the course of our field study. In this case, however, the lack of substantial policies previously, allowed us to perform a sort of 'before and after' study, although in fact our study mainly focuses on the 'before' situation.

As for the other countries, we wished at least to include some of the best-known cases. The reason for choosing Germany and Sweden was exactly the opposite of that for excluding the UK. In both countries a number of studies on the dynamics of social assistance had already been carried out, stimulated by the Bremen Longitudinal Study of Social Assistance. Thus, we could further develop these studies, while extending the data set to cover other countries/cities. In the case of France, which was selected because the RMI represents the 'new generation' of means-tested income support measures, we were rather unlucky in terms of data. Although follow-up studies of RMI recipients have been performed on a national scale since the beginning of this scheme, reflecting the concern for monitoring and evaluation of the RMI shared by scholars and policy makers, individual data covering a long time span were not available for administrative reasons. Thus, the study of social assistance dynamics had to be based on retrospective survey data, which, despite yielding important information on beneficiaries' subjective experience and assessment, are not comparable with archive data. France is nevertheless important for our study, as we will see in the following chapters, for understanding the complex polysemantics of the concept of 'social integration' and the crucial role played by local patterns of implementation of an otherwise highly centralised policy.

The countries selected do not only represent different types of welfare regime, they are also very different in terms of political tradition, demography, family arrangements, unemployment rates, women's activity rates, immigration rates, gross domestic product (GDP) levels, labour market dynamics and so on. All these aspects are, of course, crucial in defining the context in which poverty is experienced and in which social assistance policies are developed and implemented. For example, while the unemployment rate started to rise in the 1990s in all the countries studied, it did so from quite different starting points and within quite different economies. Thus, the almost 7% unemployment in Sweden in 1994 was still far below the 22% of Spain in the same year. These aspects are taken into account in the analysis in the following chapters, although they do not constitute the core of the study.

We are well aware that in many cases national estimates may differ from standardised Eurostat or OECD data due to the definitions and measurement criteria. It is a particularly intractable problem when comparing poverty rates: consumption versus income, median versus average, what equivalence scale to use and so forth. With regard to poverty in particular, there may be quite substantial differences in the rates presented in standardised comparative tables and those presented by national statistical offices or used in national studies and national policy debates. This depends both on the sources used and the means of measurement (see also Atkinson, 1998a; Krause, 1998; Commissione di Indagine sulla Esclusione Sociale, 2000). Finally, within-country variation in certain crucial dimensions (unemployment and poverty rates, and also women's labour force participation and marital instability rates) may be so great that average national rates are almost meaningless. For instance, the unemployment rates in Milan, Turin and Cosenza in 1991 were respectively 6.8%, 14% and 32%. Differences among the same cities for youth unemployment were even greater: 12.2%, 30.7% and 77%. Not even the East-West divide in Germany produces a difference of this magnitude. In fact, in 1991, the unemployment rate was only slightly lower in Halle than in Bremen – 9.7% compared to 10%. Possibly the numerous training, retraining and make-work programmes set up in order to deal with the effects of unification account in part for the difference. However, in Halle, women make up a higher proportion of the working population than in Bremen, and as they are highly vulnerable to unemployment, the two figures are only partially comparable since they refer to populations with a different gender composition. Of course, there are also important economic and social differences between these two German cities that make it misleading to apply a single common indicator. Although normally less dramatic, cross-country differences may be found in all the six countries, with the partial exception of Sweden. For these reasons – lack of sound comparative indicators on crucial social dimensions at the national level[24] and the existence of substantial intra-country differences in these same dimensions – we have resisted the temptation to present a neat table presenting national data on the relevant dimensions.

Three main criteria were used to select the cities: availability of data, within-country variation and cross-country comparability. We began with the cities for which the national teams already had access to social assistance archives, that is Bremen, Halle, Gothenburg, Helsingborg, Turin and Milan. To these, other cities were added to provide within-country contrast and cross-country similarity from the point of view of significant social and economic factors. For example, Milan and Turin have quite different social and economic situations, although they are both in the north-west of Italy and belong to the so-called industrial triangle, while Cosenza represents a case of a marginal service city in the south. Halle and Bremen have contrasting local social and economic configurations and also represent West and East Germany. It would be interesting in the future to compare social assistance patterns within, and not only across these two parts of Germany. In the case of Germany, beyond our problems with the social assistance data in Halle, it is possible that the comparative analysis was somewhat overshadowed by the East-West contrast. This may have hidden more subtle differences that we might have detected had we compared, for instance, Bremen and Munich.

Although both industrial ports, Gothenburg and Helsingborg are differentiated by the greater economic dynamism of the latter, stimulated by its vicinity to Denmark. The two Spanish cities, Barcelona and Vitoria, have analogies respectively with Milan and Turin, in that Vitoria is a medium-sized industrial town, while Barcelona is a metropolitan town with a more diverse economic basis. In the case of the French cities,

Saint Etienne and Rennes, one has a long industrial history and the other is a more service-oriented town. Moreover, these two towns have two quite distinct traditions in terms of political culture. Finally, Porto and Lisbon, like Vitoria and Barcelona, provide a contrast between a small manufacturing city and a metropolitan, commercial, service city and port.

These intra-country differences can, to some degree, be 'paired off' cross-country to design shifting clusters of cities around a common feature. Thus, we have three metropolitan towns – Barcelona, Lisbon and Milan – as against a number of medium ones; the 'traditional' manufacturing towns of Gothenburg, Helsingborg, Bremen, Halle, Saint Etienne, Turin, Vitoria and Porto, in contrast with towns of a more commercial and service orientation – Rennes, Milan, Lisbon and Barcelona. Ports such as Bremen, Gothenburg, Helsingborg, Porto and Lisbon, in contrast to towns with an economy centred around the automobile or chemical industry, such as Turin, Saint Etienne and Halle.

In the following chapter, we shall analyse in detail these, and other, cross- and intra-country similarities and differences, some of which were part of our original research design, while others emerged in the research process itself. We also discuss the differences that seem most relevant from the point of view of social assistance applicants and the patterns of implementation and performance of social assistance. Here we wish to point out that, looking at our cities as social systems in their own right, there will be more social assistance regimes than the three basic types represented at the national level, due to the existence of specific local forms. Depending on the nature of the national system – its degree of decentralisation and discretion – these local systems may simply represent variations, or be specific and quite diverse regimes. This will be the focus of Chapter Three, while Chapters Four and Five respectively, will trace how these different national and local regimes select their beneficiaries, that is their 'poor', and investigate the interplay with the local economic circumstances, particularly the labour market. We will look at how, on the basis of their selection and other criteria, they encourage or enforce certain types of social assistance 'career'.

Notes

[1] This is, for instance, the perspective from which Walker and Ashworth (1998) look at what in their eyes is the UK's 'exceptionalism' in the crucial role allocated to social assistance compared to social security. What they do not seem to be

aware of, is that there are European countries in which the role of social assistance may be negligible without it being supplanted by social security or other universal schemes.

[2] A recent OECD study (OECD, 1998a) tries to evaluate the incidence and distribution of poverty in the various social groups across the industrialised countries, on the basis of the distribution of employment among, as well as within, households. The hypothesis is that inter-country differences in the economic vulnerability of individuals and families depends largely on the one hand from differences in the distribution of employment among household members, particularly husbands and wives, and on the other hand from differences in the distribution of employment among households. Thus, for example, in Italy, as in most Mediterranean countries, occupation is strongly concentrated among male family heads. As a consequence, there is a more even distribution of employment across households than in the European average; but at the same time, there is a higher than average incidence of poor households among those whose head is in employment.

[3] A similar phenomenon may be noted in Turin, where the local system of income support provides a special measure for old, just retired people waiting for the pension office to calculate their pension benefit and set the payment process in motion. In this case, income support is paid in the form of an advance payment to be paid back once the pension benefit starts. One might wonder why the pension offices are not able to deal more efficiently, in terms of timing, with what, after all, is a perfectly foreseeable event: the reaching of retirement age.

[4] Actually, this may be too bold a declaration, in so far as one should also take into account non-take up rates. These too may depend on the way a measure is offered and implemented – the greater the stigmatisation, the higher the non-take up rate is likely to be.

[5] A recent book that has addressed the specificity of European cities is that edited by Bagnasco and Le Gales (2000). In this book, the concept of local society is central to all analyses.

[6] See for instance Bradshaw et al (1993) on child support policies, and OECD, 1998a (vols 1 and 2) on social assistance policies. The latter are two very informative studies of social assistance, respectively in Australia, Finland, Sweden and the UK (vol 1) and Belgium, the Czech Republic, the Netherlands and Norway (vol 2). A study that is very near to that presented here – in its longitudinal analysis of social assistance careers in the US, Canada, Germany and Sweden – McFate et al

(1995) – totally downplays the fact that the data belong to specific local archives (at least the German and Swedish ones), and no specific effort is made to link them to local social and demographic contexts and practices. The same observation may be raised with regard to Leisering and Leibfried's (1999) work and all the various studies based on the otherwise landmark-setting Bremen longitudinal study.

[7] See for example, Ashworth et al, 1992; Bonß and Plum, 1990; Buhr et al, 1989; Fridberg, 1993; Jarvis and Jenkins, 1997, 1998; Leibfried, 1987; Leibfried et al, 1995; Leisering and Leibfried, 1999; Leisering and Zwick, 1990; Paugam, 1997b; Shaw et al, 1996; Walker and Ashworth, 1994; Walker, 1998.

[8] This is, for instance, the conclusion Gallie (2000) draws from his analysis of a few TSER projects, such as 'Inclusion through Participation' (INPART) and 'Social Integration through Obligation to Work?' (on this see also Lødemel and Trickey, 2000), and from the proceedings of the thematic network 'Misleading Trajectories: Evaluation of Employment Policies for Young Adults in Europe Regarding non Intended Effects of Social Exclusion'.

[9] This is a caveat we introduce on the basis of the ESOPO study we present here. It is not present in the studies we are referring to, not even in the comparative ones, which should be particularly attentive to the distorting effect of the sorting mechanisms.

[10] This would remain true even if the RMI at present being experimented in a selected number of municipalities were generalised, in so far as the income threshold is so low that it is highly unlikely that middle-class households – again with the partial exception of jobless middle-class separated women and mothers – may be included in such a measure in case of temporary financial hardship. They should first exhaust all their resources, and therefore be already firmly inserted in a downward path of financial deprivation.

[11] Since January 2001, under the New Deal for Lone Parents programme, lone parents with children over the age of three must at least have an interview with a personal adviser at the local jobcentre to discuss options and ways to find a job.

[12] Recommendation 92/441/EEC of 24 June 1992, on common criteria concerning sufficient resources and social assistance in social protection systems.

[13] This process has been strengthened following the Lisbon and Nice summits in 2000, with the adoption of a European social agenda. The preparation of National Action Plans for Inclusion is part of this ongoing process.

[14] It is not by chance that, according to some comparative welfare state analysts, policies to combat poverty are considered a crucial indicator of welfare state patterns. See for example, Leibfried, 1993.

[15] That is, the amount of time during which the obligation to be available for a job is suspended due to motherhood has been shortened, although it still varies quite widely between countries on the basis of the age of the youngest child: between three years in France, Austria, Finland, and 16 years in the UK (where there is currently a debate concerning this). On the differential impact on lone mothers of policies across welfare state regimes, see Kilkey and Bradshaw, 1999; Larsen, 2000; Pedersen, 2000. For changing trends, see Millar (2000).

[16] See Eardley, 1996. In order to overcome some of the above mentioned shortcomings in comparing widely different systems, this study has used the vignettes or typical cases approach: comparing what 'identical' cases are, on principle, entitled to in a given locality (ie, reference is made by informants to the rules in a given city within a given country). Of course such an approach can greatly undermine the ambitious goal of comparing national – not only local – systems, since within-country variation may be even greater than between country ones, if there is no institutional, nationwide standard. It is the case in this study, for Italy, whose position in the different rankings constructed by the researchers might have been totally different (and worse) if another town had been chosen. In our study, we used both reference to specific towns and the vignette method, but out of an awareness that there are local welfare systems. Moreover, we use the vignettes in a twofold perspective: to describe formal entitlements, and to describe actual practices.

[17] See Guibentif and Bouget, 1997. In the first section of their book, they analyse the differences between regulations applicable in each member state; in the second section they describe the actual administration of the various schemes, from the point of view of who are the beneficiaries and how much the implementation costs.

[18] Since the minimum income typically represents a maximum threshold, and schemes pay the difference between this maximum threshold and total income available to the recipient (on a household basis), average amounts received may be much lower than maximum ones. See, for instance, the study on the amounts

paid within the various social minima in France by Amrouni and Math, 1997/ 1998. Specifically, for the RMI the mean amount is about 67% of the maximum payable. This is about the average ratio reported for Sweden in Guibentif and Bouget's (1997) work.

[19] According to the few data that Guibentif and Bouget (1997) have been able to collect on duration, it is possible that there are quite different national situations, with the Netherlands having among the longest durations (in half the cases the benefits are paid for two years or more), and other countries such as Denmark and Sweden having average durations of six months or less. More limited in the range of countries, comparative studies on social assistance recipients by Duncan et al (1995) and by Gustafsson and Voges (1998) indicate that the majority of claimants leave social assistance within a year, but remain slightly longer in Germany compared to Sweden. Buhr and Weber (1998) and Leisering and Leibfried (1999) show that the great majority of beneficiaries in Germany remain on benefit for less than a year. A similar finding is shown by Walker and Ashworth (1998) for the UK. Before the study presented in this book, however, there were no data on countries having less universal and/or less generous systems, such as the Southern European ones, and the specific dynamics below these average durations had never been fully explored.

[20] A national framework law intended to define general criteria in the area of both social services in general and social assistance in particular, as well as the respective responsibilities of State, regions, provinces and municipalities in this field, was approved in October 2000 and is now starting its complex implementation process. In this law, mention of policies against poverty as a specific responsibility of local government is made. Yet the introduction of a national income support measure – through the extension of RMI being experimented in 39 municipalities since 1998 – is subordinated to the approval of still another law, which has yet to be proposed in Parliament.

[21] In all countries there are special provisions for older and disabled people. In France, within the system of *Allocation Familiales*, there is also a special scheme for poor lone mothers: the *Allocation Parent Isolé*, which is temporary, but more generous and less stigmatising than the RMI, and has no availability to work requirement attached.

[22] When these measures also included elderly and disabled people, we considered only the data concerning the able-bodied and their children. The criteria and rules governing each measure are presented in Chapter Three. A synopsis is presented in the Appendix.

[23] In fact, the need to develop adequate comparative social indicators is newly emerging in the debates and concerns within the main international organisations. Both the OECD and the EU have started work in this field that is in the initial phase of matching tentative definitions with available data.

TWO

Cities as local systems

Enzo Mingione, Marco Oberti and José Pereirinha

Local formations, constructions of poverty and policy implementation

Our comparative analysis of anti-poverty measures and programmes has developed from the 'regulation' and 'constructionist' approaches (for example, Gough et al, 1997; Paugam, 1999). At the same time, it differs from these in that it focuses not only on cross-country variation, but also within-country variation. It assumes that, a) national systems differ in the degree to which they allow or even incentive variation and, b) intra-country variation is a result of national welfare regimes and also the way patterns of social, economic, demographic and political development at the local level coalesce into recognisable social formations. The interrelationships between the national and local modes of regulation of poverty are depicted in Figure 2.1.

In this chapter, we introduce the local welfare systems of our 13 cities, setting them in their social and historical contexts. Thus, our focus will not be specifically on the income support measures that are at the core of the ESOPO study. These will be analysed in detail in the following chapter. Here, we simply identify those features that render our 13 cities veritable social formations, thus explaining the specific features that distinguish their modes of regulation of poverty vis a vis other cities in the same country, as well as other cities in different countries. The chapter is structured into three parts. In the first, we try to give some methodological indications on how to read the local welfare set-up and its construction, analysing the historical development of the cities with particular regard to the industrial side. In the second part, we describe the current socioeconomic transformations that are creating tension, and the groups at major risk in the various cities. Finally, we consider the

Figure 2.1: The links between national and local levels concerning poverty regulation

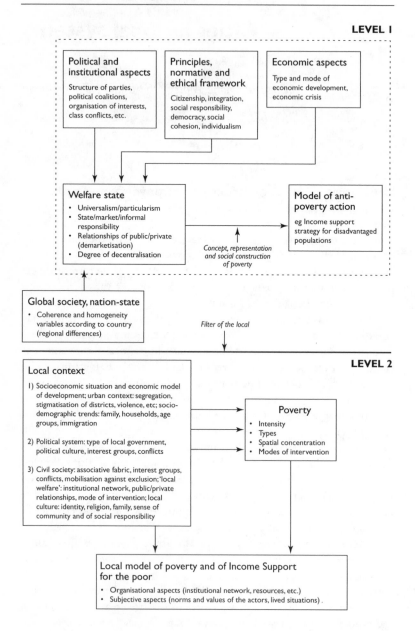

local welfare model in each city, looking at how different social actors mix. In the conclusion, we attempt to summarise and interpret local models and welfare strategies, going beyond the local differences.

In order to grasp the structure of local systems, we need to view them within the framework of national models, focusing in particular on how the latter have adapted to the actual social, economic and cultural configuration of specific cities. For this reason, it is important to take into account the various urban traditions. These can be seen in terms of their economic history, the patterns of development and organisation of civil society, the changing sets of relevant actors, as well as their demographic history and the spatial distribution of different social groups. It is the interplay of all these factors that develop the diverse commitments to welfare and different attitudes to the poor, including the division between 'deserving' and 'undeserving' poor. Local systems, in fact, must be evaluated in terms of their mix of institutional and individual actors, since diversity and complexity are playing an increasingly important role in the development of active policies based on partnerships and shared responsibility between providers and recipients.

In this context, local welfare systems can be conceived as dynamic entities in which the specific social and cultural context gives rise to a specific mix of actors involved in strategies for implementing social policies. These deal with needs and populations that also have locally specific profiles in terms of demographic and economic characteristics. At this level of analysis, the major methodological difficulty is to go beyond a straightforward description to find parameters for a meaningful comparison and interpretation of local regimes of poverty regulation. Our study begins by identifying some elements of diversity between cities in the same country and then interprets the significance and impact of this diversity in terms of typology.

For example, both the German cities, Bremen and Halle, are industrial centres that have been hit hard by unemployment due to the process of de-industrialisation. Yet there are considerable differences in the impact of this phenomenon on the population. This is not entirely explained by the features of the main local industry: the naval and port activities in Bremen, and the chemical industry in Halle. The most important difference is that Bremen is located in West Germany and Halle in the East. It is for this reason that Leisering and Leibfried (1999) also used these two cities, not so much to delineate local models, but to represent the differences between the two halves of present-day Germany. This diversity is reflected in the mix of local actors, the institutional system, and the profile and careers of the populations that have recourse to social welfare. In Halle –

but presumably also in other industrial cities in the Eastern *Länder* – there are few foreign residents, and the number has actually declined since reunification. Foreigners are consequently under-represented among welfare recipients. The employment crisis has mainly affected women and young ethnic Germans, who have to deal with an unfamiliar welfare system, while facing the consequences of equally unfamiliar labour market mechanisms. This is the result of the dual process of political unification and industrial restructuring. Vulnerability to unemployment in Bremen, on the other hand, as in other northern industrial cities in the Western *Länder*, is connected with the contraction in job opportunities for the poorly educated – above all, but not only, first and second generation immigrants – and the new wave of immigration, in particular asylum seekers from eastern European countries and the former Yugoslavia.

There are other features of the local system in Halle connected with its location: the relatively young age structure of the population, the greater propensity of married women to enter the labour market, widespread childcare services, and the still weak presence of secular and religious associations in the social welfare sector. Joblessness and income poverty, two phenomena that appeared after reunification, are addressed mostly through the large number of occupational training and work reinsertion programmes implemented as part of the large-scale investment in industrial and economic restructuring.

These brief observations offer us a first parameter for analysis of the local systems: the importance of *regional location* in determining the economic, social and institutional context. This factor plays a role of varying importance, but is especially significant in the comparison of northern and southern Italian cities. In Italy, the most evident indicator of diversity, though not the only one, is the incidence of joblessness. Thus, we need to look at the extent to which the opportunity for local employment affects the conditions and careers of those in economic difficulty. While the unemployment rate in 1995 – our first observation year – in Milan was 8.2%[1], in Cosenza it was 32.2%. In the former city, long-term difficulty in finding a job affects only a small part of the population: mainly those who pursue marginal lifestyles or who suffer from an accumulation of problems – severe lack of skills, social isolation, a criminal record, or drug addiction. In Cosenza, unemployment affects a high proportion of women and young people, as well as many adult men. In neither case are policies directed at helping those in difficulty to find paid work central to the local welfare system, but for different and opposite reasons. In Milan, once a condition of 'normality' has been restored, it is relatively easy to find a job, whereas in Cosenza attempts at job insertion rarely succeed anyway, given the scarce opportunities offered by the local labour market.

More intriguing are the differences between Milan and Turin, since they are not explained purely by the 'regional' parameter. This points to the influence of other factors in the construction of local welfare systems. Both cities are in the north-west of Italy, and both have a long and well-entrenched history of industrial development. However, industry in Milan has long been more diversified and more oriented towards the international market. The tertiary sector developed earlier and there is a high concentration of financial activities[2]. Although Milan, like Turin, was a point of attraction for various waves of immigration in the postwar years from the south of Italy as well as the north-east, this did not result in clear-cut, highly visible forms of spatial segregation within the city. The industrial history of Turin, on the other hand, has been dominated by a single company: Fiat. As a consequence, its population was, and still is, heavily dependent on the strategies and fortunes of this company. There is a much higher percentage of working-class families, whose numbers were swelled by the hundreds of thousands of immigrants, who until the 1980s came to the city for work, especially from the south. Notwithstanding the number, or possibly because of it, integration of southern immigrants was slow and difficult, giving rise to spatial segregation in the hastily built social housing, which created whole neighbourhoods. Interestingly, the new waves of immigrants, now from the Third World and Eastern European countries, seem to be following the same spatial pattern. However, the current economic context is totally different. While Fiat remains Turin's major industry, its role as employer is declining and the emerging features of the local labour market (with its higher demand for advanced technological skills and highly educated labour force) risk leaving both the traditional working-class and the less skilled new immigrants with diminishing opportunities (see Martinotti, 1982; Negri, 1982; Bagnasco, 1986).

These differences in the economic and social history of the two cities are reflected in the institutional mix of actors intervening in welfare practices. The fact that social policies in Turin are more generous and universalistic than in Milan and comprise, above all, active measures for occupational training and job insertion, is not a function solely of the higher current rate of unemployment (in 1995 the unemployment rate was 14%). It is also due to a different tradition. The municipal authority plays a strong role in dealing with problems arising from the need to integrate large groups of – often poor – immigrants, as well as coping with the outcomes of Fiat's industrial and labour market policies. Other features are the systematic involvement of trades unions in the implementation of policies, and the importance of Fiat's direct interest in the local system. In a national context where income support measures and job insertion policies remain marginal, the municipality of Turin has a long tradition of job insertion and training programmes targeted at the most vulnerable social groups. These are used either in combination with or as a temporary alternative to income support measures, especially for long-term unemployed people, low-skilled young people and, more recently, disabled people and those suffering from drug addiction.

Similar contrasts may be found between the French cities in the ESOPO sample, Rennes and Saint Etienne, although the factors that emerge are different from the previous cases. Rennes has never been an industrial city. It developed on the basis of tertiary and administrative activities linked to the public sector, in parallel with development in new technologies and cutting-edge industries. The working-class has never been culturally, politically or numerically important. In addition, the modest role of major industry in the economic development of the city means that there has never been a large influx of immigrants. We are therefore looking at a local working-class recruited essentially at the regional level. The city is also the centre for a major regional university, which attracts many students (one inhabitant in four is in higher education), and there are many young graduates. By contrast, Saint Etienne, which is an old industrial mining town, has been seriously hit since the early 1970s by the dismantling of its economic base, and faces a much more difficult social situation. Unemployment problems seem to be connected, on the one hand, with the decline in job opportunities for young people – especially those of foreign origin with few qualifications – and, on the other, with the difficulty that older blue-collar workers who have been made redundant have in finding another job. A considerable proportion of these are immigrants who came to work in the mines and manufacturing industry. The employment crisis is therefore affecting not only the first, but also the second generation of immigrants. Those most affected by the employment crisis also tend to be concentrated in social housing districts.

Compared to Saint Etienne, the population of Rennes is, overall, both younger and better educated. There are more middle and senior managers, fewer blue-collar workers and foreigners. Unemployment is low, women have a higher activity rate, and there is a lower concentration of poverty. These features have an impact on the profile of social assistance beneficiaries, and there is a considerable difference in the intensity and forms of poverty in the two cities.

From these examples, two important factors emerge regarding methodology, and allow us to go beyond both a purely descriptive level or an interpretation that tries to fit everything into a national model of welfare and poverty. Firstly, we have identified the existence of a 'regional factor', and secondly, the influence of social divisions and heterogeneity.

The former is highly significant, as we have already pointed out, in the case of the German and Italian cities, but also in the Spanish cities of Barcelona and Vitoria, in so far as they belong to two different autonomous regions. The different regional locations are less important for the French cities analysed in our study, and also for the Portuguese cities of Lisbon and Porto; although Porto is in the centre of a region characterised by dynamic small and medium-size agricultural activities and traditional industries that have been more open than those in Lisbon to the recent trend towards decentralisation. Only the two Swedish cities, which lie in the same coastal region in the south-west, are unaffected by the regional element.

The second factor to emerge from the comparisons between Milan and Turin, and also Rennes and Saint Etienne, is related to the question of social homogeneity/dishomogeneity. There appear to be three different models. The first one is the model of Turin and Saint Etienne, which are cities where social divisions and segregation are important. The situation reflects the interplay between the social divisions that developed during industrialisation, and the process of de-industrialisation. These features are found too, though in different versions, in Bremen and Vitoria. The second model is that of Milan, which represents a case of heterogeneity developed in a complex way over a long period. In their own fashion, Barcelona and Lisbon are close to this second model. Finally, there is Rennes, where a high level of homogeneity has persisted over time. Though in different situations, Halle and Porto have similar characteristics.

In Cosenza, social homogeneity is the result of lack of change and of economic marginality. The Swedish cities on the other hand constitute mixed cases. Whereas they started out with strong social and cultural homogeneity, sustained during industrialisation by the development of universalistic welfare, this is now complicated by the impact of Third World immigration.

Within the social homogeneity/dishomogeneity dimension, three distinct elements play an important role: the demographic composition of the population in terms of age and gender, the distribution of occupational and educational groups, and the characteristics of the immigrant population. All three are crucial in defining patterns of vulnerability to poverty, as well as in shaping collective ideas about who the poor are.

Demographic and market transitions have contributed to the creation of a number of highly vulnerable social categories within the able-bodied – the long-term unemployed, precarious workers, marginalised immigrants, discriminated minorities, socially isolated individuals and single mothers. These categories are not evenly distributed in the cities examined in this study. There is, above all, a distinct difference between the cities in Northern and Central Europe and those in Southern Europe. In the former, the critical issues relate to Third World or Eastern European immigrants (or, in France, their naturalised progeny)[3], the increasing fragility of marriages and the social isolation of a growing number of individuals. In the south, the impact of immigration and break-up of the nuclear family is less pronounced. Immigration from less developed countries is more recent and still represents only a relatively small percentage of the population. Rates of divorce and births out of wedlock are rising slowly from very low levels. But the employment crisis is having a noticeable affect on the living standards of many families (above all those supported by a single earner) and on the chances of employment for an increasing number of the young and women.

Milan and Turin, although they belong to Southern Europe, lie close to the midpoint between the two syndromes. Both cities have more immigrants and a higher fragility of marriages compared to the Italian and Southern European average. Particularly in the case of Milan, where joblessness has never reached worrying levels, and insecure and informal jobs are not widespread as the main source of income for individuals and households, poverty is for the most part linked to social isolation of family-less low income older people. It also affects young and middle-aged adults, who for some reason have broken their family ties and social networks, and most of all it hits foreign immigrants.

Another important difference exists between the cities with a strong industrial tradition, an established working-class and a trades unionist culture, and those that have never attracted traditional Fordist industry, but are administrative, financial or commercial centres. This contrast is found in four of the six countries in our study. The exceptions are Sweden, where both Gothenburg and Helsingborg have a similar tradition as harbour towns[4], and Germany, where both Bremen and Halle are industrial cities. Saint Etienne, Turin, Vitoria and Porto have a stronger manufacturing tradition than Milan, Barcelona, Lisbon and, to a lesser degree, Rennes. The latter, in fact, are also administrative, financial and commercial centres, and have a more diversified employment structure and culture.

Within this classification, the case of Cosenza remains isolated, being more similar to cities in the less developed regions of Spain and Portugal. The city's population, as well as its unemployment rate, swelled due to immigration from the rural countryside, where small farmers could not produce enough to survive. Unemployment worsened further once the restructuring and de-industrialisation processes in northern Italy in the 1980s and 1990s radically reduced the emigration outflow, without there being any development of locally based enterprises.

The more markedly manufacturing complexion of some of the other cities has a dual effect on the welfare context: the changes in industry, which lead to greater economic and social vulnerability, and the local culture and mix of actors involved in welfare provision. Manufacturing, port or mining towns with a Fordist tradition have been more severely hit by industrial restructuring and a contraction of job opportunities. Rates of unemployment are generally higher than the regional average and, above all, reinsertion in work is difficult for those with poor vocational skills or chequered work and contributory biographies. All this is taking place in areas that up to 30 years ago were drawing in large numbers of workers from outside – foreign immigrants or migrants from less developed regions – radically altering the conditions in which local welfare operated. In the space of one generation, welfare efforts have had to switch from dealing with problems connected with the social integration (rather than occupational integration) of newcomers, to tackling the persistent difficulties of redundant workers or second-generation immigrants in finding work. In the north, these are frequently foreigners or naturalised citizens, and in the south are from less developed regions and rural areas. In both cases the poorly educated are the most affected. At the same time, these areas are receiving new waves of immigrants who are experiencing even greater problems of integration than their predecessors. In some of these cities, such as Bremen, Gothenburg and Helsingborg, the steady influx of asylum seekers and immigrants from Eastern Europe and the former Yugoslavia has significantly altered the traditional balance of local social assistance[5].

As to welfare culture, the Fordist industrial tradition led to a greater focus on measures favouring work insertion. In addition, secular and trades union associations have supplanted the traditional charity traditions to a greater extent than in other, more diversified, cities. This is particularly evident in the case of Turin, compared to Milan. In fact, in the former city, notwithstanding the presence of a long-standing tradition of religious institutions working with less privileged groups[6], there is also a widely shared consensus that the municipality and public sector should take the lead in providing social assistance and developing social integration measures. Further, a strong trades union culture tends to bolster the universalistic orientation of the local welfare programmes. In Milan, on the other hand, at least since the 1970s, the municipality has taken a residual role in social assistance, leaving space for charitable institutions such as Caritas and San Vincenzo.

The role of trades unions should not be under-evaluated in Southern European cities. Where there is a wide divergence in welfare programmes at the national level, cities with an industrial and trades union tradition tend to have more generous and more universalistic social assistance measures than the sometime richer but traditionally more socially heterogeneous ones. This is the case of Vitoria and Turin with respect to Barcelona and Milan.

City size – metropolitan versus medium-sized cities – certainly has an important influence in shaping local social formations, as well as the concentration of vulnerable social groups (see for example, Castel, 1995; Mingione, 1997; Reyneri, 1996; Sassen, 1991, 1996). In our study, however, it does not appear to have a particular role in the formation of local welfare systems. Possibly this is due to the fact that the three metropolitan cities in our sample – Milan, Barcelona and Lisbon – are all located in Southern Europe, where there is the highest intra-country diversity in local welfare systems. This makes it difficult to fully test the importance of city size within intra-country, as well as cross-country comparisons.

The local construction of poverty

Local profiles of the poor in a historical perspective

The nature of the recent economic transformation varies considerably among the cities. It depends largely on the industrial structure determined by their economic tradition and on developments since the Second World War. Another influence is the varying impact of current processes of industrial transformation and 'tertiarisation'. Geographical location and the relationship with international trade and foreign capital are also important factors in explaining the diversity between cities, resulting in different degrees of vulnerability to poverty and social exclusion. We should, therefore, look firstly at the formation of the cities' economic and employment structures and at the recent changes taking place.

Some cities (such as Barcelona, Milan and Saint Etienne) have an industrial tradition going back to the 19th century, or even further. Other cities (Rennes and Turin) were regional administrative and service centres until the beginning of the 20th century, undergoing intense industrialisation only in the inter-war period. In this case, whereas Turin became an important mono-industrial automobile manufacturing centre, the major role of Rennes, both socially and economically, remained that of capital of Brittany and university town, despite the location of the Citroën manufacturing plant. Halle, on the other hand, developed a strong industrial specialisation in export-oriented chemical production in the postwar socialist period, and subsequently faced a crisis after reunification. Cosenza is a weakly industrialised city in a relatively undeveloped regional context, where it has the role of administrative and service centre. Finally, the other cities (Gothenburg, Helsingborg, Lisbon, Porto and Bremen) have benefited from their coastal location, which provided favourable conditions for economic development as trading and manufacturing centres, with specialisations ranging from shipbuilding to chemicals.

The economic changes that occurred after the Second World War were crucial in shaping the economic structure of all the cities in the early 1970s, affecting their employment characteristics, as well as their class and urban structure. Some experienced an economic boom induced by the process of industrialisation, which led to a growing demand for labour and created a new working-class in the manufacturing industry. But the patterns of industrialisation occurring in these cities were quite different. In some (Turin and Saint Etienne), it was based on large-scale manufacturing, which meant that they became the location of mass production factories, although there were also numerous small and medium-sized industrial firms. Particularly in Saint Etienne, these smaller businesses are now playing an important role in new developments in the local economy. Milan extended its already wide industrial mix and intensified its role as the financial and advanced economic services centre for Southern Europe. Halle became one of the most important export-oriented chemical centres in Eastern Europe. Vitoria, which started out as the centre of a dynamic export-oriented agricultural district, began to attract foreign investors and became very dependent on the international market. The same occurred a decade later in Porto. Other cities (Barcelona, Lisbon, and until very recently Porto), following their long industrial tradition, developed a manufacturing sector based mainly on small or medium-sized factories within the context of an economically influential metropolitan area. Barcelona had a Fordist period when it became the location for Seat and related industries in the 1960s. This, however, happened late enough to allow the survival and development of a strong system of small and medium-sized industries. Other cities (Gothenburg, Bremen and Helsingborg) were able to combine, in a relatively balanced form, the emerging industrial sector with their traditional commercial and service activities (although the first two specialised in shipbuilding, which became a factor of vulnerability in the 1980s). Still others followed a different pattern, either focusing on their tertiary sector vocation, with only weak industrialisation (Cosenza), or benefiting from industrial decentralisation policy and setting up high-technology industries integrated with an upgraded tertiary sector (Rennes).

Those cities which based their postwar industrial development on heavy industries (Turin, Bremen, Saint Etienne and Vitoria), as well as those which followed a more complex industrial pattern (Milan and Barcelona), experienced a growth of population with a significant increase in the number of blue-collar workers and a strong polarisation of the labour market. Social integration occurred through work, but was not accompanied by a spatial or cultural integration. This led, in some cases, to the creation of densely populated working-class districts within the city (Saint Etienne, Turin, Vitoria), or in suburban areas (Milan, Barcelona, Bremen). In the long run, the first type of concentration turned out to be more divisive and segregated than the second. The Swedish cities too had a tendency to social polarisation and segregation, but this was attenuated by the decreasing income inequalities, at least up to the beginning of the 1990s. In contrast, in a city such as Rennes, where economic growth was mostly based on innovative and dynamic industries and a strong, well developed tertiary sector, spatial integration did result. Here, a weaker working-class enabled the development of a more homogeneous and non-polarised social structure, dominated by a large class of white-collar workers, who had a strong influence on the urban development of the city. Up until German reunification, the least segregated and divided city in our sample, as might be expected, was Halle. In recent years the situation seems to be slowly changing, as newly affluent strata, highly skilled white-collar workers, the self-employed and professionals, move out from the old social housing districts to refurbished buildings or new suburban districts. This leaves behind in declining urban districts the population most prone to difficulties. Finally, Cosenza in the 1970s was still coping with a wave of urban growth produced by the decline in traditional agricultural activities in the surrounding region. Local industrialisation remained weak, and this created a large marginalised population with unstable employment in the building industry or services, housed in low-quality dwellings in the new suburbs.

After the oil crisis of the 1970s – but rather later in the case of Halle and the Portuguese cities – the transformations in the economy had important consequences for the industrial and employment structure of all the cities, as well as their class composition and demographic structure. These transformations have modified the way in which poverty occurs and revealed two areas of risk that both lead to vulnerability: the level of unemployment (and hence the difficulty of finding a job) and the existence of both old and new minorities or immigrant groups. These two phenomena interact with changes in the family situation, which also affect the labour offer: increasing participation by women (particularly mothers) in the labour market, together with growing marriage instability. The latter is weakening the male breadwinner model on which the economic survival of women and children and the welfare systems in Central and Southern Europe were based (and to a large degree still are)[7]. To a lesser degree, the increasing independence of young people within the family tends to weaken the traditional family model. These changes are in general far more pronounced in Northern and Central European cities, than in Southern Europe. However, both Turin and Milan have marital instability rates more similar to Germany and France than southern Italy or Portugal. Furthermore, the impact of all these changes differs, of course, according to the starting level. Thus, marital instability has little impact on the economic insecurity of women and children, or on the number of women in the labour force in the Swedish cities and in Halle, where there has been a high proportion of working women for decades. On the contrary, in other cities marital instability has been a serious cause of vulnerability for women and children, and one of the reasons for the increase in the number of working women.

Let us now analyse these dimensions in each of the 13 cities, starting with changes in the occupational structure and employment opportunities.

During the decade 1981-91, the number of jobs in the manufacturing industry fell by 26% in Turin and 36% in Milan. In the same period, there was a growth in service employment, due partly to industrial restructuring and partly associated with new developments in advanced financial and economic services. These features, characteristic of post-industrial economies, have generated a twofold trend: a rise in unemployment and the diffusion of insecure low-wage jobs in services, together with an increase in the number of white-collar workers in low-skilled, precarious jobs with low earnings. The increasing polarisation of employment is also reflected in the spatial concentration of vulnerable social groups and in the poverty associated with unemployment (affecting women and young people especially), insecure jobs and low wages. A similar period of economic crisis began in Vitoria in the 1990s. After Spain joined the EEC in 1986, the effect was a rise in long-term unemployment due to the loss of jobs in manufacturing for the low skilled (thus generating unemployment among middle-aged workers) and the lack of jobs for women and young first-time jobseekers. The considerable growth of the service sector in Vitoria, especially in the period 1985-90, was insufficient to provide jobs for the growing numbers looking for work (the unemployment rate in 1995 reached 12.6%).

Saint Etienne entered a period of economic crisis in the early 1970s. This derived from endogenous factors – the decline in the industries that had led its postwar development – and exogenous causes connected with its geographical location. It suffered from its proximity to Lyon, which proved more attractive for the more dynamic high-tech industries and services. Those hit most by unemployment were the less skilled workers (rates of unemployment reached 13%). But, unlike Milan and to some extent Barcelona, where the decline in manufacturing employment was offset by expansion in new advanced sectors, in Saint Etienne the increasing precariousness of the labour market affected not only the traditional working-class, but also young people (in France and Southern Europe even the more skilled faced problems in finding jobs).

In Halle, the crisis in employment in manufacturing occurred after reunification (in 1995 the rate of unemployment reached 16.2%). It involved women and young people on a massive scale, although this was partly attenuated by huge investment in active employment policies and by the departure of a large number of foreign residents (Cubans and East European guest workers).

Gothenburg and Bremen, with relatively similar industrial structures based on shipbuilding, were affected differently by the wave of industrial restructuring. In both cases, it led to a considerable decline in manufacturing employment, the drastic scaling-down of shipbuilding and the development of new industrial sectors. In Gothenburg, the protectionism of the Swedish economy together with large investments in new sectors requiring a highly educated and skilled labour force, as well as the fact that the city is a major university centre, delayed the employment crisis until the early 1990s and attenuated its impact. Nevertheless, there has been rising unemployment since then, mostly affecting young adults (aged 18-24) and migrants. In Bremen, the employment crisis began in the early 1980s, but struck again in the 1990s, becoming far more severe (in 1995 unemployment rates were 13%, against

7.6% in the Swedish cities). Long-term unemployment is affecting the very young, poorly skilled labour market entrants, middle-aged and senior workers and the new wave of migrants and asylum seekers who tend to have badly paid, precarious jobs. Helsingborg has a recent history similar to that of Gothenburg. Its importance as the main trading link with Denmark and its small size protected it from being more seriously hit by the decline in the chemicals industry. But at the same time, these factors, together with the fact that it is not an important university centre, have made it less attractive for the development of new high-tech industries and services.

Vitoria, the capital of an agricultural province within an industrial region, achieved a balance of employment in the industrial and service sectors in the mid-1980s. The creation of the regional Autonomous Government in the city in the 1980s generated public employment. However, the industrial recession in the early 1990s produced large numbers of unemployed people, some of whom were workers who had come to Vitoria during the rapid urbanisation of 1960-80, others are their children. These internal migrants originate from the south of Spain. Their level of formal education is generally low, and they tend to concentrate in three districts of the city, remaining weakly integrated with the local Basque culture.

A distinctive employment pattern is found in Barcelona. This city suffered economic decline in the late 1970s, when the traditional manufacturing sector suffered economic difficulty. The first phase of the industrial crisis, which hit the textile sector in particular, reduced income-creating opportunities for the working-class, and the most vulnerable became jobless, with little chance of finding new jobs. This led to a high level of unemployment by the mid-1980s. However, the economic recession in Barcelona had a far less serious effect on employment than in other Spanish cities. This was due to a number of factors, including the diversified nature of industry, the city's location in an industrial metropolitan area with sectors that attracted large amounts of foreign capital, and the development of local policies to support economic restructuring. Moreover, as in the case of Milan, the growth of the service sector, aided by a diffused informal sector, has made it possible to keep unemployment in check over the last decade – those at risk being mostly young entrants and middle-aged people (in Barcelona unemployment, to date, never exceeds 10%).

Cosenza finds itself in the opposite situation. As already mentioned, the city is located in an underdeveloped region in the south of Italy. It is characterised by a weak industrial base and an extensive tertiary sector, which absorbs over 80% of the employed population, involving mostly public and traditional services. The creation of a new university on the outskirts of the town in the early 1970s, while helping many young people to pursue higher education without having to leave the region, did not succeed in attracting investment and high technology enterprises. The decline in local industrial employment since the early 1980s (due partly to cuts in public investment and shrinkage in construction activity), together with the end of migration abroad or to other Italian regions, caused a very high (over 30%) unemployment rate, mostly among young adults, male and female. The majority are first-job seekers who have little hope of obtaining regular employment, given the poor prospects of the local labour market. But they also have little incentive to move, given the higher cost of living in the richer Italian regions, and the possibility, if they remain in Cosenza, of participating in a 'household economy', where partial incomes from different sources, including socially assisted jobs and jobs in the informal market, are pooled and shared.

Unlike Cosenza, the other cities where the public and private service sector is dominant, such as Rennes (where this sector employs almost 70% of the total working population), Lisbon or Porto (the centre of an important metropolitan region), were less affected by the crisis in the industrial sector. Between 1980 and 1990, the unemployment rate in Lisbon remained constant (7.3%), and in Porto even declined (6.9%). Rennes was affected to some extent by industrial stagnation after the mid-1970s, when rising unemployment hit mainly women and young people. However, in the long run these employment difficulties were counterbalanced by the development of high-tech industries and services based on specialised education, promoted by the importance of the local university (as in the case of Milan and Barcelona, unemployment never exceeded 10%, even in the worst period). Young adults (aged above 25) with relatively high levels of education still have difficulty in finding a good long-term job and apply for the *Revenue Minimum d'Insertion* (RMI), which gives the programme a particularly unusual shape, as will be discussed later.

Employment problems thus contribute in very different ways to the local construction of poverty: from their extremely limited role in Milan to their devastating impact in Cosenza. Rennes and the Swedish cities are affected to a limited extent by unemployment, due not only to the local economic development model, but also to effective and innovative social policies. Then there are Barcelona and the Portuguese cities, where unemployment is not very high and where there are, in any case, ample opportunities for jobs in the informal economy. All the other cities are seriously affected by the employment crisis, though none so severely as Cosenza (both in terms of the level and of the local actors' inability to activate policy responses).

This picture now needs to be re-examined in the light of the second area of risk – the presence of vulnerable groups of migrants or other minorities. These too are unevenly distributed among the cities: ranging from Bremen with the highest level to Halle with the lowest. The two Portuguese cities, Rennes, Cosenza, Barcelona and Vitoria also have relatively few foreign immigrants and minorities, although in these cities the number of foreign residents has been increasing in recent years. Milan and Turin also fall in an intermediate position. The number of immigrants from developing countries is rising fast, and they face insecure employment, as well as serious housing and social insertion problems. At the same time, the least educated second-generation immigrants from southern Italy face similar difficulties. This dual trend is more marked in Turin as it has a larger traditional working-class, some of whom are recent immigrants from the south, low skilled and very near the poverty threshold. To a lesser extent this dual trend also exists in Milan. In this respect, Saint Etienne is similar to Turin. The population most at risk are those of North African origin with French citizenship. These workers were attracted by the industrial expansion of the 1960s, and then made redundant and marginalised (Paugam, 1999) through the process of industrial restructuring. The situation is different in Bremen and the Swedish cities, since the majority of industrial immigrants have not been given citizenship and now mix with new waves of asylum seekers and recent immigrants. Here, as pointed out by Leisering and Leibfried (1999), for West German cities in general and Bremen in particular, foreign immigrants (mainly of Turkish, Yugoslavian, North African and East European origins) constitute a relatively high proportion of residents (over 10%) and now constitute a majority of the local poor.

Finally, let us briefly look at how marital instability and the lack of family support affect the local construction of poverty in the cities. This is in fact a two-sided problem. The impact of demographic transformations (the number of one-parent families, isolated single-person households, increasing individualisation, marital instability and so on) depends not only on the level of marriage and family 'frailty' and the level of welfare assistance provided by family and kin. It also depends on the degree to which it is possible for individuals – lone mothers, the young, the frail elderly – to set up a household of their own and to claim resources in their own right, not only on the basis of family and kin membership. It depends, therefore, on the degree of 'de-familisation' (in access to income and care) allowed by the State and the market (see Hobson, 1989; Orloff, 1993; Saraceno, 1997; Esping-Andersen, 1999). In cases where frailty is high, but individual entitlements are low, both in the market and the welfare state, the lack of family-kin support may have devastating effects on the seriousness of poverty, as noted for the ghetto poor in the USA (for example, Katz, 1993; Massey and Denton, 1993; Wilson, 1987, 1993, 1996). Vice versa, as indicated by the differing incidence of poverty among lone mothers in the various countries (for example, Lewis, 1997b; Pedersen, 2000), a high degree of marital instability and a high degree of individualisation of rights and responsibilities can occur without causing high rates of poverty either for women or for children. This is possible if women have a high rate of participation in the labour force and support is available for those in need (through social services and income support). Only where mothers do not work and social assistance income support is stigmatised (as in the UK and the US) or unavailable (as in many Italian cities), can marriage break-up represent a serious economic risk. In this case, the availability of family-kin support may make a crucial difference. At the same time, the extended or prolonged expectation of family solidarity may result in poor families being overloaded with demands. This then leads to the phenomenon of 'familisation' of poverty: where the whole family is made vulnerable through the need to support its members, and individuals fail to become financially and socially independent.

Saint Etienne and Halle are probably the cities where a high level of family instability combines most unfavourably with a lack of public support, but for different reasons. In Saint Etienne, the adult children of immigrant workers are unlikely to live with their parents or to receive kinship support, and also find it difficult to get stable, adequately paid work. In these conditions, it is difficult for the local RMI programmes to deliver sufficient training and work insertion contracts. In Halle, a family tradition that developed in the socialist period based on easy divorce, high female participation in the labour market and limited kinship help, finds it very difficult to cope with the unemployment that followed German reunification[8].

Bremen, Turin and Milan are in an intermediate position: a relatively marked tendency to individualisation and marital instability is creating new risks for socially isolated individuals and lone-parent households. In Bremen these risks are countered by relatively generous local welfare, but as yet there are few incentives for mothers of young children to enter the labour market. Milan has the advantage of a favourable labour market situation, although middle-aged low-skilled lone mothers returning to work may have to accept low paid jobs in the traditional service sector. There is generally a sharp division between 'the employable' and 'the unemployable'. The latter includes not only very low-skilled people, but also young people without families, and adults of both genders whose personal history or lifestyle puts them outside the acknowledged norm: for example, drug addicts, mentally ill people, former prison inmates. The situation in Turin for those without family support seems more difficult than in Milan from the point of view of market resources, but is eased to some extent by social assistance policies. Since the early 1980s, these have targeted lone mothers (plus older people and children) as a special deserving category of beneficiaries, although underlying these policies there is a legally based expectation of family-kin solidarity.

In Rennes, Barcelona and Vitoria, family instability and lack of kinship support appear to be less widespread, although lone parents are fast on the increase, as in the northern Italian cities. In the case of Rennes, the growing number of single parents is protected, at least in part, by local social policies and individualisation of entitlements. In Barcelona, the importance of family and kinship support is combined with a large and dynamic informal labour market. Vitoria is more similar to Turin, but marriage break-up and social division in the city are certainly less serious, in part as a consequence of a much smaller population.

The various combinations of areas of tension (Table 2.1) shape the clustering of the cities. It differs, at least in part, from that suggested at the outset. In certain respects, Halle and Cosenza are alike, even though the former is an industrial centre and the latter the least industrialised city in the ESOPO sample. Both are characterised by serious employment problems that affect, almost exclusively, the local population. In both, local welfare is weak, though for different reasons. In Halle, the combination of a recently established welfare system – still little used – and generous work insertion programmes, limits social assistance to income support. In Cosenza, the underlying problem is a scarcity of resources and employment opportunities in the face of widespread need. In the former case, the local welfare situation is the result of the 'shock' to the system caused by reunification, whereas in the latter case the situation is dictated by a long history of immigration from rural areas and a lack of industrial development. The system has adapted to chronic forms of economic difficulty which was rendered more acute with the end, in the late 1970s, of mass emigration and the contraction in manufacturing. But whereas in Halle there is only weak family support and a highly

Table 2.1: Impact of socioeconomic factors on the local construction of poverty in the sample 13 cities

Cities	Unemployment/ poor jobs	Immigration/ minorities	Weak familiy ties versus family support
Barcelona	Intermediate	Low	Intermediate v High
Bremen	High	Very high	High v Intermediate
Cosenza	Very high	Low	Very low v High
Gothenburg	Intermediate	High	Very high v Very low
Halle	High	Very low	High v Intermediate
Helsingborg	Intermediate	High	Very high v Very low
Lisbon	Low	Low	Very low v High
Milan	Very low	Intermediate	High v Intermediate
Porto	Low	Low	Very low v High
Rennes	Very low	Low	Intermediate v Intermediate
Saint Etienne	High	High	High v Intermediate
Turin	High	Intermediate	High v Intermediate
Vitoria	High	Low	Intermediate v High

individualised context, in Cosenza both family-kin and informal support are quite strong, leading to 'familisation' of poverty.

There is also a similarity between the two cases with relatively few employment problems: Milan and Rennes. In both cities, de-industrialisation has been balanced by the growth of the tertiary sector; in neither are immigrants or minorities central to problems of poverty, even though they are becoming increasingly important in Milan. The two cities are also similar in terms of the weakening of family support, although not to the degree found in Scandinavian and English-speaking countries. However, in a certain sense, the institutional responses are opposite in the two cities: Rennes is one of the pilot French cities in the development of new public social policies, whereas in Milan the local authority is neither very generous nor innovative. Innovation in welfare is left to the initiative of the third sector, with the municipality acting mostly as a financing agent. Here too, it is clear that strong similarities in the local construction of poverty are not automatically reflected in the local welfare set-up.

We then have four cases – Bremen, Saint Etienne and the Swedish cities – in which the vulnerability of immigrants and minorities is decidedly a priority[9]. Problems of job insertion are combined with the difficulty of social integration, notwithstanding the support offered by families and communities, which for most immigrant groups maintain a strong role of solidarity. These are four industrial cities where the transformations of the employment structure have been far-reaching. In Bremen, and to a lesser extent in the Swedish cities, the immigrant-specific dimension of poverty has been further heightened in the 1990s by new arrivals, especially asylum seekers.

The case of Turin is rather similar to the four cities mentioned previously, in so far as the issue of immigration has been a long-standing feature of both the specific demography of poverty and the issues facing social assistance policies, although the features and origins of immigration changed dramatically in the 1990s: immigrants no longer arrived from the southern Italian regions, but from North Africa and, more recently, from the Eastern European countries. Possibly this explicit need to deal with social integration issues (and not only poverty) explains the relatively integrated approach to social assistance in this city, and its propensity to innovation and systematic rethinking of its policies.

Immigration (mostly from North Africa) also plays an important role in Saint Etienne, but in a way that renders this city unique in our sample. Not only do many of the immigrants, as everywhere in France, have French citizenship, but they also have their own representatives and associations that negotiate with the municipality on matters concerning social policy. Thus, they are not only an important group of beneficiaries but also, at least to some degree, a partner in their implementation.

Immigrants and minorities do not constitute a significant problem in the Spanish and Portuguese cities. Vulnerability due to unemployment affects mainly the local population, as in Halle and Cosenza. However, unlike Halle, social welfare is still heavily dependent on family-kin solidarity and a network of, mostly religious, charities. Unlike Cosenza, not only can the beneficiaries more easily integrate formal employment opportunities with informal ones, but at the time of our study the Spanish cities had already developed a kind of universal, last resort minimum income scheme, in addition to family support and traditional charity. Thus the risk of 'familisation of poverty' due to overburdening is somewhat reduced. The Portuguese cities, which at the time of study seemed more similar to many Italian ones with their lack of a universal minimum income, were already moving towards the introduction of a minimum income scheme. This was inspired, like the Spanish one, by the French RMI, although the income threshold was set at a much lower level.

Institutional structure and welfare mix in local systems

The analytical framework

We now direct our attention to the way in which social assistance measures, such as minimum income benefit, become structured between the public sphere, the third sector (intermediate organisations and the Church) and private responsibilities.

The local form of anti-poverty strategies reflect the type of economic development, political system and culture in the specific city or region. These bring into play concepts of integration, citizenship, public action and local community, and the way that they are defined at the local level. These are, therefore, determining elements in defining 'local systems of welfare' in the wider sense, that is as anti-poverty strategies constructed locally. The structure of the local fabric has a substantial effect on the 'efficiency' of an anti-poverty strategy. At least, it constitutes an essential element to take into account in interpreting local situations, although these are also shaped to a greater or lesser degree by national regulations and welfare cultures.

Figure 2.2 synthesises the heart of our approach and the way in which we present each local context. It should also act as a reminder that, as far as the treatment of poverty through welfare is concerned, it is important not only to capture the relations between the State, the market and civil society but also to go more deeply, attempting to define the forms and dynamics of each of these three dimensions. For the first, rather than simply talking about 'the State', we need to examine public and institutional regulation and to explain its local roots, how it is organised, its extent and the way it intervenes (linking these with the other two dimensions). Although the ESOPO project did not deal in detail with the second aspect, the market, it should be noted that this is constructed differently from one country to another, and even from one region to another. Its capacity for social integration also, demonstrably, varies a great deal. Many resources may be integrated or harnessed by the workings and logic of the economy. As a result, the capacity of the market to produce poverty also depends on the way in which the economy is organised in a given cultural and social context (one only has to think of cities within the so called 'third Italy' area).

The third and final dimension, civil society, which was revealed by our research to be fundamental, is actually split in two. On the one hand, it relates to the content and internal organisation of the third sector, on the other hand to the way in which family-kin responsibilities are

Figure 2.2: The structure of local welfare systems

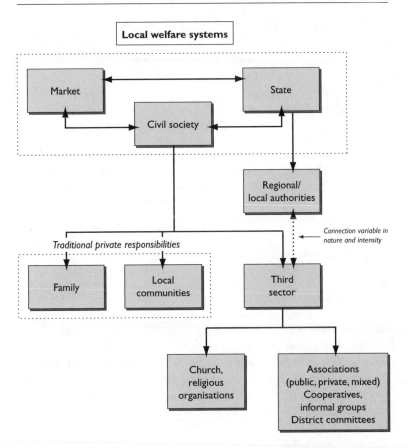

institutionally regulated and practically played out. These two sub-dimensions rest on various elements. With regard to the family, we may point to patterns of organisation and stability, the cultural models shaping its gender and intergenerational roles and patterns of solidarity, legal regulations concerning expected financial responsibility towards family and kin; with regard to the third sector we may point to the presence, strength, size, visibility, ideological outlook of non-profit and volunteer associations and groups, as well as of the Church organisations. In addition to these, attention must be paid to the growing, but differential role allocated to non-profit enterprises (social cooperatives and the like), both in providing services and in creating job opportunities for vulnerable workers. This dual role of the third sector may develop within forms of explicit partnership with local governments or through some form of implicit division of responsibilities.

Our presentation of the different local contexts therefore aims both to give a precise account of the social framework within which the anti-poverty strategies operate, and to bring out the complexity and diversity of local configurations dealing with poverty.

The diversity of local models of welfare

Table 2.2 summarises the main characteristics of each local model: in the interplay of the role and institutional organisation of the public sector, the role of the third sector and of family and informal networks. The specific measures that we have studied in the ESOPO project, which will be analysed in Chapter Three (and synthetically described in the Appendix), must thus be set within this broader context.

Gothenburg and Helsingborg

These Swedish cities are characterised by their economic, social and cultural homogeneity and by the fundamental role of public regulation in the local welfare system. The strong local autonomy of the Swedish welfare system does not translate into major differences between the institutional systems concerned with the administration of minimum income benefit in the two cities. This homogeneity is greatly indebted to the strong institutionalisation of social citizenship at the national level, and to a widely shared consensus on the crucial role of the welfare state in defining what Swedish citizenship is about. It may also be amplified by the similarity between these two cities and, possibly by their geographical proximity.

This homogeneity is reinforced by the hegemony of public regulation and, above all, by the low mobilisation of local resources connected with the third sector, which could otherwise introduce differences at a local level. In other words, in the Swedish case, strong decentralisation and local autonomy in a largely homogeneous cultural and territorial context does not produce great diversity in local systems of anti-poverty strategies. In both Gothenburg and Helsingborg, programmes and actions connected with minimum income benefit come essentially within the public sphere, placing few demands either on the third sector or on family-kin responsibilities.

However, the strong institutionalisation and bureaucratisation of the local system does not result in a uniform treatment of claimants. Actions

Table 2.2: Dimensions that play a part in the local construction of welfare, in the field of social assistance for disadvantaged populations

	Institutional organisation	Participation of the third sector and role of informal responsibility
Gothenburg Helsingborg	• Central role of municipal authorities, although the State remains present through financing, setting of criteria and implementation of complementary provisions • Unlimited resources	• Hegemony of public social services • Marginal role of associations and/or religious institutions • Low demand on family obligations
Rennes	• The State is mainly responsible, but relies on local authorities. The city council is at the centre of the local strategy within a relatively integrated local institutional system. Distribution of responsibilities on a territorial (neighbourhood, district) basis under the control of the city government • Unlimited resources	• Third sector associations and volunteer groups called upon to set up accompanying measures and more generally support systems, but with weak decision-making and negotiating powers • Marginal role of the Catholic Church and religious associations • Low mobilisation of informal responsibilities
Saint Etienne	• The State is mainly responsible, but it relies on local authorities for implementation. • The local system is fairly fragmented. The central actor is the *Département*. The division of tasks between city and *Conseil Général* (Département Council) is based on social categories suffering from insecurity, not on administrative boundaries • Unlimited resources	• Third sector associations and volunteer groups called upon to set up accompanying measures and more generally support systems, but with weak decision-making and negotiating powers • Marginal role of the Catholic Church and religious associations • Low mobilisation of informal responsibilities
Bremen	• Highly decentralised to *Länder* and municipal authorities • Unlimited resources	• Important role of associations in emergency action or in particular spheres (care needs, housing, psychological support, etc) • Charitable and religious organisations are also very active among their own members • Encouragement to mobilise family obligations, linked with the logic of the family dimension of welfare

continued

Table 2.2: Dimensions that play a part in the local construction of welfare, in the field of social assistance for disadvantaged populations (contd)

	Institutional organisation	Participation of the third sector and role of informal responsibility
Halle	• Highly decentralised to *Länder* and municipal authorities • Unlimited resources	• Active participation of associations in support, information and emergency services • Modest role of the churches and religious associations • Limited demands on family obligations
Milan	• Responsibility of the municipal authorities • Fragmented, selective, not very extensive network of public institutions • Limited resources	• Decisive role of traditional religious associations (*Caritas* and *San Vincenzo*) • Formal involvement of associations and social cooperatives • Recourse to family obligations • Presence of an informal sector in the economy
Turin	• Responsibility of the municipal authorities • Fairly dense, well-organised public institutional network • Limited resources	• Modest role of religious charities • Formal involvement of associations and cooperatives • Mobilisation of family obligations • Presence of an informal sector in the economy
Cosenza	• Responsibility of the municipal authorities • Disorganised, poor, patronage network of public institutions • Low level of resources	• Participation of associations and welfare cooperatives with few resources • Strong demands on family obligations and informal community networks • Widespread, but poor, informal sector in the economy
Barcelona	• Strong regional and local autonomy • Public sector is important, but not extensive or well-organised	• Charity (*Caritas*) has maintained an important role, but is losing influence • Significant recourse to extended family obligation • Important presence of an informal sector in the economy
Vitoria	• Strong regional and local autonomy • The institutionalisation of social services is fairly established	• Charity intervenes for the most excluded • Mobilisation of extended family obligations
Lisbon Porto	• State (national government) responsibilities • Low level of resources	• Essential role of charities at district level (especially Santa Casa da Misericordia in Lisbon) • Low participation of other types of associations • Mobilisation of family obligations • Recourse to the informal economy

are individualised, but are clearly related to the hegemony of public regulation. The short time that people normally stay on minimum income benefit is largely explained by the existence of a wide range of training and job insertion programmes, together with unemployment benefits that may be earned through virtually any job experience, including socially assisted jobs, in a relatively dynamic labour market. The welfare system is all the more efficient because the population involved is culturally homogeneous and well informed. However, these features are increasingly being called into question by the presence of immigrant populations whose needs and cultural understandings may differ from those of Swedish natives. This, in turn, could lead to a partial de-bureaucratisation and stronger demands on third sector associations.

Rennes and Saint Etienne

The French situation is similar to the Swedish one in the central place it gives to public regulation in organising income support, its strong institutionalisation and low mobilisation of intermediate organisations. However, the French system is less decentralised, and applies to urban contexts that differ considerably from one another, economically, institutionally and culturally. Political traditions and cultures, modes of development and institutional networks, population profiles, and the nature of poverty in the various cities, are other phenomena that oblige us to take into account specific local features, even when presented with a national, top-down policy such as the French RMI.

The humanist Christian Democratic political tradition in Rennes has contributed to developing a highly interventionist culture in the social sphere[10]. The political and cultural development of the city has been driven by the middle and upper strata of those working in the service sector. This led very early on to the promotion of social and cultural policies, and there is consequently a dense public network of social services that relies on strong inter-service collaboration. A combination of elements, such as the diffuse and strongly integrated institutional network designed to combat exclusion, and a well-developed tradition of development-based community social work[11] largely explains why the RMI has been integrated into a local system that was already well structured.

Strong public regulation and a tradition of institutionalised intervention (within the framework of a diffuse social work culture) lead to an efficient system, but one which marginalises the more informal intermediate organisations, especially if they do not fit into this highly institutionalised framework. Thus, although present, religious institutions and charitable and humanitarian associations are not central to the Rennes RMI strategy. The role of social cooperatives and third sector enterprises is also fairly limited. Job insertion contracts are negotiated directly with local market enterprises and monitored by the municipality social workers. The lack of demand on the third sector, together with the dynamism and efficacy of social assistance measures, point not only to the degree of comprehensiveness of the local welfare system, but also to its good integration in a local economic and cultural context where it finds its partners also in the market. This in turn is helped by the fact that poverty and social exclusions do not yet constitute a severe social problem.

Saint Etienne, by contrast, is facing a severe social crisis made more visible by the fact that the social categories affected by the employment crisis are mainly concentrated in social housing districts. Worst hit are the first generation immigrants who came to work in the mines and industry; but employment problems have spread to the second generation. Yet the weakening of working-class resources, including traditional forms of mutual support, did not automatically lead to the development of specific strategies by the municipality. Before the introduction of RMI, the social policies introduced by the municipality, particularly in the area of social exclusion, were not on as large a scale as in Rennes. This low level of involvement on the part of the municipality was partly compensated for by the initiative of third sector associations. Even now, these are more involved than those in Rennes in implementing and following up the RMI. Associations are called on to check on claimants and to carry out part of the work of integration. However, they are not in a position to make decisions or to negotiate with the main public actors. Overall, therefore, the system is less municipally based and less institutionalised than in Rennes. Moreover, the typical Fordist working-class institutional and political culture puts a premium on forms of organised class-based solidarity rather than community-based ones. This limits the development of a shared approach in social work and collaboration between different services and associations.

The paradoxical consequence is that, although the actors are more diversified across the public/private divide, Saint Etienne's local welfare system, compared to Rennes, seems to be more rigidly organised around the administration of RMI, and less capable of innovation. Social work is still organised on more conventional lines and mobilises fewer political, human and organisational resources.

Bremen and Halle

Germany has a highly decentralised system that confers great responsibility on the *Länder* and municipal authorities. As in Sweden and France, anti-poverty welfare systems in German cities are characterised by specific public regulation, although with a greater degree of local autonomy in assessing needs and defining the amount of support. Moreover, they have far more active institutional links with a vast network of intermediate local organisations – trades unions, occupational or religious groups[12]. The existence of a dense network of associations of this type, all contributing to social assistance, is the distinguishing feature of German welfare. Since the Middle Ages, assistance to the poor has been organised according to a division of labour between municipal authorities and charitable and ecclesiastical associations. The diversity of associations involved at the local level thus adds to differences in the pattern of public provision allowed by the federal system. The outcome is the existence of specific local systems of welfare, albeit with common basic rules and criteria.

Since reunification, a new difference has been added: that between Western and Eastern *Länder*. The extension of the West German welfare system to the *Länder* of the former East Germany has produced only partial homogenisation. Not only were there contrasts in economic conditions, but the expectations of the population, the professional culture in social services, and the actors involved in civil society also differed greatly as a result of these regions' postwar history. Substantial differences remain in the concept and organisation of anti-poverty policy in the two parts of Germany.

Halle has faced a phase of transition between the two systems of social protection and, in a broader sense, social organisation. However, an imprint of the former system remains. This was a bureaucratic structure that did not have to deal with mass unemployment or poverty; it also largely marginalised volunteer and religious associations. In the former Democratic Republic, the public sector was hegemonic – volunteer or non-profit associations were less numerous, not highly 'professional' and used very little. Even though the network of associations and charitable organisations in Halle is becoming more extensive and involved in welfare provision (especially the *Volkssolidarität*), it has not yet reached the level and diversity of the network in Bremen.

Bremen appears to be better equipped with public institutional networks that are fairly well integrated, and can also count on a well-developed social work culture and a wide range of third sector resources. Third sector organisations constitute a welfare system in its own right, which is closely interlinked with public social provision in spheres as diverse as housing, healthcare, psychological care, leisure activities and school education. Moreover, the local authorities in Bremen have developed a series of training and job insertion programmes that are quite successful. Concern over integration, the prevention of social exclusion and the formation of ghettoes seem to be the main motivating forces behind welfare policies. These give less emphasis than in Halle to the recipients' duties, but stress their willingness and capability to cooperate. They also try as much as possible to avoid the creation of forms of segregation in the city. Thus, for instance, assessment of needs can be fairly generous if this means allowing a family to remain in a more expensive apartment in a middle-class neighbourhood instead of being moved to a cheaper, but more segregated, neighbourhood.

Milan, Turin and Cosenza

Notwithstanding a long tradition of socialist local governments since the postwar years and until the early 1990s, as well as the existence of an ample range of benevolent lay and religious institutions that cater for the less privileged, since the 1980s and early 1990s public social assistance in Milan has been relatively meagre and short-term. There is no specific focus either on social integration or job insertion. Although a wide range of social services provides assistance for families in difficulty, particularly those with children, social exclusion and poverty do not command sustained or integrated attention from the municipality. Income support measures seem to be conceived for people perceived as passing through a short spell of bad luck, or too marginal and beyond hope to deserve sustained effort. Thus, the poor and socially excluded are left to the care, evaluation and discretion, of private, non-profit, charitable, and mainly religious, organisations. These often compete with each other, and for public money. Caritas and San Vincenzo are among the most important institutions in this field, but there are also many other smaller groups and institutions. The growing influx of immigrants over the last 15 years has further intensified the role of these associations, since immigrants have difficulty in benefiting from public social protection services, either because they lack entitlement or because they do not know their rights.

As in other Italian cities, the growth of the third sector, particularly in the form of social cooperatives, has in recent years been directly stimulated by national, and particularly municipal, authorities as an instrument for implementing their welfare policies. Local governments tend to contract out social services while at the same time granting fiscal and contributory benefits to social cooperatives that employ people belonging to disadvantaged social groups. In Milan, this encouragement of a welfare mix is occurring within an institutional and cultural framework in which the public sector has no (at least no longer) well established and acknowledged leading cultural or political role.

Social integration has long been a high priority concern for local government in Turin, a city now characterised by cultural and ethnic diversity. In the past, this was due to the presence of a large working-class – partly constituted of first and second generation internal immigrants – with its vulnerabilities, but also its institutions and culture. This same concern, and the focus on the integrating virtues of a steady job and a work ethic, was also shared by some of the religious orders that operated in the city since the beginning of the 20th century and which became famous for their work with the underprivileged youth, creating the first professional training schools. Turin was also one of the few Italian cities in which the controversial experiment of the 'workers priests' developed during the 1950s. All this has consolidated into a tradition of both public responsibility for social welfare and inter-institutional cooperation, including cooperation with third sector and religious associations, which has lasted through the years and through changes in political coalitions (Negri and Saraceno, 1999). The city and its welfare system are now having to deal with the problem of integrating immigrants within the context of a post-Fordist employment crisis.

Social welfare in Turin commands larger resources than in other Italian cities, is better organised and less fragmented. It strives to achieve integration with training and work insertion programmes. There is an overall stronger institutionalisation of the system as a whole, which has more numerous provisions, and a higher amount of the minimum income benefit based on a more universalistic orientation than in Milan. The role of religious and charitable organisations, although important, is on balance more modest than in Milan, and tends to integrate public policies, rather than substitute them. There is a large and growing use of social cooperatives through contracting out or within a clearly defined strategy of partnership. In this case, the public sector maintains a leading role not only financially, but also culturally. Social dialogue is a systematic feature of policy making.

Cosenza represents a different situation yet again, but one that is very common in southern Italy. In a context where poverty and unemployment are widespread, and given the absence at national level both of a decent universal unemployment indemnity and of a minimum income provision, the scarce local resources are mainly used for patronage purposes or, at best, with a high degree of discretion. This applies to the political system as a whole, where electoral consensus is sought through the redistribution of public resources either directly (through subsidies) or indirectly: patronage facilitates access to national schemes, such as invalidity benefits or socially useful jobs. Not only social assistance, but social policies in general are almost non-existent: very few social services exist, for instance, for children, families or older people. Financial assistance is limited to an occasional, derisory lump sum, since the objective is to award it to all those who apply. The benefit may be paid out once a year, at Easter or Christmas, and is subject to a high degree of discretion, recalling ancient forms of charity.

In a situation of economic stagnation and large-scale recourse to the informal economy, welfare relationships depend to a large extent on bargaining and the exertion of pressure. Networks of 'recommendation' are therefore essential, reinforcing the logic of patronage, which penalises those who do not have this particular type of social capital. The scarcity of public resources and poverty of the local economy is matched by the poverty of civil society, also in terms of the range of actors involved. Local party leaders are the main mediators of available resources. Although some religious charitable organisations, parishes and a few secular voluntary organisations offer support, the main welfare institution remains the family, including the extended kinship network. When emigration was the main way out of unemployment, this reliance on family solidarity meant that a number of local households lived off the remittances sent back by those who had emigrated. This resource is no longer available, since emigration has practically dwindled to nothing. Economic restructuring in the traditional destinations of emigration, Northern Italy and Central Europe, has changed the quality of labour demand.

Currently, the situation of Cosenza is characterised by increasing insecurity at a time when traditional patronage approaches to the redistribution of public resources are being challenged, without other changes in the situation in view.

Barcelona and Vitoria

In recent years, Barcelona has experienced a decline in the traditional working-class and an increase in service sector employees, with a rising proportion of temporary contracts. The diminishing presence of the working-class in the city has, moreover, been reinforced by the 'suburbanisation' of factories and workers' housing. At the same time, a new group among the poor are Third World immigrants, although they are less numerous than in most Southern European cities. In Barcelona they represent less than 1% of the population and most do not apply for minimum income support as they are employed either in the formal or informal economy. The extensive informal economy as well as the expansion of temporary jobs means that although job insecurity has increased, more income opportunities are available.

The regional or *Comunidad Autónoma* (Autonomous Community) government introduced a welfare law in 1984 and became responsible for the application and management of the minimum income programme (*Programa Interdepartamental de Rentas Minima de Insercion*: PIRMI) in 1990. However, implementation of the programme at the municipal level has been the responsibility of the city's social services. Prior to the introduction of the Autonomous Community programme, Caritas played a major role in taking care of the poor. But since the minimum income programme was established by law, this Catholic institution has dealt with only 10% of cases, although it retains an important role in catering for the most needy. Other voluntary organisations take care of an even smaller share. The Autonomous Community is in charge of organising, checking and guaranteeing the efficiency of the services and management of the programme. The city council is responsible for welfare planning, prevention schemes and the promotion of social assistance programmes. Within the city, each district decides the number of social care centres and deals with emergency welfare demands. Since 1992, there has been a joint welfare plan in order to coordinate public and private welfare activities in the city. There is a strong presence of private and religious third sector associations, mobilised by the public administration on a model fairly similar to that of Turin.

Voluntary associations are broadly involved in social work, and intervene on a large scale among immigrant populations. At a time when the city is going through a process of tertiarisation, with relatively high levels of unemployment in the industrial sector, the city seems to have succeeded in establishing a relatively well-institutionalised system of social assistance. Public services, originally designed for marginal groups with health problems, have been both upgraded and renewed, and are integrated with an active (mostly religious) third sector. It may happen that the same household applies for income support both to public and private services with little risk of being found out. Given the small amount of money provided by public social assistance to recipients, there may even be a shared understanding among social workers that this, as well as recourse to the informal economy, is necessary if people are to survive. This kind of understanding is less likely to occur in either Turin or Vitoria, where public income support is more generous, but control on means and behaviour is stricter and 'cheating' is less condoned.

As in Barcelona, poverty in Vitoria affects around 9% of families and is visibly concentrated in the inner city as well as a suburban district. The poor tend to be either long-term unemployed people or young people looking for a job. In order to provide these groups with income support and improve their chance of finding work, the city council has developed a relatively well-coordinated programme that involves job insertion in publicly subsidised employment. The overall local welfare system is rather complex and with a higher role for public institutions and levels of government, which in turn require a higher degree of formalisation of rules and procedures. Specifically, three levels of government are involved in the financing and implementation of social services in Vitoria: the Basque Autonomous Community, the provincial government (*Diputacion Foral*) and the City Council. Other non-governmental institutions, such as Caritas, perform subsidiary tasks, but the voluntary sector is far less developed than in Barcelona. The relatively generous minimum income benefit in Vitoria makes recipients less likely to search for complementary sources of income, and more likely to depend exclusively on public assistance.

Lisbon and Porto

Of all the cities in our study, the Portuguese ones have certainly experienced the most drastic changes in recent years. They have moved from a charity-based management of poverty and insecurity that stressed the role of the family and community, to an institutional form of regulation that is administratively highly organised, and where social partnership is both expected and regulated. However, even after the introduction of the nominal minimum income scheme (RMG), which was still in an experimental stage at the time of this study, income support in Portugal is quite low and does not allow broad-based coverage or a genuinely institutional treatment of poverty. This in turn has two consequences: it allows a highly selective and discretionary approach to assistance, leaving much space for subjective assessment by social workers who have significant discretionary powers. It also leaves ample room (and need) for intervention by traditional charities, which may act as partners or as substitutes for public intervention. As their distribution and degree of organisation is not uniform across the various cities, they may increase local differences.

These phenomena were more evident at the time of the study, since the RMG was not yet implemented at the national level.

The two cases in the ESOPO sample, Lisbon and Porto, indicate well the crucial, as well as ambivalent role played by well-organised private non-profit associations in the face of a still weak public sector in the area of social assistance. In Lisbon, in fact, the main actor in delivering both publicly and privately funded social assistance is *La Misericordia*. This is a nationally organised religious fraternity that also exists in other cities. However, in Lisbon it is the main partner of the municipality, on behalf of which it administers income support as well as social assistance in general. It is a large organisation with trained personnel, and represents a resource that is lacking in Porto, where it is not compensated for either by a more developed public sector or by the presence of other as reliable third sector associations. Thus in Porto, social assistance is more reduced than in Lisbon, while sharing the same discretionary features. Yet, the very organisational strength of La Misericordia in Lisbon, and its professional and cultural tradition on what social assistance and social work are about, may render it more difficult to develop an innovative and entitlement based approach.

A concept of welfare tied to charity from religious institutions tends to produce submission to arbitrary decision-making by organisations, outside the control of the individual. As a result, negotiation and bargaining are not central to assistance relationships, which are often rather passive in the face of the administration and its procedures. From this point of view, the introduction of a more clearly regulated and objective measure, the RMG, with its dual stress on entitlement and activation, may represent a major cultural break both for public and private social services, social workers and beneficiaries. The 1999 Annual Report on the implementation of RMG suggests as much (*Commissão Nacional do Rendimento Minimo, 1999*).

Towards a comparative interpretation of differences in local welfare systems

As might be expected, it is more difficult to interpret the local level of analysis in terms of welfare and poverty models than the national one. Certainly, some common trends may be detected, both in the processes of 'marginalisation' with which policies are confronted at national and city level, and in the policies themselves. Among these are the growing focus on activating measures and the stress on social partnerships and welfare mixes. Yet the social and cultural specificity of each city remains the main factor in shaping these same trends. As Dahrendorf maintains (1995), "reactions to globalisation will differ in spite of the fact that the global market requires the same positive qualities from everyone. Moreover, since the success of these common trends depends largely on local resources and actors, they may further increase cross-city differences within the same country. At the same time, they may reduce the contrast between cities located in different countries where there is a similar social and economic profile and range of actors.

The bi-dimensional diagram in Figure 2.3 indicates where the cities in our sample stand in relation to these common trends. The horizontal axis represents the degree to which public policies and measures constitute an institutionally-defined social right, the vertical one the degree to which individualisation and market expansion has produced autonomy from non-institutional support (for example, family and kin, charities or informal support)[13]. These two dimensions underlie most welfare state research, albeit in different ways. Within a given country, each local welfare system offers its own unique combination of these two trends, according to the resources available and the understanding of poverty and rights.

Figure 2.3: Distribution of ESOPO cities according to their level of institutional support and the degree of autonomy from family and community support

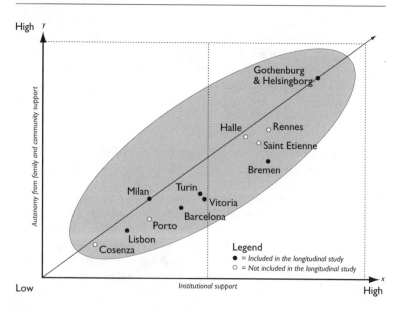

At the bottom left of the diagram lie the cities where the public welfare system draws on limited resources (institutional, financial and in terms of human capital), and therefore does not offer developed, comprehensive intervention to help the poor. This is usually complemented by wide-ranging assistance provided by non-governmental institutions, as well as by family and kin. In this position are found cities in countries that have no nationally regulated minimum income scheme and different kinds of local measures in favour of particular social categories. The degree of generosity depends both on city policy and on the category: an arrangement that leads to a relatively high degree of discretion. In this context, the role of local government is crucial not only in adapting policies to the local situations and encouraging social innovation, but also in defining entitlements.

At the top right of the diagram, we find the opposite case – a high level of institutionalisation with centralised control of a relatively large supply of resources (financial and human capital). This is reflected in comprehensive intervention for beneficiaries, taking into account their specific personal needs. It is a combination that leaves relatively little room for family and community intervention. The level of individualisation is high, but protected by universalistic state intervention – contrary to what would happen in a more market-oriented system (which would be located in the top left quadrant). It tends to strongly institutionalise cooperation with non-profit and volunteer organisations, and reduce the degree of discretion left to social workers. At the same time, it can encourage a bureaucratic approach to social assistance, with little flexibility and space for innovation, particularly if the local authority concerned has little scope for defining and implementing policies.

The cities investigated in our study are distributed on an ellipse around the diagonal linking the two poles[14]. This is not surprising, since the evolution of the two variables is, at least partly, correlated to the historical development of local welfare systems. The more state intervention moves towards developing a universalistic capacity to meet the needs of individuals (ie towards the top right of the diagram), the more it withdraws responsibility from family, charity associations, and so on (possibly absorbing them in a subordinate role). Where state intervention has remained subsidiary, resources and responsibility for support have been left to the unevenly structured world of family and informal intervention. In the centre of the ellipse lie the mixed cases[15] where private institutions have kept a share of resources and responsibilities, even though there exists an established and universal public support system. This mixed situation is well illustrated by the German cities. With respect to the

Swedish cities, the German ones are less citizenship-based. Public support for individuals, particularly for young people, is subordinate to the inability of family members to provide, and private charity institutions maintain an important role. The latter, however, is much less important here than in Southern European cities, which are found close to the bottom left corner.

As we shall show in Chapter Four, the degree of institutionalisation of support also has an impact on the selection of users. In cases at the top right of the diagram, even those in temporary difficulty (unable to pay the rent for a few months or to find the money for a vocational training course) can make use of public assistance, whereas the systems at the bottom left select only individuals and families suffering from very serious difficulties. The mixed cases, located in the centre, are more generous than those in Southern European cities, but are often selective, partly by virtue of the stigma connected with dependence on public welfare.

The diagonal is not strictly based on an evolutionary approach and does not automatically reflect the economic strength of the local community. For example, though per capita income in Milan is one of the highest in our sample, this city is located towards the bottom left of the diagonal.

The diagram also indicates various 'auxiliary' factors, such as the degree of rigour of controls or discretion exercised in welfare practices, as well as the role played by private social assistance associations. These will be analysed in greater detail in Chapter Three. What is essential to underline here is that different positions on the diagram on the whole indicate different rationale behind public income support programmes and, consequently, different parameters used for assessing the effectiveness of or dependence on public welfare. In the cases near the bottom left[16], the general rationale is one of limited intervention, centred on family subsidiarity, complemented by private and informal contributions. It can thus be assumed in these cases that public intervention alone will never resolve the problems. The duration of the assistance is almost always simply a function of the access rules, and its continuation does not automatically indicate dependence or ineffectiveness.

On the other hand, in the cities near the top right of the diagram, which have relatively homogeneous social situations and strong, compact and long-lasting political coalitions (Esping-Andersen, 1990)[17], public intervention is seen as being comprehensive and independent of the family and social situation of the recipient. It is assumed that it should be able alone (or together with other non-monetary public welfare programmes) to resolve in the shortest time possible the financial problems faced by individuals. Continuing dependence is taken to point to a programme's ineffectiveness. The mixed cases located in the centre of the diagram are more complicated. Here, intervention does not disregard the family or social situation of the person in difficulty, so its success depends on the correlation between the type of intervention and the type of recipient – a correlation that varies considerably from city to city[18].

In order to understand how local welfare programmes are currently functioning, and with a view to future developments, we need to consider two further aspects not shown in the diagram. These are the relationship between income support and social insertion activities, and the role played by third sector institutions, with particular attention to associations and bodies that are expanding their range of intervention in the face of a growing disparity in needs.

Except for older people and people with disabilities (and in some countries, such as the UK or the Netherlands, lone mothers), income support in the golden age of the welfare state was seen as a temporary measure. It enabled survival between two jobs or in a period of slack employment. For this reason, the systems that developed then did not address the issue of job insertion or recipients' responsibilities. Yet today, all countries are moving towards situations where social conditions are increasingly heterogeneous and unstable. Under these conditions insertion (and exclusion) are becoming important issues in local welfare practices, as is the recourse to third sector actors as insertion mediating agencies and acknowledged social partners in public policies.

This dual development – concern for social integration and the involvement of social partners, especially from the third sector – has been given explicit form in France through the introduction of the RMI (and subsequently in the Spanish 'Autonomous Community', and in Portugal). The RMI now being introduced experimentally in Italy follows the same principle. Furthermore, these two dimensions have become part of the official social policy discourse of the European Commission, and are at the basis of the action plan against social exclusion launched at the Lisbon Summit in March 2000.

The challenge of social integration is forcing all cities to move towards comprehensive public intervention, and also to establish new relationships between the institutionalised, bureaucratic forms of public action and the more flexible, informal ways of dealing with social problems. This is not without effect on the way we perceive poverty and exclusion. It affects the responses to both poverty and exclusion, and how we assess their dynamics, as well as the consequences for the social groups concerned. It should also make us very careful in our use of the 'classic' typologies of the welfare state and modes of poverty regulation, which are generally built around the formal institutional characteristics of regional or national systems. More specifically, by limiting the analysis to the interplay between the two axes shown in the diagram – degree of citizenship entitlement and degree of de-familisation – as is prevalent in comparative welfare state research, we do not account for the actual working of welfare systems, at the national or at the local level.

Certainly, it will not suffice simply to factor in the third sector. Under this label lie the most diverse actors and institutions. In fact, the intermediary structures involved in the local systems of the 13 cities in our study range from large national institutions – such as Caritas or La Misericordia – to small volunteer groups. Moreover, there is the whole world of social cooperatives and the like, as well as the non-governmental organisations (NGOs), which are non-profit organisations, but are nevertheless on the market, and often on the public market. In certain cases, an association may be fully integrated within the institutional public apparatus and equivalent to a semi-public institution. This is particularly so in Germany, given the principle of subsidiarity which is prevalent there (Schultheis, 1996b). Other associations are still highly autonomous and act essentially outside the local public domain, according to a rationale of assistance based on filling the gaps left by public intervention (as in Milan, for example). One also finds a great diversity in ethnic representation, and the importance of ethnic groups and associations in social integration activities – a role that is limited in France, but much more important in Germany and Sweden, due to active public support[19].

A more careful analysis will allow us to see in a less mechanistic light the links between, for example, the central role of the family, integration in the local community and a strong presence of the Church and religious institutions in the field of social assistance. A mechanistic approach would make a clear distinction between traditional ways of fighting poverty or modes of solidarity and the more modern forms. Our analysis, on the contrary, shows that tradition and modernity come together to produce original arrangements that cannot be reduced to old-style oppositions or rigid models.

The same is true with regard to religious institutions and networks, given that the relationship between state and church varies considerably from country to country. Depending on the local context, religious institutions may intervene only in urgent cases of extreme exclusion or act as full partners of the local institutional apparatus (Bremen, Milan, Lisbon). They may confine themselves to traditional-style actions and charity work on behalf of 'the poor' (Lisbon), or act almost like a social service with professional staff and a proper financial and organisational structure (Bremen and Milan).

These elements bring us, therefore, to see the lines along which the different local configurations are evolving in less linear and homogeneous terms. It is by no means certain that we will witness a generalised fostering of the process of institutionalisation (a slide towards the top right of the diagram). Original re-compositions involving either the third sector or other kinds of local resources could make their appearance.

Current innovations in the relationship between public intervention and the third sector therefore tend to fall within three different modalities, characterising the way in which the third sector institutions are being incorporated within the modernising public welfare systems. In France and Sweden, this has gradually led to the marginalisation of traditional private charity organisations. However, the centralised French approach is more rigid than the decentralised Swedish one. In the latter, it is easier to set up new local third sector organisations to act as intermediaries between the needs of immigrants and various ethnic groups and the local state welfare apparatus. In the case of Germany, their incorporation has made private organisations subordinate to public intervention, but they retain an important complementary role and also receive substantial public funding[20]. In Southern Europe, third sector institutions have maintained a considerable degree of operational autonomy, even when they obtain public funds. The three modalities are thus expressed differently in the local contexts and impact differently with the present changes.

Notes

[1] Rates of unemployment have decreased substantially in northern Italy since 1995. In Milan in 2001, the unemployment rate is 3.4%.

[2] Already in the 19th century Milan lay at the heart of one of the two main industrial areas of the Austro-Hungarian empire: Lombardy and Bohemia. It soon became Italy's most important and dynamic industrial and financial centre, acting as a magnet to continual waves of urbanisation from the last decades of the 19th century onwards. Alongside expansion in manufacturing, with multifarious specialised types of production, financial and commercial activities oriented to international markets became firmly established. As a result, there is little social division or segregation in Milan itself. Areas of segregation and urban decay are distributed patchily across the entire territory, but are more concentrated in the outlying periphery. Social inequalities spread out from the wealthy prestigious city centre to the working-class districts in the northern industrial suburbs.

[3] Halle is an exception, as the percentage of foreign-born population in the city is low and few are welfare recipients. With respect to the new wave of asylum seekers, the French cities seem less affected in comparison with Bremen and the Swedish cities.

[4] Gothenburg is much larger and has a strong shipbuilding and car assembly tradition, while Helsingborg combines its role as the main ferry link to Denmark, with a specialisation in chemicals.

[5] In 1993, financial support in Germany for asylum seekers was transferred from 'social assistance' to a separate system (Leisering and Leibfried, 1999, p 190).

[6] Mention should be made of the youth training institutions created at the end of the 19th century by Don Bosco and the Salesian religious order. These lasted through the last century, and have been joined by a number of other institutions, often international, created by religiously-inspired individuals and groups working in various areas of social vulnerability and exclusion: disabled people, drug addicts, prostitutes, AIDS bearers and so forth.

[7] The term 'third Italy' was coined in the 1970s to describe the social formations typical of central and north-east Italy, characterised by numerous small firms, medium-sized towns, high cultural and political homogeneity and social stability (in contrast to both the heavily industrialised regions and the less developed regions). The characteristic feature is a combination of a high entrepreneurial propensity and extended family networks that has led to territorial-based productive specialisation. See, among others, Bagnasco, 1977; Becattini, 1989; Brusco, 1986, 1991.

[8] See for example, Lewis, 1997a; Sainsbury, 1996. It has been pointed out that in Southern Europe the male breadwinner model is better understood as a kinship solidarity model, since interdependence between generations well beyond childhood and beyond the nuclear household is taken for granted (for example, Naldini, 2001; Saraceno, 1998a, 2000).

[9] The fact that local assistance programmes are not overloaded by demands for support is a consequence of two contingent factors: people are not yet familiar with them and the temporary nature of a large number of special retraining and job insertion programmes.

[10] In Bremen, for instance, the proportion of new immigrants among social assistance beneficiaries already in 1989 represented almost half of the recipients (Leisering and Leibfried, 1999).

[11] Social workers are numerous, and they work on many different aspects of integration and anti-poverty strategies. This is indicated by the fact that the rate of formal commitment to RMI-linked 'integration contracts' in Rennes is more than three times that in Saint Etienne (75% and 24% of claimants respectively).

[12] Three examples will suffice to demonstrate the city's capacity for innovation in the social sphere: a) the first version of RMI was tested in Rennes; b) this city is where the main innovations relating to the implementation of RMI are now taking place (for example, the introduction of community job placement workers); c) the council of the *Département* (the Conseil Général of Ille-et-Vilaine) introduced a 'youth' RMI in Rennes in 1999, anticipating a possible extension at the national level (which however never occurred).

[13] The main organisations are: Deutscher Caritasverband (Catholic), Diakonisches Werk (Protestant), Arbeiterwohlfahrt (industrial sector), Deutscher Paritätischer Wohlfahrtsverband, Deutsches Rotes Kreuz (Red Cross), Zentralwohlfahrtsstelle der Juden in Deutschland (Jewish) and Volkssolidarität (in the East). These are either religious or trades union and occupational organisations.

[14] The position of each city on the graph was agreed upon with the local research team taking into account all the material collected for the ESOPO study: institutional regulations, patterns of implementation, experiences of the beneficiaries. Thus, alongside the analysis of legal rules and criteria, the results of interviews with beneficiaries and social workers have also been taken into account to locate each city. The allocation of positions is the result of comparative assessments on all these dimensions.

The position on the Y-axis takes into account the extent to which individuals and households needing support are (legally or informally) expected to rely on family and/or kin. The higher levels of autonomy from family-kin protection are at the top, while the more marked forms of dependence are at the bottom.

The position on the X-axis takes into account the generosity and comprehensiveness of the protection provided by the institutional intervention of public welfare for people in difficulty. Higher levels of public protection are on the right, while a lower level is on the left.

[15] It should be kept in mind that in the ESOPO study we did not include cases where processes of individual responsibility are left predominantly to market forces.

The position of Lisbon and Porto refers to the period prior to the generalisation of RMG. Probably they would now be located higher on the institutional support axis, although remaining low in terms of the degree of de-familisation and independence from charities and informal networks.

[16] The concept of mixed cases has been used for the TSER European research on unemployment and social exclusion coordinated by Gallie and Paugam (2000) with reference to France and Germany in particular, but also including the UK.

[17] These cases, which all belong to the South European welfare model (see Ferrera, 1993; Mingione, 1997; Paci, 1989), are characterised by a high level of fragmentation, heterogeneity and 'particularism'. Fragmentation can be understood in a dual perspective: firstly, fragmentation in policies and in target groups; and secondly, geographical fragmentation of social policies, which leads to significant intra-country differences in social citizenship (and consequently intra-country heterogeneity).

[18] The particular combinations experienced by Scandinavian countries (and cities) could occur since the population was fairly homogeneous in terms of culture and expectations. With the presence of new immigrants, the level of homogeneity is decreasing and expectations are becoming more diversified.

[19] In this sense, the diagram shows three different kinds of development that refer mainly to the Scandinavian; South European and Continental patterns. If the UK had been included, we would have also seen another pattern, mainly characterised by a level of institutionalisation that is lower than the Swedish and German cities, but higher than the Southern European ones. It also has high levels of individual autonomy and responsibility connected with participation in the labour market (higher than the German cases) – located in the top right quadrant of the diagram, although more towards the left of the diagonal. Only US cities would be located in the top left quadrant (see Mingione, 1997).

[20] Strategies including ethnic minorities are very different, depending on the institutional framework. For instance, in France the question of representation of ethnic minorities has never been put on the political agenda. As French citizens, they have not been represented as ethnic. Conversely, in the United Kingdom, ethnic minorities have been included in an active policy of favouring specific ethnic minority interests in a context of racial discrimination and recognition of cultural differences (Bulpitt, 1986; Weil, 1991). Other northern-central European countries have followed the British example rather than the French 'Republican state culture' model.

[21] In Germany, for example, the Conference of All Churches produced a unitary document on welfare intervention, which facilitated public coordination of the sector in different areas and explains how it has been possible to rapidly revitalise religious organisations in the East German *Länder*.

THREE

Income support measures for the poor in European cities

Yves Bonny and Nicoletta Bosco

Introduction

Within the framework outlined in Chapter Two, this chapter focuses in particular on the income support measures for the able-bodied poor adopted in the countries and cities examined. Our aim is twofold: firstly, to reconstruct in detail the mode of construction and implementation of the measures in order to understand their impact and significance for the life chances of beneficiaries; and secondly, to develop a basis for comparison, allowing us to go beyond the specific features of each case study and integrate them within a more general picture.

In order to do this, we need to take into account the multiple dimensions and levels involved in the actual implementation of a programme. These include the selection of the beneficiaries, the perspectives and options offered by the programme to those involved and its consequent social significance. The only way to understand the effective range of a measure and its impact on poverty is, in fact, to reconstruct the whole set of regulations applied in the social treatment of poverty. Three levels of contextualisation are crucial.

The first, and most obvious one, has already been dealt with in Chapter Two. It concerns the socioeconomic and social-demographic background within which the measures are developed and implemented. This plays a decisive role, most notably in the employment prospects offered and the selection of beneficiaries. With respect to the dimensions mentioned above, it contributes to the definition of the profile and the image of those affected by income support measures. The profile will differ considerably according to the dominant forms of economic activity, whether the city is flourishing or in decline, the structure of the population by age-group, the importance of immigration, the attractiveness of the city for surrounding populations, and so on. At the same time, the economic conditions shape the perspectives and options open to the actors. The accompanying programmes included in the various systems of social protection – including training courses, funded job schemes, and so on – obviously cannot be isolated from the employment situation specific to the local context, that is the level of unemployment, types of job skill in demand, wage levels, the possibility of working part-time, and so on. The strategies developed by the beneficiaries of income support programmes, and the way that they experience their situation, will depend on the distribution of poverty and the employment prospects of the city concerned.

Second, income support measures take place within a specific cultural and political universe, which plays a major role in the social construction of poverty and the response provided. Poverty has no univocal interpretation, inasmuch as we are not dealing with a reality independent of a social framework. As mentioned in the introduction, the very notion of poverty involves a number of social representations, both in relation to the qualification of situations and persons and the definition of the forms of social intervention considered appropriate in face of the acknowledged poverty problems. No objective standard of living indicator can tell us whether or not a given person will be regarded as poor by his/her community, if support will be provided and if so how, if this will lead to stigmatisation, and so on. In order to know this, one needs to reconstruct the whole web of meanings that shape the notion of poverty in a given social universe. This will depend on prevailing economic conditions, but also on political structures and dominant cultural and ideological representations. Thus, if we speak of *exclusion* in some countries, the *underclass* in others and *marginalidad* in others still (see Fassin, 1996), this is not simply a question of terminology, but refers to three very different social constructions of poverty. One cannot study poverty and resulting measures independently of the social universe that names it and gives it meaning. This is always social, historical and dependent on the systems of reference[1] that guide those involved in the struggle against poverty, from the politicians who pass the laws to the social workers who intervene in concrete situations. In this regard, there are very significant differences among the countries and cities studied.

Third, one cannot understand the exact range of a programme unless one locates it within the whole social protection context where it takes place. By this we mean not simply the public system of social protection, but also informal forms of protection connected with primary solidarity. These two modes of protection are not independent. We therefore need to understand how primary and secondary solidarity[2] relate to each other, at the cultural and ideological level, the institutional and legal level and also the practical level, since these will shape the distribution of responsibilities between public actors, associations and interpersonal and family solidarity. The different configurations translate into cognitive and normative models that structure the actions and representations of the actors and define their respective expectations.

We need in particular to understand the exact scope of the measures and the way they fit into other programmes. Each system of social protection forms a whole, so most of the characteristics of a single programme cannot be understood in isolation. As mentioned in Chapter One, a specific measure finds its public and its effective range partly through the way it relates to other elements of the public social protection system (for instance, unemployment allowance or family allowance), and partly through different regulations (for instance, regarding the minimum wage). Thus, in different policy contexts, the able-bodied 'public' benefiting from social assistance income support will be smaller or larger, with greater or lesser disadvantages in relation to the labour market, and even a more or less accentuated specific gender and/or age profile. It will depend not only on the national and local social and economic situation, but also the overall system of income protection. This in turn has important consequences for the impact of a given measure.

There is, in our view, a considerable advantage in focusing on the local level, without necessarily embracing a 'localist' perspective. In particular, it avoids imposing an inappropriate concept of 'welfare state'. This is especially important in countries in which social policy is not standardised at the national level, and where there are consequently still large regional or even municipal variations. It allows us to examine measures belonging to very different institutional forms side by side. It also avoids stressing the contrasts that may exist between national and local regulation of poverty on the sole basis of the formal organisation of the schemes. In fact, aside from the official institutional set up, even in countries where social policy is not highly centralised or standardised, there may nevertheless be similarities between cities for cultural and historical reasons, or due to the economic and political situation. These factors can play a major role in the construction of homogeneity at the national, or at least the regional level[3].

Conversely, in countries endowed with uniform national institutional schemes, the 'local' approach allows us to emphasise the existence of variable modes of implementation and very different degrees of mobilisation of actors. The local level is not simply a *locus* for the application of rules and bureaucratic procedures whose meaning is obvious. It plays a crucial role in the way a measure, even though centralised, is concretely translated into the actions, decisions, relations, resources, and so on, which define a certain type of intervention.

Finally, the local level is particularly relevant in the present context of devolution, especially in connection with integration measures, which are increasingly being used in income support programmes[4]. The ambiguity of this evolution has been underlined by a number of analysts (for example, the European Foundation for the Improvement of Living and Working Conditions, 1999). The decentralisation of public action, motivated by the greater flexibility achieved, the personalisation of follow-up and mobilisation of local actors and resources, may actually engender major disparities. This is due to the great variations that exist in the investment by local actors, particularly locally elected representatives, in the implementation of integration policies[5]. Analysis at the local level is therefore essential to permit the examination of the network of actors concerned and the logic of their intervention. It enables us to bring to the fore any blockages or synergies that may explain those disparities, as well as the types of supra-local regulations which help to preserve uniformity in the programmes and equity of treatment despite decentralisation.

The local welfare configurations approach implies that the systems have been analysed and compared on the basis of their actual patterns of implementation, rather than just their formal and institutional characteristics. We have tried in particular to identify any divergences between legislative or statutory texts and decisions taken in the field. This enables us to determine the actual treatment of applicants and beneficiaries in the cities studied, and thus evaluate not only the differences between the cities, but also the sources of these differences (official texts, professional cultures, local political orientations, and so on)[6]. Homogeneity at the legal level can hide profound differences in the way policies are implemented de facto and similar outcomes may arise from very different processes. To take a particularly revealing example, while the leaving curves for Milan and Helsingborg are surprisingly similar, the reasons are very different. In the former, the rapid exit from the programme can be attributed to the scanty benefits and their limited duration, while in the second it is due to a particularly generous benefit scheme coupled with numerous programmes for employment assistance and the development of professional qualifications. In other words, the meaning of 'entering' and 'leaving' a scheme is not at all the same in the two cases. We may conclude that these curves *as such* give us no indication about the nature of the measure or its effectiveness in making people independent and enabling them to get beyond the initial condition of poverty.

In order to understand the way the policies really function, we also closely examined the characteristics of the various measures – the institutional framework of which is synthesised in the Appendix. They were examined, as we have said above, both with regard to their formal, legal features, and at the level of their implementation. Further, the beneficiaries' perspective was also taken into account in order to assess the actual impact of a given measure on their lives. Through a number of interviews conducted in each city with former and current beneficiaries[7], we tried to capture their objective life conditions within each local context, as well as their subjective perception of their poverty situation, the measure they were (or had been) benefiting from and the social services that dealt with them.

In order to analyse such diverse material and fully exploit the potential of our approach, we developed a multidimensional model constructed on an inductive basis from the 13 cities studied[8]. Unlike analytical models that focus on purely formal differences, or those deduced a priori without practical verification, our objective was to identify differences from within. We therefore did not try to develop a typology as such. Of course, the eight dimensions selected in our model are not independent of each other, and it is possible to identify certain polarities representing typical forms. For instance, familiar contrasts, like that between Northern and Southern Europe, can be recognised. It is also possible to rank the cities, for instance, according to the degree of institutionalisation of policies against poverty. This being said, it seemed important to preserve as much as possible the full diversity these dimensions contain. They can too easily be obliterated in a typology, which tends to rigidify contrasts, and group together in an often questionable way heterogeneous dimensions in a single type, forcing all the cases into a limited number of configurations. On the basis of a detailed analysis of the local contexts, presented in Chapter Two, we have tried to stress the diversity of possible positions on each dimension studied, whatever the convergence that can be established in other respects.

The preference given to a comparative structural analysis, as opposed to the construction of a typology, in the strict sense of the term also allows us to bring out original features of each local welfare configuration. For example, if one were to draw up a typology on the basis of the degree of institutionalisation of policies against poverty, Barcelona would lie in an intermediate group, together with other cities that are 'in transition'. However, this would fail to catch one of the original characteristics of the Catalan experience, which is the attempt to draw on the collective sense of solidarity to activate the proximity resources (that is, neighbourhood, formal and informal community associations) that are still very much alive in Spanish society. This is particularly significant in view of the many problems generated by the 'negative individualism' associated with highly centralised social protection systems, built on a rigid distinction between secondary solidarity, linked to public intervention, and primary solidarity (see Gauchet, 1991; Castel, 1995; Astier, 1997, on the notion of 'negative individualism').

One of the numerous problems we had to face in developing a comparative framework was that there was not always a single programme applying uniformly to all situations of poverty and treating them in a uniform way. In many cities, treatment varies according to the categorisation that is applied to an individual or a household. This can sometimes mean that different measures apply to different groups of people. It is difficult to ignore all these variations, as they are quite often significant. A closer analysis, however, showed that beyond the very real differences in treatment according to the category of claimants, these measures also have a number of cross-category characteristics. These were important enough to allow the identification of a common underlying model of income support also in the cities that use a categorical approach. The category-based distinctions are certainly a crucial dimension of this model, but they do not spoil its coherence, which justifies a general comparative analysis (obviously this assumption can be misleading, especially in contexts that have high scores concerning discretionary power).

In the following paragraph, we present the different dimensions of our structural analysis. After this, we describe the welfare measures in the 13 cities in the ESOPO project, trying to combine an emphasis on the specific local features with a comparative analysis. Chapter Three closes with a series of diagrams representing the different local configurations on the basis of the selected dimensions. These complement Figure 2.2 in Chapter Two, in so far as they include more dimensions, but focus only on income support measures[9].

The various dimensions of income support

For the sake of simplicity, we have used a model in which a limited number of dimensions are considered, although we try to take into account all relevant sources of variation. In a number of cases, this has forced us to put together within a single dimension aspects that were analytically distinct. When this is the case, we have indicated the different aspects involved and specified in the next section (Local patterns of income support compared) how these affect each city.

The major dimensions in our study concern three aspects: (a) the *dominant orientation* within which the measures can be placed, (b) the *conditions of access to and protraction of economic support*, and (c) their *content*. The local welfare configuration of each city is represented graphically in Figures 3.1-3.6 at the end of the chapter. Scores have been attributed to each of the selected dimensions, and a local welfare 'shape' drawn in the form of a polygon, constructed by linking the scores for each dimension. Since the dimensions selected are themselves multidimensional, the scores have to be considered as combined qualitative evaluations of each dimension.

Dominant orientations

Bureaucratic regulation versus discretionary power

Bureaucratic regulation concerns decisions taken in strict pursuance of the rules/laws (whether local or national), whereas discretionary power refers to the margins of manoeuvre allowed to social workers in granting access to benefits. This may include the choice of the kinds of measure applied, the duration and amount allowed, and the renewal and protraction of benefits. Discretionary power may result from the lack of clear rules or be actually written into the regulations in acknowledgement of the complexity and diversity of need. Discretionary power can thus take on very different meanings within the local contexts. Social workers can sometimes have a wide margin of manoeuvre in assessing the needs of people claiming economic benefits, apart from the categorisation of need provided by the law. But discretionary power can also be due to the absence of a unifying legislative and/or regulative framework. This is sometimes replaced by sub-local non-written rules employed by social services, resulting in a high degree of variability of decisions, even within a single social work office.

Discretionary power and bureaucratic regulation characterise general orientations typical of two different cultural models. On this basis, we can position each local welfare configuration on a continuum (see the horizontal axis in the diagram of Figure 2.3 in Chapter Two) ranging from a highly bureaucratic approach, where interaction and negotiation play a limited role (as in Helsingborg and Gothenburg[10]) to an approach in which negotiation, and even personal relations between social workers and perspective beneficiaries are crucial for granting and obtaining support (Lisbon and Cosenza). In Cosenza this sometimes leads to what can be defined as a patronage system. This polarity can also affect various aspects of benefit allocation, including access and the renewal and duration of benefits, but also their contents and generosity, in so far as social workers are allowed to choose among measures that can differ in length or generosity.

The score attributed to each city in our sample reflects the answers to the following questions: does the claimant, having the required characteristics for each local context, have guaranteed access to income support, or can social workers apply their personal opinion regarding the deservedness of the individual? Can they use their discretionary power for controlling the access (or renewal)? Can they choose among different measures or are they legally bound to apply given rules? Cities where the prevailing model of intervention is one of bureaucratic regulation will have higher scores in this dimension. Lower scores mean a high degree of discretionary power in applying the rules.

Family obligations versus collective solidarity

The poles of family versus collective solidarity (see the vertical axis in the diagram in Figure 2.3 in Chapter Two) represent two very different models of solidarity. Family orientation implies a model where family obligations and responsibilities make up for the lack of adequate public services, or where public intervention is admitted only when the family and its safety net are not sufficient, or defined as being inadequate. Collective solidarity, on the other hand, refers to situations where rights are highly individualised and guaranteed by universalistic procedures and public obligations.

This dimension also includes the regulation of so-called 'obliged kin' (for example, the extended family members who have legal responsibility for providing financial or other support) and, more generally, the relevance of family (including kin) obligations within each context. Where family-kin members are still considered the main providers, public support represents the last resource to which individuals and families can turn in case of need. It is well known that one of the strongest features of welfare systems in Southern Europe is the central role assigned to the family in supporting individuals well beyond childhood, and sometimes irrespective of cohabitation.

Once again, the orientation with regard to solidarity has implications for both objective and subjective experience. While giving primacy to collective public solidarity has the advantage of ensuring everyone minimal protection, it also tends to discharge the family group from any sense of responsibility with regard to its members. This in turn can generate a kind of 'negative individualism', in which a person's poverty is combined with a lack of social ties. Conversely, although giving primacy to family solidarity may facilitate social integration, it leaves part of the population unprotected and may also result in an overall impoverishment of the family when it is crushed by multiple demands for support that it has not sufficient resources to meet. This can become even more problematic when family relations are strained or non-existent. In this connection, we can observe real discrepancies between laws and behaviour, particularly in northern Italy. Here the legal priority given to family solidarity is increasingly in contradiction with cultural transformations tending to individualise relations within the family. Thus, we have assigned a low score to Turin because, even though the responsibilities of 'obliged kin' are defined by a national law, and further enforced by a local law, they are not usually applied by social workers when they involve non-resident kin. The medium value assigned to Halle means that this condition is applied only sometimes, and at the social worker's discretion.

Universal versus category-based orientation

Regarding the various anti-poverty measures, there is an important contrast between those with a universalistic orientation and those that target defined groups of able-bodied poor on the basis of a notion of deservedness or priority. Targeting may coexist with a high degree of national and local institutionalisation, or vice versa a high degree of fragmentation and discretion. Thus, this contrast may not be adequately captured in the bi-dimensional diagram Figure 2.3 in Chapter Two.

Universalism does not imply flat homogeneity, and within the universalistic orientation we do not necessarily find uniform treatment. Distinctions may be made between different categories of applicants or beneficiaries; but the principle behind such distinctions is 'to treat different cases differently', without any evaluation of deservedness being implied. By contrast, in the category-based orientation there are explicit or implicit evaluations of deservedness/undeservedness. Of course, when we consider concrete cases, the distinction is rarely as clear-cut as that. Even in places where a minimum level of support is considered a right, we often find an implicit evaluation of deservedness/undeservedness, especially with regard to able-bodied poor.

In France, for instance, non-normative evaluation is recent and corresponds to a retroactive interpretation of the category-based logic applied before the RMI (*Revenu Minimum d'Insertion*, or minimum income for integration) was introduced. The philosophy followed then was aimed at distinguishing the 'deserving' from the 'undeserving' poor. One had a right to social assistance if one was unable to work, such as an invalid, a disabled or older person, or was exempted from the obligation to work (as in the case of single parents with a child below the age of three; see Castel and Laé, 1992, pp 10-11). The introduction of RMI represented an acknowledgement that even able-bodied adults with no serious mental or physical disability preventing them from working, or without heavy caring obligations, could deserve support when in need. Yet, even today, there remains in France some notion of deservedness (for example, lone mothers of very young children, who benefit from a special measure) and undeservedness (young adults below the age of 25, who are excluded from RMI if they do not have children of their own).

Conversely, in a case such as Turin, the fact that it is allowed to provide support 'according to need', even to individuals in officially less deserving categories[11], somewhat relaxes the categorical nature of the local system in the direction of a greater universalism. However, too strong an element of discretion in interpreting regulations may undermine this more universalistic approach, since there is too much scope for variability. Thus, the social assistance system in this city encompasses various, rather than a sole model of support (Bosco et al, 1999).

People's experience of the situation differs profoundly depending on whether income support is explicitly associated with a concept of deservingness, or whether it aims to provide an appropriate form of support without imposing any value judgement. Whereas the former case is based on some notion of merit, the latter is based on the idea of a legal right[12]. In relation to the universalistic dimension, we assigned a higher score to cities where, within the programmes provided for the able-bodied, social workers were not allowed to choose between treatments of greater or lesser generosity on the basis of a notion of deservedness or priority.

Conditions of access and protraction of economic support measures
Selectivity

Selectivity can refer to two different characteristics. The first concerns the existence of income thresholds and therefore implies assessment. In almost all the ESOPO cities people have the opportunity to claim for benefits if their personal (or household) resources fall below a certain level[13]. Within this means-tested logic, however, the resources taken into consideration for purposes of assessing entitlement can vary greatly[14]. Income thresholds below which entitlement is granted may vary according to the target population, or the household composition (particularly its age structure). Or, in some places, they may be the same for everyone claiming benefits. Selection criteria have a profound effect on the characteristics of those who have access to the system. The more severe the means-testing, and the lower the income threshold, the more serious the problems of recipients. The following two chapters analyse in-depth how this affects both the characteristics of beneficiaries and their welfare 'careers'.

The second aspect of selectivity results from the presence or not of a tight budget constraint. Inadequate resources can mean that the system is unable to protect people in need. The degree of selectivity will depend on how much funding has been allocated to the welfare programme, and will directly condition the rate of acceptance of applications. As a scarcity of resources leads to high selectivity, this limits the number of claimants who can accede to benefits, and risks undermining the principle of financial aid as a right. For example in Milan, even though municipal regulation established a principle acknowledging universal entitlement to a Minimum Living Allowance, the number of beneficiaries and amount of the benefit depend on the resources made available each year in the municipality budget. Consequently, the certainty of entitlement is subordinated to the discretion of social workers and the will of the governing political coalition.

Moreover, the impact of selectivity on people's objective and subjective experience should not be underestimated. The more selective a programme – at both levels – the more negative the general portrait of the beneficiary population, and the more difficult it is for them to become independent and socially integrated. This explains why the duration of income support – when not set by administrative or legal rules, as, for example, in Milan – seems to increase with the rigour of selection. It is also why the beneficiary population's perception of the measure is likely to be more negative when selection is more rigorous, since the measure then seems like a form of charity for the most marginalised, inducing in beneficiaries a feeling of personal failure.

Recipients' duties

This dimension includes a range of aspects concerning the duties required of recipients of economic support and the way that these are handled by social workers. The kind of duties may differ considerably. They may involve simply the formal willingness to look for a job (that is, being enrolled at the employment agency), or the obligation to perform some kind of job – or to be trained for a job – in exchange for the benefit, or involvement in social integration/activation activities. As many authors point out (European Foundation for the Improvement of Living and Working Conditions, 1999; Gough et al, 1997) there has been a shift in recent years towards the principle of workfare, even though there is no consensus regarding its definition[15]. There is a subtle distinction between 'pushing' factors (which suggest somehow punitive or disciplinary elements) and 'pulling' factors in the form of incentives or activation strategies (Heikkila, 1999). The logic on which such duties are based is twofold and varies according to the local context. On the one hand is the idea that receiving subsidies can produce passivity and dependency in the able-bodied poor and that these perverse effects must be hindered by introducing compulsory work training or job experience. On the other is the assumption that the able-bodied do not totally deserve support or, at least, that they must 'earn' it by behaving according to social expectations. Where this second attitude prevails, recipients become more indictable if they are unwilling to comply. It can sometimes happen (as in Vitoria and Turin) that 'social integration' or 'activation' measures are profoundly ambiguous: for example, training programmes are offered more as a way of controlling the beneficiaries than for their relevance for professional integration. This engenders passive attendance, simply to avoid sanctions.

There are differences not only in the demands made on applicants, but also in the way they are enforced, often depending on the category to which recipients belong. However, in general, the greater the degree of undeservedness perceived, the higher the pressure and control (that is, longer procedures for preventing fraudulence, more frequent home visits or contacts with social workers, and so on) exercised before granting benefits or prolonging recipiency. Some support measures entail no precise demands, either because the general profile of beneficiaries suggests that they will fail on the job market, or because there are few resources for setting up social and professional integration programmes. In these cases – Portugal is an example – such demands, when they exist, are left to the discretion of social workers, who can choose to use their networks within the informal economy to find reinsertion opportunities.

Often recipients are 'obliged' to seek 'reinsertion', in the terms defined by social workers and/or by institutional rules, as a counterpart for receiving benefits, with little room for negotiating what they are willing to do, or under what conditions. The main idea is that beneficiaries must 'do something in return' for social assistance. Benefits may be discontinued or reduced if this requirement is not fulfilled. The question is then how strictly the notion of obligation is interpreted and applied: what is an 'active' job search or a 'reasonable' job offer, what forms of pressure are exerted and what sanctions or penalties applied for non-compliance? Our research demonstrates that in the cities whose measures stress the notion of receiving 'something in return', different positions are adopted – weak pressure in the two Swedish cities, steadier pressure in Halle. This has a strong effect on beneficiaries' objective and subjective experience.

Since this dimension stresses the idea of 'obligation', in attributing scores to each local context we have considered both the presence of an obligation (to work or to follow courses) and the extent to which benefits are cut (in amounts or duration) when recipients are unwilling to comply.

Contents of the measures

Generosity

This dimension cuts across all the others, in so far as it involves the income thresholds, the equivalence scales, the amount of the benefit, its duration and the possibility of renewing it, as well as the presence of accompanying measures and linked benefits.

The question of generosity is highly controversial within the European discourse on welfare reform. A general definition of adequate generosity could be that benefits should provide the possibility of staying above the poverty threshold. But this is far from being accepted everywhere, because of the idea that if benefits are too generous they could discourage people from looking for a job (see Geldof, 1999). Moreover, to appreciate the real impact of the sum granted, it is important to situate the measure in its social, economic and cultural context. This means taking into account the cost of living and also the state of the local job market – in particular, wage levels as compared with the benefit granted – as well as unemployment rates and the type of jobs potentially accessible to welfare beneficiaries. From this perspective, we might hypothesise that in Halle a relatively favourable benefit level, combined with not very enticing employment prospects, would encourage people to stay on welfare. But this does not automatically follow because, among other things, the cultural variable – in this case, the importance of paid work in constructing personal identity – plays a crucial role. The more one's self-image is built around paid work, the less one can envision oneself on permanent or long-term income assistance. In other words, the less one can settle into what might be called the 'welfare mentality'.

Next, we need to evaluate what percentage of a beneficiary's total resources are represented by welfare payments. Here the relevant rules are those concerning the recipient's work-earned income. With the aim of facilitating access to full professional activity, certain measures make considerable allowances for money earned through work, others do not. This of course has a considerable impact on available resources (and on the length of time benefits are paid). Then there is the possibility of obtaining undeclared complementary income in the 'informal' economy. This varies from one local situation to another, depending on the local labour market, the size of the informal economy, and the degree of institutional control on the latter. Finally, there is the weight of private solidarity – assistance from the recipient's network of kin and friends or from charitable associations – compared to public solidarity. Once again, we observe great variation among the different cities. In some, the welfare benefit constitutes the recipient's only resource (Sweden), whereas in others family solidarity and the informal economy play an essential role in most recipients' living conditions (Barcelona[16] and Turin).

All these considerations concerning the generosity of income support have been simplified in order to allow the definition of a single score for each city. Thus, in order to define this dimension, we have decided to use a very rough index that has been calculated on the basis of the answers to the following questions:

- Will the receipt of income support enable a household (in this case with one member only) to reach the poverty line?
- Does the equivalence scale used to equalise different household sizes stress individual needs or expect a large degree of household sharing?
- Are housing costs covered?

When the answers to these questions are affirmative, the score given is high. We have in fact assigned 10 points to the Swedish case. The scores of all the other countries (or cities) have been weighted in relation to the Swedish standard[17].

Duration

Here we are concerned with the presence (or absence) of specific *time limits* on the receipt of benefits for individual recipients or categories of recipients (not the actual duration, which will be discussed in Chapter Five).

The variability of time spent on welfare is a very complex question, strongly influenced by the general features of local welfare systems and their cultural meaning, but also depending on labour market conditions, on patterns of family and kinship solidarity, and on the presence of charitable associations. Duration does not have a linear relationship with a lack of selectivity or generosity. In cities where beneficiaries are in situations of extreme poverty and the services themselves have only limited resources, low benefits sometimes go together with long-term duration (for example, Lisbon), even if the amounts are so small as to make no significant difference in the recipients' conditions. In other cities, such as Milan, low amounts can go together with short duration, and benefits may be interrupted after a defined period, even if the recipient is still in a situation of need. This does not occur in Sweden, France and Germany, and to some degree in Turin (see endnote 11). In these cities, in fact, once recipients have been acknowledged as such, they can receive benefits as long as their need persists.

We have assigned a high score when there is the possibility of continuing to receive financial support as long as recipients meet the criteria governing access to assistance.

Activation measures

The concept of activation refers here to the positive non-financial incentives or opportunities offered to recipients, who are free to choose whether to participate or not in programmes that provide some sort of training, education, employment services or work (Heikkila, 1999). This dimension therefore involves the combined evaluation of a range of actions and programmes aimed at improving the situation of the beneficiaries, over and above income support. In this regard, we can distinguish between 'social aid' and 'professional integration' activities[18].

The evaluation of this dimension cannot be performed in absolute terms, and implies taking into account the kind of beneficiaries involved, as well as their perceptions. Given the orientation of the ESOPO study, which concerns the able-bodied, we decided to allocate greater weight to forms of action aimed at encouraging professional integration. While considering the average profile of beneficiaries and the local economic situation, we have compared the measures on the basis of the forms of activation in place for the able-bodied, and assessed to what degree they contribute to improving their situation and chances of overcoming poverty.

A particular problem at this level is posed by the institutional and organisational set-up of the different welfare programmes, which vary considerably from one city to the next. The most significant distinction concerns the relationship between income support and training or employment programmes. In some cities the latter are integrated within the income support measure, in others they are separate – the social welfare office providing the financial support and the employment office coordinating the programmes related to professional integration. For this reason, we have tried to evaluate the quality of activation measures on a global level, focusing attention not so much on the formal content of each measure, or the institutional and organisational set-up, as the whole set of programmes available to beneficiaries aimed at their professional integration[19].

Three aspects of activation programmes seem particularly relevant: how much they offer (beyond the monetary aspect), how effective they are, and how much personalised assistance they provide. The first refers both to the variety of help offered and its appropriateness for improving the recipients' situation, either in social and psychological terms, or in terms of training and professional qualifications. Effectiveness can be measured by looking at the usefulness of the programmes for getting beneficiaries off welfare (and more generally out of poverty), given their profile and the local context. Personalisation refers to how finely the proposed help is tuned to individual situations, as this seems to be an essential condition of successful integration.

Local patterns of income support compared

Helsingborg and Gothenburg

The Swedish system of social protection is well known for its comprehensiveness and generosity. Even though Sweden has experienced many changes since the mid-1970s that have affected the financial basis of its welfare system (decrease in the rate of growth, higher unemployment, important influx of refugees), it has been able to maintain a high level of social protection for its citizens.

Social assistance plays a small role in Sweden's social security system, which relies on universal and contributory benefits. In 1990, 53% of social security expenditure was financed by the public authorities, 45% by employer's contributions and 3% by insured persons. The universal, non-contributory citizens' pension left few older people receiving social assistance. Other social benefits, such as parental insurance and fairly generous unemployment benefits (in a country with high activity rates for both men and women), explain the very residual role of social assistance. Moreover, all other means of support need to be exhausted before claiming social assistance.

The welfare system operating in Helsingborg and Gothenburg, as everywhere in Sweden – the *Socialbidrag* – is distinct from all others in our study due to the philosophy underlying Swedish anti-poverty policy.

This rejects the idea of a minimum income in favour of the more generous concept of 'a reasonable standard of living'. The welfare benefit constitutes a universal right, and the maximum threshold of resources for eligibility is relatively high. As a consequence, some beneficiaries receive the welfare payment as a complement to job-earned income or other benefits that total less than the fixed maximum. It should be noted, however, that Sweden has one of the toughest means-tests of the OECD regarding the treatment of income and assets. Notably, all sources of revenue are taken into account (including savings) and easily sellable assets (like a car) have to be sold after a certain time on welfare, unless they are deemed essential to getting or keeping a job. This, together with other factors (lack of information, shame, unwillingness to put oneself under the control of social workers, sources of income judged sufficient to make ends meet during short periods of relative poverty, preference for other solutions such as family help, and so on), explain the great discrepancy between the population whose income is below the threshold and the number of people actually receiving welfare assistance (estimated in certain studies to be only 20% of that population).

Entitlement is based on legal residence in the country. This has resulted in a dramatic increase in the proportion of legal immigrants receiving social assistance in the last decade. In 1993, foreign-born residents represented 10% of the population, but 25% of social assistance recipients. As a result of immigration, the proportion of the population receiving cash assistance increased from six to eight per cent during the 1990s. The other major group receiving social assistance is the young. In 1994, 63% of the recipients were single and mainly young people (who are entitled individually to the benefit once they reach the age of 18, even if they still live with their parents). Couples with children and lone mothers each represented 15%.

The measure is marked by a strong principle of public collective solidarity, with the result that no rule of subsidiarity in relation to the family group intervenes except for the expectation that spouses and cohabiting partners support each other, and parents support their children under 18 years of age. Younger children are sometimes entitled to benefit in their own right, if it is shown that living with their parents would pose a problem. The role of voluntary agencies is also very limited.

Social assistance is locally organised and, at least in part, locally financed; but the central level, with the aim of promoting geographical equality, tries to minimise local differences. At the time of our study, and until recently, this aim was pursued through recommendations issued by the

National Board of Health and Welfare (*Socialstyrelsen*). However, the legal power of these recommendations and the range of variability allowed, became controversial and new standardisation guidelines came into effect on 1 January 1999, reducing the discrepancies between municipalities in the amount granted.

The monetary benefit is generous – the highest of all the cities studied for all household compositions. It is supposed not only to cover all basic needs, but also the cost of personal care (for example, insurance, washing and cleaning), recreational pursuits (for example, a daily newspaper, local travel), and social contacts. This standard amount is supplemented with the coverage of actual housing costs, provided these do not exceed a maximum level fixed by each municipality. On top of this, additional payments can be granted on an individual basis in order to respond to all reasonable requests, such as medical and dental treatment or travelling costs to search for a job.

Benefits are granted for an indeterminate length of time, as long as the recipient's resources remain below the fixed maximum and they are actively looking for a job (they must be registered at the employment office). However, beneficiaries seem not to be too closely surveyed on this last point, firstly because the unemployment rate is growing, secondly because social workers have large caseloads, and finally because the welfare and employment offices are not tightly coordinated[20].

The profoundly individualistic orientation of the Swedish system of social protection means that all beneficiaries are treated as uniformly as possible. More specifically, little or no distinction is made in the treatment of men and women, even for women with young children. The breadth of childcare public services provide implies in return that women recipients minimise their childrearing activity. Much more is expected in the way of job seeking on the part of women with young children than in the other countries studied[21].

The programmes designed to socially support and professionally integrate recipients are many and varied, as Sweden traditionally has very active policies in favour of training and employment. According to an OECD study (1999), Sweden was the country with the highest proportion of the GDP spent on 'active measures', as opposed to cash assistance payments. Most of these measures are implemented by the local employment offices under the aegis of the national government. Social assistance is thus limited in scope and in many cases beneficiaries switch over from welfare to another programme. The feeling expressed by many recipients was that they were only moving about within the system – back and forth between social assistance, periods of paid training, spells at protected jobs, and unemployment benefits – raising the question of how efficient and relevant all these programmes are. However, the fact shown by our comparative analysis that, on average, people leave the programme much more quickly here than elsewhere (even if this is associated with a non-negligible proportion of re-entries), does indicate that the Swedish programmes are in comparative terms quite efficient.

The relationship between beneficiaries and social assistance services is an impersonal 'service-user' type. Beneficiaries have rights that the service applies in a highly bureaucratic fashion. Personal contact is limited and marked by the relational distance characterising administrative management, especially for people without social problems. Even the individualised handling of situations, whether regarding additional payments or training and employment programmes, does not significantly modify the nature of this relationship, given that the management of individual situations is highly structured with precise instructions that leave relatively little room for discretionary power. Nor does the frequent rotation of personnel facilitate a more personal relationship with beneficiaries.

This relational pattern has been partly internalised by beneficiaries, who often expect little more from social workers than the financial support provided (social workers are not usually in charge of training and employment programmes) and are satisfied with an impersonal relationship. Still, many – and especially single mothers with children – complain that they do not get enough practical information or support and are not listened to attentively.

There are very few differences between the two cities studied, which is an indication that, although the administration of social assistance is decentralised, the national regulations, together with a shared consensus over its meaning and underlying values, are effective in maintaining a large degree of homogeneity throughout the country. The only clear difference at the time of the study concerned the amount granted, which was higher in Helsingborg, especially if paid only for a short time. Gothenburg had already applied the new national regulations, which establish that some items previously included in the calculation of the standard amount (for example, furniture, household utensils) should now be handled on an individual basis. Labour-related programmes were until recently run by the State and not the municipalities, again tending to lessen local differences. In these times of high unemployment, however, the active role of municipalities has grown here, like elsewhere, and more significant differences might develop in the future.

Bremen and Halle

The German welfare system is often identified as a typical case of an insurance-oriented system, meaning that most benefits depend on a contribution to a specific social insurance programme and are earnings related, aiming at maintaining the standard of living of the recipient. The system is divided into three main branches: the first gives security against old age, unemployment, invalidity, maternity and death of the main earner. This branch is based on contributions, although there are non-contributory schemes for civil servants, soldiers and the judiciary. The second branch gives compensation to victims of crimes and in cases of war injury: these programmes are non-contributory. The third branch covers social assistance and has traditionally occupied a residual position, the overall system being built around full-time employees and a male breadwinner model. Its aim is to provide a supplement to existing benefits for those who cannot contribute (or do not contribute enough) to the social insurance programmes.

Until recently, after the economic boom of the postwar period, poverty was treated as both a marginal and shameful phenomenon (Paugam, 1996; Schultheis, 1996a). Although the situation has changed considerably in recent years, due notably to economic changes at world level and the reunification process, these cultural views seem to persist. This may explain why the non-take up rate in Germany is particularly high in social assistance (various studies estimate the rate at between 33 and 50 per cent).

The main social assistance programme, the *Sozialhilfe*, has two elements: *Hilfe zum Lebensunterhalt*, or general assistance, and *Hilfe in besonderen Lebenslagen* (assistance for people in special circumstances), directed at disabled people, people without health insurance and anyone with special needs. Pensioners whose earning-related pension does not reach the subsistence level may receive an income-related social supplement to bring it up to the social assistance threshold. Moreover, people who have exhausted unemployment compensation can claim Unemployment Assistance for a period (this is based on combined insurance and assistance criteria).

Sozialhilfe is administered by local authorities and funded by these and the *Länder*. Anyone resident in Germany can receive social assistance, although there are specific qualifications required for immigrants. EU citizens who have been working in Germany can receive benefits for up to six months (after losing their job), but after that they have to leave the country. Similarly to Sweden, an increasing number of recipients are immigrants, but also refugees and asylum seekers. In 1992, 50% of families receiving assistance were not of German nationality.

The number of recipients of social assistance has increased dramatically over the last two decades (over 150%). This rise is attributed to unemployment, which is more acute in the former East Germany. In 1992, 5.8% of the total population was receiving social assistance, 62% of whom were women. Single householders and lone parents (mainly women) were the largest groups of recipients. However, increasing unemployment is also bringing young people into social assistance.

The general welfare measure – *Hilfe zum Lebensunterhalt* – is similar to the Swedish one in several respects, being a national measure managed at the municipal level and thus decentralised. It constitutes a universal right to which access is determined on the basis of a fixed maximum amount of resources. There is a basic benefit, plus various additional amounts – namely for rent – that are determined on an individual basis, but within strict regulations. It is granted for an indeterminate length of time, as long as the recipient's resources remain below the established threshold, and applies the principle of 'something in return' by demanding that beneficiaries look actively for work or participate in training and employment programmes. Finally, the relationship between professionals and beneficiaries is first and foremost an impersonal service-user one, centred around the financial benefit.

In what respect does the German system differ from that in the other countries? First, income support is conceived as subsidiary to family solidarity when it comes to access and protraction. This means that parents have financial responsibility for adult children living with them and vice versa (in some cities this also applies to non-cohabiting parents and children). Along the same lines, alimony comes before public assistance in the case of divorced persons, giving rise to bureaucratic and legal collection practices that are sometimes painful for the applicant – a fact that discourages many from applying.

This 'familistic' orientation is likewise reflected in a still quite salient cultural and social model that has very deeply rooted assumptions concerning the gender division of labour and the private nature of childrearing. Public childcare services are among the least developed in Europe, and mothers of young children are treated quite differently from other beneficiaries. The German system makes special financial provisions for mothers of children under the age of three, which may be collected concurrently with the minimum income payment. Moreover, the requirements of actively looking for work and accepting any reasonable job offer are suspended for lone parents of children under three and applied with great leniency for single mothers with older children. In this respect, the German measure is radically different from its Swedish counterpart. The only point in which it is profoundly individualistic is in relation to equivalence scales, which are quite generous. This represents a major difference in orientation compared to other countries, which otherwise share the German familistic approach. The equivalence scales applied in Spain in cities such as Barcelona and Vitoria, assume a much higher degree of sharing and saving within the family, and are therefore far less generous, reflecting concerns opposite to those in Germany (see Schultheis, 1996b).

The German system is less generous than the Swedish one not only in terms of financial support, but also in training and employment programmes, which are less dynamic than in Sweden. Furthermore, when it comes to social, as distinct from professional, integration, the principle of subsidiarity comes into play: priority is given to mutual assistance groups and other non-governmental organisations, which have a vast field of action and are partially financed by the State, thus reducing the field of overtly public intervention. Consequently, even more than in Sweden, in the eyes of its beneficiaries, public social assistance boils down primarily to its financial component.

It should be emphasised that administrative agents in both Bremen and Halle have heavy caseloads. This results in limited information being provided to beneficiaries, limited availability of professionals and little time for individual attention, of which many beneficiaries complain. When comparing the two cities, one has of course to take into consideration the tremendous impact of the reunification process on the citizens of Halle. The local characteristics regarding the implementation of welfare assistance and the way it is experienced by recipients and non-recipients alike must be linked to the major structural and cultural changes that have occurred in recent years. To mention just a few aspects: before 1989 unemployment virtually did not exist and poverty was much less of a problem than today. Lone parents were stigmatised much less, and the activity rate among women was about 91%. It is now around the West German level (60%), while a number of social benefits for mothers (like very cheap public childcare centres) have been dropped.

Against this background, we can observe that the actual implementation of the measure seems more favourable to beneficiaries in Bremen than in Halle. First, in the latter town the principle of subsidiarity is applied more strictly: parents and adult children who do not live together are in some cases declared financially responsible for each other, which is not the case in Bremen[22].

The second difference concerns attitudes towards the principle of 'something in return'. In Bremen, emphasis is placed on the idea of a voluntary commitment, especially in the matter of assisted employment programmes (*Hilfe zur Arbeit*). These are quite numerous and relatively efficient (it is estimated that two out of five recipients who participate in work schemes find a 'normal' job afterwards), and the rare penalties imposed for not participating are light, although after a certain time on the programme some pressure is exerted. The notions of obligation and sanction intervene far more often in Halle in order to save money and to combat a perceived tendency of recipients to settle down into being on welfare in a city where unemployment is over 20%.

Last of all, beneficiaries are received differently in the two cities. While Bremen is relatively well endowed with social assistance centres, Halle has only one social service centre for an estimated 12,000 beneficiaries. This is reflected in the interviews with beneficiaries conducted in Halle. Many complained of the bad physical state of the offices, overcrowding, waiting in the halls, and lack of organisation.

Rennes and Saint Etienne

The French system of social protection has been built around a system combining social insurance provisions for the employed and their families, and social assistance for poor persons unable to work (invalids, disabled and older people), or otherwise exempt from the obligation to work, such as single parents with a child below the age of three (Castel and Laé, 1992, pp 10-11). Analogous to the German one in many respects, the system is possibly more complex and fragmented. In addition, benefits addressed to families with children play a much greater role in France than in any other of the six countries.

Social insurance is divided into several schemes based on occupation and categories of workers. The *Régime Général* provides coverage for sickness, work-related injuries, maternity, the family, old age and death. Specific schemes exist for farmers, civil servants, railway workers and miners. Supplementary social security schemes also include a supplementary pension. Besides these, France has a highly fragmented social assistance system, due to the existence of several programmes designed for specific circumstances. There are seven social minimum benefits including the *Revenu Minimum d'Insertion* (RMI), the *Allocation de Parent Isolé, Allocation de Solidarité Spécifique, Minimum Vieillesse, Allocation Veuvage, Minimum Invalidité* and *Allocation aux Adultes Handicapés*. Whereas the RMI is targeted at those not eligible for any other scheme, the other six are targeted at specific populations. There is also a complex interaction between the various social programmes.

In the French context, the fragmentation of programmes requires a closer look at each one. Three programmes that are outside the scope of our study (*Minimum Vieillesse, Allocation aux Adultes Handicapés* (MAH) and *Minimum Invalidité* (MI)) cover respectively: the population over the age of 65 (or 60 if disabled), people with disabilities, and people who are sick or disabled through a non-work related accident. These programmes include resident immigrants. However, whereas to receive the *Minimum Vieillesse* a person needs to have 10 years residence, for the MI no specific length of time is required.

Two family-related programmes are the *Allocation de Parent Isolé* (API) and *Allocation Veuvage* (AV). The first is a benefit for lone parents and the second for widows less than 55 years old. The API is more generous than the RMI, but it has a time limit (or age of child limit) and the claimant cannot reside with a member of the opposite sex. The AV is for widows who are rearing or have reared children. It excludes the self-employed (only farmers are included) and is financed through social security contributions. While these two programmes are means-tested, there is also a complex system of universal benefits paid for children, which is administered by the *Caisse d'Allocations Familiales*, and represents a substantial integration to the income of families with children.

One other programme, *Allocation de Solidarité Spécifique*, is a state benefit for the unemployed whose entitlement to unemployment insurance benefits has expired. Beneficiaries must be under the age of 65 and have worked for five years out of the previous ten. This programme is mainly directed at long-term unemployed people. It is financed two thirds by the State and one third by contributions from civil servants.

One of the principal features of welfare provision in recent decades is the blurring of boundaries between social insurance and social assistance. This can be seen for instance in the gradual widening of social security benefits to include the unemployed as well as people who are too poor to make financial contributions. At the same time, non-contributory and means-tested social benefits, such as the RMI, are being introduced, marking a radical departure from the insurance principle.

As new forms of poverty developed during the 1980s due to unemployment and social precariousness, the distinction between the deserving and the undeserving poor gradually lost its relevance. At the same time, it became clear that an attempt to divide poverty into different categories made little sense when they consisted of an increasingly heterogeneous population. It was in this context that France set up a universal minimum income system (the RMI, *Revenu Minimum d'Insertion*) in 1988. The guiding principle is that every individual whose income is below an objective maximum level has a right to the RMI, regardless of the reasons for their poverty. The RMI, however, was not designed to replace the existing social minima that had developed over the years to cover specific types of situations. Its aim was more to 'fill in the holes' of existing welfare provision. The RMI thus has a somewhat residual role, as it is subsidiary to a host of category-based measures that already make up a form of minimum income for many people (and indeed are often more generous than the RMI).

The French social system emphasises the principle of individual entitlement and national responsibility, over family membership and family solidarity. Yet, there is an age limit: applicants must be over 25, unless they have children or are pregnant. The main reasons given for this minimum age are the preservation of family solidarity, the danger of 'disincentiving' young people from working, and the existence of a policy of social and professional integration aimed especially at the 18 to 25 age group. Another reason cited is the cost that would be involved in extending the RMI to all persons over the age of 18. Yet, the 18 to 25 age group is undergoing serious difficulties, and the question of extending the RMI to cover them is regularly discussed. Immigrants are eligible, provided that they have been resident in France for three years.

The RMI is a national measure whose financial characteristics for the most part do not vary from city to city. In contrast to the Swedish and German cases, no portion of the financial benefit may be individualised. It varies only according to household composition and resources. Only the added housing benefit varies: according to the level of the rent and up to a maximum amount. However, since this maximum is rather low and therefore frequently reached, one can hardly speak of individualised treatment in this case either.

The RMI is granted for an indeterminate length of time. It involves a notion of mutual commitment, rather than 'something in return' – therein lies its originality. Recipients commit themselves to participating in activities that they help to define, aimed at improving their situation. The agreement is formalised by the signing of an integration contract, which implies that in return the community will develop suitable proposals for integrating the beneficiary. The integration contract involves no firm obligation, because its objective is not so much to constrain the recipient as to support people as they try to achieve their projects. Penalties are applied only in cases of manifest bad faith. Integration is either social (for example, regarding housing, health, hygiene, treatment of drug or alcohol addiction) or professional, depending on whether or not the recipient is fit to work. Contracts are signed for periods between three months and one year and may be renewed as often as deemed relevant. The focus on integration activities, moreover, implies institutional cooperation among different local actors, (public, non-profit, private; for example, enterprises), who are responsible both for providing resources for the integration contracts (temporary in-work experiences, training, and so on) and for implementing them.

The fact that there is an institutionalised connection between financial benefit and integration activities plays an essential role in the relationship established between professionals and beneficiaries. While the delivery of benefit is handled by bureaucratic procedures, as in Sweden and Germany, this is not in theory the core of the beneficiary's relation with the social service professionals, which is focused on integration activities. The personnel in charge of receiving beneficiaries are not the same as those who manage the delivery of the income allowance. Their job is to inform beneficiaries of their rights and to assist them in administrative procedures, as well as to meet them regularly to see how the integration activities are proceeding. This facilitates personalised follow-up. The recipient's perception of this relationship is conditioned therefore by how attentively their case is actually followed and how useful the proposals and projects for achieving integration are.

Issues of access and financial benefit are managed by a national organisation and there is no margin for local action. Above and beyond local demographic and socioeconomic conditions then, any variation with regard to this overall framework has to do with integration policy. The only other possible source of variation concerns additional forms of support, either financial or in kind, which may be attributed by municipal or departmental social services. In Rennes, for example, welfare beneficiaries may use public transportation free of charge, whereas this is not the case in Saint Etienne. This was the only difference we were able to observe at the level of income support.

Integration policies, on the other hand, differ considerably from one municipality to the next. Though orientation and funding are fixed in a national regulatory framework, such policies are essentially applied at the local level. Modes of social intervention in Rennes, for example, are much more dynamic than in Saint Etienne. The city of Rennes has set up special personnel to receive welfare beneficiaries and has specially trained local integration workers (as distinct from social workers), who assist beneficiaries in all matters of professional integration. Moreover, the high level of inter-institutional coordination in Rennes has allowed for the development of quite diversified offers in the domain of professional integration, whereas Saint Etienne has been characterised for many years by institutional compartmentalisation and much less active recipient follow-up (although the situation was improving at the time of our study). The interviews conducted confirm that follow-up in Rennes is more attentive, personalised and efficient than in Saint Etienne. Overall, Rennes is one of the most dynamic of the cities studied.

Barcelona and Vitoria

The Spanish welfare system seems to present a strange combination of precariousness and relatively limited exclusion. In fact, despite a high proportion of households (between 15 and 25 per cent) living below the poverty line – defined as 50% of the average equivalent family income (estimated during the 1980s and early 1990s) – and despite high unemployment rates (about 20% in the mid-1980s, and again since 1992), Spanish society seems to display a relatively limited degree of social exclusion. There are few homeless people, lower and decreasing crime rates than in other European countries, low infant mortality, and low rates of single person and lone-parent households (Laparra and Aguilar, 1997). The presence of high integration levels depends on various factors, including family solidarity[23], that make it possible to reduce the impact of unemployment and job instability (according to official statistics, one third of the labour force had a non-permanent job at the time of our study), which encourages the various household members to adopt combined strategies.

The Spanish social protection system, as in other Southern European countries, offers greater protection to older people (aged over 65), people with disabilities (invalidity greater than 65%) and, in general, to those more unable to work than the able-bodied poor. At the same time, among the able-bodied, it protects those who have suffered from precariousness in their working history (insufficient contributions during their working life), more than those who for some reason have been excluded altogether from the labour market (persons who have never succeeded in finding a job).

Income support measures for the poor – *Ingresos Minimos de Insercion, Renta Minima de Insercion* or *Salario Social* – have developed at the regional level and the laws that regulate this kind of measure vary greatly in the 17 *Communitades Autonomas* (Autonomous Communities)[24]. Since there has been a high discretionary power in implementing the national guidelines, these programmes have not been developed in the same way or to the same degree across the country. The main differences concern the fact that in some regions benefits can be legally claimed as a right, while in most cases the regional governments grant the benefit at their own discretion (Laparra and Aguilar Hendrickson, 1997, p 528).

In five regions (Andalusia, Asturias, the Canaries, Castilla-Leon and the Basque country), there are workfare programmes with an obligation to accept job offers. These measures aim to encourage labour market insertion, and involve the obligation to sign a social insertion contract. They are very different from one region to another, and in some cases claimants may be asked to work within social services assisting older people and/or people with disabilities. Six regions have legally established temporary social interest jobs (*Emplejo Social Protegido*) as a compulsory alternative to benefits[25].

The Basque[26] and Catalan systems – the *Plan Integral de lucha contra la Pobreza*, which includes the IMI *(Ingreso Minimo de Insercion), the Ayudas de Emergencia Social* (AES) and other accompanying measures in Vitoria, the PIRMI or *Programa Interdepartamental de Rentas Minimas de Insercion*, which includes RMI *(Renta Minima de Incercion)* as well as emergency and accompanying measures in Barcelona – share the same cultural inspiration. Claiming benefit is considered a right and all those who are entitled should obtain it. The reference unit for this kind of support is the household (which must have been formed at least one year before applying for benefit). Benefits are given to persons between 25 and 65 years old. As in France, it can be given to younger households if there are children or people with disabilities needing care.

The basic amount granted is identical to the monetary level required for admission to the benefit and is quite low (lower in Barcelona than in Vitoria). Moreover, in contrast to Germany, the equivalence scales are rather unfavourable for large families. In Vitoria, however, the basic amount is systematically supplemented with an additional sum granted on an individual basis, with the aim of covering part of the rent and current housing expenses. In Barcelona there is no additional amount, but at the beginning of the period of assistance, social workers can give money to pay debts incurred up to that moment. In this respect the cities are vastly different: whereas in Barcelona the basic amount is usually not enough to live on, in Vitoria it is generally sufficient to stabilise living conditions at a minimum level. It should be noted, however, that family solidarity and the informal economy (which is much more developed in Barcelona) enable many beneficiaries to pull together different types of resources.

In both cities the benefit is designed for one year, but it can be renewed as long as the condition of need persists[27] and as long as the beneficiaries meet the criteria for attribution, which include a 'something in return' obligation, most often in the form of a signed integration contract. The main difference with the French RMI concerns the compulsory participation in integration activities.

Evaluating the situation created by this kind of benefit, concern that financial support given to the poor might discourage the search for a real job seems unfounded. The many programmes set in place to help beneficiaries to get out of welfare, together with the low amounts granted, render it difficult to argue that it creates a culture of dependency. It should be added that, at least among the beneficiaries interviewed for this study, being on the measure was considered by recipients more a privilege than a stigma.

With regard to the accompanying measures[28], there are courses in elementary education, professional training, reorientation and refresher courses. The same kind of courses are offered to most beneficiaries: they have not proved diverse or differentiated enough to suit recipients' profiles. Such courses are usually more appropriate for the most deprived recipients – among them immigrants[29] – namely because they ensure re-socialisation and improve their self-confidence; but are less suitable for people whose main problem is lack of an adequately paid job.

In addition to these courses, the municipality of Vitoria has reserved many low-qualified temporary jobs, such as cleaning or concierge work, for welfare beneficiaries. It can happen that people get off the programme because they obtain such a job, keep it long enough to be able to collect unemployment insurance, then when they exhaust this, return to social assistance if they do not find anything else. In Barcelona, the job offer is much less institutionalised or institutionally controlled than in Vitoria, and getting a job has more to do with the social workers' personal initiative.

The relationship of recipients with social services and social workers differs greatly in the two cities. In Vitoria a rigorous surveillance system has been put in place, with the aim of checking recipients' resources, prevent fraud and ensure that the obligation to look for work is respected. This has a direct effect on social workers' practice: although they regularly meet beneficiaries, they must fulfil numerous bureaucratic procedures and are consequently often not available to follow-up beneficiaries, either to give them moral or psychological support or integration assistance. Beneficiaries are often critical of the service and personnel, though some declared that the pressure social workers exerted on them ultimately had a positive effect.

In Barcelona, on the contrary, social workers tend to have an extremely understanding attitude towards beneficiaries, giving them much advice on job openings in both the formal and the informal economy. They are not strict about the 'something in return' obligation, or about declaring income sources from which the recipient is known to benefit, as long as they do not exceed a certain amount. Such treatment expresses the social workers' intention to practice a kind of local justice in the face of a measure they judge insufficient – an attitude that understandably wins a very favourable judgement from beneficiaries, who are otherwise quite critical of the financial sum allotted and the kind of professional integration projects proposed. The other side of the coin is that this situation can lead to high discretionary power, collusion and consequently mistrust and manoeuvring.

Milan, Turin and Cosenza

The social security system in Italy is highly diversified and follows a corporatist model. Schemes are earnings-related and separately funded. However, there is also a Public National Health System, established in 1978, covering all citizens and legal residents for medical care. Old age pensions are contributory. People whose contributory record has reached a minimum period, but is not sufficient to qualify for the minimum pension, may have it integrated on the basis of a means-test for the individual or the couple (*Pensione Integrata al Minimo*). A *Pensione Sociale* provides a means-tested pension for people over the age of 65 who do not benefit from any of the other pension schemes[30]. Invalidity pensions and invalidity allowances are of two kinds: one is provided to those who have become disabled during their working life; the other is for those who were born disabled or became so while not in the labour market. The latter (*Assegno di Invalidità Civile*) is means-tested.

Another item in the social security system are the different kinds of unemployment benefit. There are two main types of unemployment benefit. One is granted to workers made redundant due to a decline in business (*Indennità di Mobilità*) and the other to involuntary unemployment in the case of individual dismissal. The first is much more generous (about 80% of the previous wage) than the second (30% of the previous salary). Young unemployed people, and people of any age (mostly women) without prior work experience, are not entitled to unemployment benefit or any other type of benefit within the social security system. Finally, there is no universal system of child allowances. Means-tested family allowances (*Assegno al Nucleo Familiare*) are paid only to wage workers, since these benefits are partly financed through contributions[31].

There is no nationally regulated means-tested income support, except for older people (*Pensione Sociale*) and people with disabilities (*Assegno di Invalidità Civile*). Since 1977, the State has transferred responsibility for social assistance to the regions and the municipalities. In the absence of a national law regulating rights and duties in social assistance (and social services provision)[32], many regions introduced regional laws on social assistance. Not all regions, however, have such a law. Moreover, there is diversity within regions as well as between regions in the access criteria to social benefits. The consequence of this is a highly locally differentiated system of social citizenship.

Eligibility requirements for means-tested income support (with the exception of those nationally regulated) are defined locally and mostly defined in categorical terms. In general, they privilege older people and people with disabilities and children, in that order[33]. Conditions of eligibility are more restricted for the able-bodied than for older or severely disabled people. The able-bodied need to be ready to take a job if offered or accept jobs of public utility. As in Germany, benefit is not officially payable when there are relatives legally liable for any member in the claimant household. Unlike Germany, the range of 'obliged kin' is quite wide, including brothers and sisters, parents and children in law, uncles/ aunts and nieces/nephews. However, in real life this requirement may be overlooked. The amounts paid vary substantially among regions and among cities. Some groups receive more generous benefits, as is the case for pensioners and disabled people, whereas the able-bodied (including lone mothers) are less generously treated and often totally excluded from any income support measure.

The great heterogeneity of the support measures available (in some municipalities there are none at all), and the even greater heterogeneity of their modes of implementation, underlines the need to be extremely careful in analysing differences and similarities among different cities. For example, if we consider the minimum living allowance, Minimo Vitale (MV), which is provided in the three cities examined, Turin, Milan and Cosenza, we find three very different situations. In Milan and Turin, this allowance is paid to all citizens who do not reach a minimum income threshold considered essential to live on. In Milan, it is conceived in principle as a social right, but is implemented with a high level of discretion. In Turin, the discretionary power is low, even though from a legal point of view receiving income support is not considered a right, and people denied the benefit cannot claim for it before a court. In Cosenza, the MV is a category-based two year measure reserved for single mothers that, due to its limited impact (given the small number of lone mothers) and atypical nature, cannot be compared with the allowances in Turin and Milan. A more general measure, though as we shall see quite limited, which is applied in Cosenza is the Assistenza Economica. In order to be able to compare broadly similar measures, we have looked at the MV and basic income for food needs (Minimo Alimentare, MA) in both Turin and Milan, and the Assistenza Economica in Cosenza.

Generally speaking, the minimum living allowance (MV) is equal to the minimum contributory social insurance pension level and there are local equivalence scales to take account of different household sizes. In Milan, however, there is no clear connection between the amount and household composition. The amount paid and entitlements vary greatly between Milan and Turin, but there tends to be a basic distinction between the treatment of older or disabled people – who usually receive the amount necessary to bring them up to the minimum social security pension level – and the treatment of able-bodied applicants, which is much more discretionary.

Different groups receive different levels of benefit. For example, pregnant women and lone parents may have their income made up to the social pension level with a supplement for rent, although for a limited period. For other groups of recipients, income support is less generous. In general, the benefit is higher in Turin than in Milan (where it is even lower than in Barcelona). Moreover, in Milan[34], those who fulfil means-tested conditions are not automatically entitled to a monetary subsidy and their 'right' in fact depends on the constraints of the city social welfare budget. This is not the case in Turin, where discretionary power tends to be exercised through a more rigorous control of resources and a prolonged waiting time for the renewal of benefit for applicants deemed undeserving. Discretionary power may also affect which of the two benefits is granted (the MV is for food, clothing, general and social life expenses, while the MA only covers expenses related to food, and is therefore less generous). Such power means that the first meeting with the social worker is crucial and that the applicant's negotiating skills can make a difference. Furthermore, in both cities family solidarity is given primacy, increasing selectivity for admission to either of the measures.

In Turin the full amount of MV is paid to able-bodied claimants for a maximum of one year. If their need persists after that, they may continue to receive support, but at a lower rate (MA instead of MV). In Milan, the period of payment is in practice always limited in time (3-6 or 12 months), but again there is a disparity among different welfare offices catering to different categories of beneficiaries. While the assistance provided for adults in need (the UAD service) offers short-term allowances, that for lone mothers (the SSMI service) offers medium-term allowances, and that for older people (CADA service) long-term payments. In both cities, the amount received by able-bodied recipients is generally insufficient to live on and must be supplemented with income from the informal economy, family assistance, or private help from charities.

Neither MV nor MA are conditional on taking job offers or participation in public work projects; but able-bodied recipients must demonstrate their availability for work, which usually means that applicants have to register with the unemployment office. In both Turin and Milan some kind of temporary job for people 'at risk of marginality' is provided: for example, the so-called *Borse Lavoro* (job grants), which last for a period of six months and subsidise employers, or *wage support*, a financial contribution to firms that employ young people in need indicated by the social services, or *introductory apprenticeship*, work experience for young people in need. In Turin there is also a wide recourse to *Cantieri di Lavoro* and socially useful jobs, which provide publicly funded temporary work in the public and private sector (these are protected jobs for unemployed people that help connect them to the labour market with activities of social utility, under laws 55/84 and 608/1997).

The situation in Cosenza is totally different from the above. The economic assistance for the poor (*Assistenza Economica*) does not provide sufficient financial resources even for the most elementary living expenses: the yearly amount is similar to the lowest monthly amount in Turin and Milan (about Ecu120). The inefficiency of the measure is further compounded by a series of administrative and organisational deficiencies. Notwithstanding the negligible amount, three levels of need (and of benefits) are distinguished in the regulations. Access to the first amount – designated for ordinary situations – is granted automatically to all those whose revenues fall below a certain level. The two other types (particular cases and exceptional situations) are specified in the regulations, but their content is not formally defined. Criteria to distinguish 'particular' situations have been established informally by the municipal social service in its daily work.

In this poverty-stricken context, where unemployment is above 30%, beneficiaries are provided with no training or job-search guidance and nothing is demanded of them. Relations with social workers are generally very poor, and characterised by laborious bureaucratic procedures and checks that beneficiaries deem humiliating and offensive, given the absurdly low benefit paid. Moreover, many respondents said they had witnessed preferential treatment that had nothing to do with applicants' real needs. They often feel that social workers have no empathy with them and do not give them accurate information about the benefits they could obtain. At the same time, some of them make an effort to use the informal negotiation process to their favour, to obtain additional advantages.

Lisbon and Porto

The Portuguese social security system is very recent in comparison with the vast majority of European social systems. Only in 1984, with the publishing of the Basic Law of Social Security (*Lei de Bases da Segurança Social* 28/84) did the principles upon which the new system would develop become clear. This basic law represents an enormous simplifying effort, reducing the numerous former regimes to two, enhancing the administrative rationalisation and improving the visibility of rights and duties of beneficiaries and employers, not to mention the State.

The law is based on the idea of the 'universal right to social security' and the main aim is the protection of workers and their families, and the protection of persons suffering from the lack or loss of means of subsistence. Since there were still very few measures covering people of working age, a new non-categorical benefit[35] – the National Minimum Income – was added to the non-contributory system in 1996. At the time of our study, it had been operational only in some municipalities for a short time.

Here we shall examine the measures operative in Lisbon – *Subsidio Mensal* – and Porto – *Prestações Pecuniárias de Acção Social* – before the application of the new minimum income programme, which is at present going through a trial period and for which we lack empirical data at the local level. Neither measure can be considered as a right, since entitlements depend on subjective evaluation by social workers and on resources of the welfare services.

In Lisbon social assistance (even after the introduction of the new measure) is run by a religious organisation, the *Santa Casa da Misericordia de Lisboa* (SCML), which although state-regulated, has its own funding sources and enjoys a great deal of autonomy of action. In Porto social assistance is managed by the Regional Centre for Social Action, a public structure that also has a high degree of autonomy. In both cases the measures are in theory applied to all persons living in poverty, but in practice they are highly selective and category-based, though the categories are not well defined.

In practice no maximum level of resources is taken into account in deciding who is admitted to the programme. Even though in Lisbon the SCML has defined a household income threshold, this is usually totally disregarded and the decision is essentially based on how the social worker evaluates the situation. The criteria on which judgement is based call into play a great deal of unregulated discretionary power. The factors considered may include the applicant's personal resources, basic expenses (rent and associated expenses), help available from other sources such as family, friends, neighbours, and charity organisations, the urgency of a given case, the social worker's empathy for the person and how they judge the person's attitude, and the funding actually available.

In both cities, the amount given is generally low and constitutes only a portion of a person's overall resources. There is no precise definition of the monthly amount and there is no clear relation between household composition and amount granted. Benefits are granted without a maximum duration, yet there are wide differences in the implementation. Single mothers with children, and children in general, have priority. In Lisbon limits on duration seem less strictly enforced than in Porto, where the city's resources are much more limited. This difference also shows up in the average length of time on welfare, which cannot be explained by differences in the structure of opportunities in the two cities – over 30 months in Lisbon, and much shorter in Porto (see Chapter Five).

Action to promote the finding of new employment is left primarily to the social worker's personal initiative. The limited resources do not permit an efficient monitoring beyond giving information on training programmes and job possibilities. It should be underlined, moreover, that due to the high degree of selectivity and the extremely negative profile of beneficiaries and their family entourage, few beneficiaries are actually in a position to hold an ordinary full-time job. When people go off the programme, it is rarely because the problem of poverty has been resolved, and there is a high risk that those who do leave welfare will come back onto it later.

Beyond the social assistance measures, other initiatives have been introduced in the last few years at the local level in order to combat social exclusion. Among these the Local Initiatives of Development and Job Creation should be mentioned. These aim to create jobs by supporting the creation of small businesses. Employment policies are partly covered by initiatives organised at the national level (but locally implemented) in the context of the *Programas operacionais do IEFP* and partly at the local level (*Iniciativas local do Emprego*).

Two studies performed in the city of Lisbon (Cardoso, 1993; Silva et al, 1989) indicated that a significant number of demands for social assistance had no response from the existing institutions. Some institutions face serious financial constraints, which means that only the demands of the most needy are satisfied. Moreover, in some cases the demands are addressed to the wrong institutions. Given the fragmentation of institutions, each with its own 'public', it is not always easy for beneficiaries to find out which one they should address. Cardoso in particular points out that a significant percentage of poor households in Lisbon (52% of the population investigated) do not ask for social assistance, either because they do not know of the existence of the services (42%) or they have a bad opinion about their efficacy (32% of cases). Another reason is the stigmatisation effect of social assistance, which leads some people to refuse the assistance they might be entitled to.

According to our research, recipients' relations with social services are characterised by dependence, strongly coloured with fatalism and subjectivism (but not patronage or 'clientelism', as in Cosenza). Against this common background, however, there are differences between the two cities. In Porto relations are strongly affected by the extreme selectivity with which applications are considered, by the utter opacity of decision criteria and the absence of explanations for decisions, and finally by a caseload that precludes any personal follow-up. Many of those interviewed said they had stopped going to the service centre, either because their requests for assistance had been repeatedly rejected or because they had been taken off the programme without explanation. Evaluation of both services and social workers was generally quite negative. In Lisbon, on the other hand, we observed a dissociation in people's minds between social services as such, judged negatively due to the laborious administrative procedures, lack of information, and so on – and social workers as people, who are often judged positively for their monitoring activity, support and dedication in making use of available funds.

The following figures constitute an attempt at graphically summarising this analysis of the different income support systems, in all their variety and complexity. They should also offer a visual map for better interpreting the results of the study on social assistance careers presented in the next two chapters.

Figure 3.1: Swedish cities

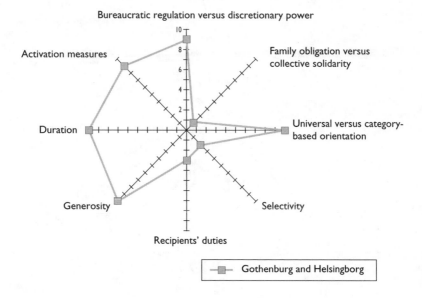

Figure 3.2: French cities

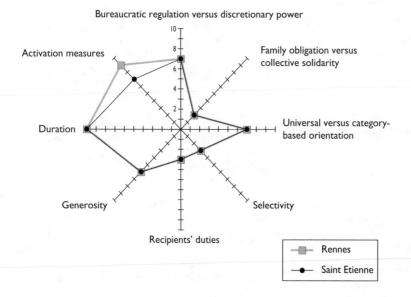

Figure 3.3: Italian cities

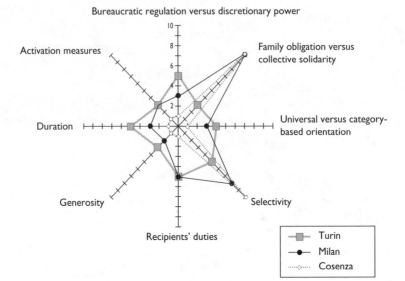

Figure 3.4: Spanish cities

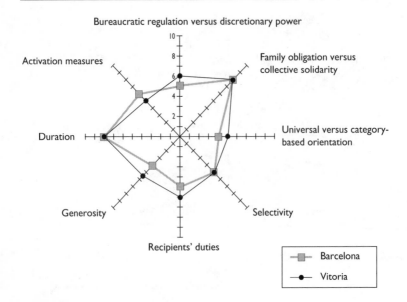

Figure 3.5: German cities

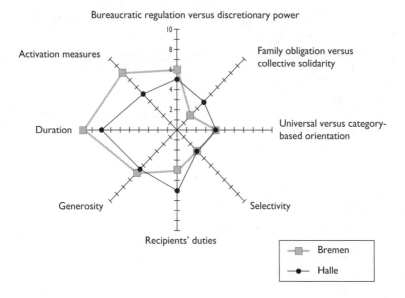

Figure 3.6: Portuguese cities

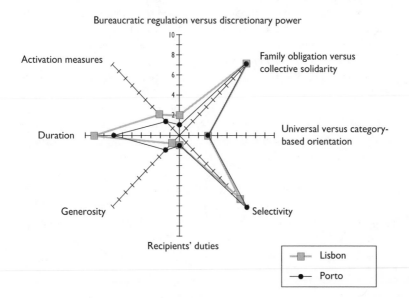

Notes

[1] The concept of '*référentiel*' is frequently used in public policy analysis in France. See, notably, Muller and Surel, 1998.

[2] Primary solidarity refers to the form of solidarity connected with family or friendship, as well as neighbourhood relations, and implies a personal acquaintance. Secondary solidarity, on the other hand, refers to more abstract social relations, inasmuch as they apply to 'anybody' within a given universe of reference (for instance, the city, the country). They cover both private forms of solidarity, like those implemented by religious associations, and public forms, whether at the State, regional or local level.

[3] It is important to underline that in the ESOPO study this homogeneity is also due to the choice of the cities. Thus, the choice of Turin and Milan for Italy, and Barcelona and Vitoria for Spain, brings to the fore important similarities. It would, however, be a mistake to extrapolate from this the existence of a clear-cut Italian or Spanish welfare state. For Italy, the counter-example of Cosenza is fundamental in this regard. A similar contrast would have emerged in Spain had we included in our sample a city from the south, for example, from Andalusia.

[4] Even those countries where integration is not at the heart of their income support programmes are experiencing a move in this direction. Thus, in Germany, a 1993 law requires that local administrations develop labour opportunities for those out of work, notably the young, in the form of general interest jobs or funded labour contracts. For an international comparison on the link between welfare and work, see Commission of European Communities, 1997; European Foundation for the Improvement of Living and Working Conditions, 1999; Gough et al, 1997.

[5] In France, it is estimated that the ratio for access to public employment programmes between the 10 most dynamic departments and the 10 least dynamic ones is 3 to 1. See Charbonneau and Landais, 1996.

[6] We resorted to the 'vignettes' method (see for example, Bradshaw et al, 1993; Finch, 1987; Marradi, 1996). More specifically, we presented a number of social workers in each city with possible 'cases' of need and asked them what was available in their city in principle, and what would occur in practice.

[7] Twenty-four interviews were conducted in each city in 1997, half with former and half with current claimants. For the French cities, in addition to these in-depth interviews, we also carried out a general survey on beneficiaries.

[8] Our approach draws its inspiration from Franz Schultheis' text: "La famille, une catégorie du droit social?: une comparaison franco-allemande", in *Comparer les systèmes de protection sociale en Europe*, vol 2, Paris, MIRE, 1996, pp 203-34.

[9] As with Figure 2.3 in Chapter Two, the proposed scores for each dimension have been agreed with local researchers, on the basis of local rules and patterns of implementation, with the validation of social workers within each local context. Scores from 7 to 10 indicate a high level for that specific dimension, 6 to 4 indicate a medium level and 3 to 2 indicate a low level. Score 1 means that the dimension is absent or irrelevant.

[10] This does not mean that the Swedish cities have absolute uniformity in decision making, only that in comparison with the other local contexts considered they can be positioned at the left side of the continuum (for intra-country diversity in Sweden, see Gustafsson et al, 1993).

[11] In the city of Turin, the possibility of renewing benefit for the entire period of need for the able-bodied poor is established not in the general regulation approved by the municipality government, but in a *circolare* – an interpretative document – from a lower legal administrative level. This means that social workers have considerable leeway in interpreting the regulation (see Bosco et al, 1999).

[12] This explains why the use of the term 'right' in the interviews both with social workers and with beneficiaries may be equivocal. It may be meant in the sense of deservedness, that is, to have a right to assistance given a particular itinerary and situation. This must not be confused with the legal meaning of having one's rights recognised and getting what one is entitled to.

[13] Except in Porto, where at the time of the study there was no income threshold and a subjective evaluation of need had to be made by social workers.

[14] For example, in Turin property ownership (except when the accommodation is suitable for the needs of the household and inhabited by it) or registered assets (for example, motor vehicles not used for work or required for health reasons) are still considered grounds for ineligibility.

[15] The debate also concerns the effectiveness of measures that make up the workfare programmes. According to Hanesch (1999, p 81; see also Cousins, 1997) these programmes are "only successful to a limited degree in reducing poverty and social assistance through integration into labour market .... They may succeed in reducing the numbers of unemployment benefit and/or social assistance claimants without increasing public expenditure in the short term, but they may do so at the cost of increased social exclusion and greater public expenditure in the long term".

[16] Laparra and Aguilar Hendrickson (1997) speak in this connection of a situation of "integrated precariousness".

[17] For example, in the case of Bremen we have considered the average monthly disposable income in 1993 (Vogel, 1997) to be Ecu1,138. To obtain a kind of monthly poverty line for a single person household, we took 50% of this amount. In the case of Germany, this threshold is equal to Ecu569 per month. We then calculated the amount of the highest benefit given to a single person household (Ecu270) and to a seven person household (Ecu1,604). We calculated the ratio W between each benefit amount and the 'threshold' (0.47, 2.8). We defined two scores for Bremen, for a single person household and for a seven person household, as follows:

$$\text{Bremen score} = \frac{\Omega \text{ of Bremen} * 10}{\Omega \text{ of Sweden}}$$

In this way we related the Bremen values to the Swedish ones, considered to be equal to 10, as they were the highest among our cases. Finally, we calculated the average of the two scores obtained for Bremen, and used the same procedure for calculating the value for each context. It must be remembered that the amount of benefit is considered without extra money for housing, but where such integration is not provided, the final score is equal to the average score minus 1. Obviously if we choose a different family size in order to calculate generosity (for example, a household with five persons instead of seven), we obtain different values. The decision to consider a seven person household was taken in order to consider the extremes and consequently the functioning of the equivalence scales, even if this family type is less common, especially in northern countries. According to the calculation with a smaller family size, the values for generosity are higher for France and Germany, while there are no great differences for the other countries.

[18] Again, the sense of activation can sometimes also include a punitive or restrictive side, the so-called 'activation by sanctions' (see, European Foundation for the

Improvement of Living and Working Conditions, 1999). We are not dealing with this meaning here, since we have already discussed it in considering what we have called 'recipients' duties'.

[19] This classification is, however, essential in order to understand the relative significance of the number of recipients benefiting from each measure and, above all, the dynamics of programme entry and exit. If this aspect is not taken into consideration, we may make the mistake of thinking that the fact that people exit a given welfare programme quickly means that it is highly efficient in terms of job integration, whereas it may just mean that the recipient has moved from one support programme to another. This is the so-called 'carousel effect', with participants moving from one measure to another without ever reaching the 'real' labour market (Hanesch, 1999).

[20] Sweden is distinct from the other countries in its very strong work ethic. Whereas the interviews seem to indicate that no heavy direct pressure is exerted on recipients by the social services, this must be situated in the context of strong social and cultural pressures (Paugam, 1996).

[21] This implies that there may be major discrepancies between expectations built into the institutional framework and the cultural representations with regard to women working outside the home shared by some immigrant populations, particularly in the case of mothers of young children. It is an issue social workers have only recently started to address.

[22] Nonetheless, the maximum level of resources corresponding to this obligation is fixed at a fairly high level. See the comprehensive table in the Appendix presenting the national and local institutional frameworks.

[23] It should be noted that in Spain, unlike other European countries with a minimum income scheme, maintenance obligations for family members not living with the applicant are not taken into account when assessing the needs of their household (Guibentif and Bouget, 1997, p 19). In other words, obligations are enforced when assessing resources, but not when assessing need (that is when assessing the overall costs supported by applicants).

[24] All means-tested programmes – which also include *supplementary benefits to minimum pensions, non-contributory pensions* and *unemployment subsidies* – affected 10.9% of the Spanish population in 1992. Persons included only in the anti-poverty programmes were a very low proportion of the total (0.1%). Moreover, despite the fact that in 1995 Spain was the only country in Southern Europe that

had already implemented minimum income policies over almost all the country, expenditure on these benefits represented the lowest share of GDP and lowest level of protection for all family typologies (MISSOC, 1996).

[25] Even though this kind of job insertion is the closest to real working life, these contracts are often too short to be helpful, and so they tend to be a way of legitimating the benefit payment, rather than being a path towards achieving better chances in the labour market (Laparra and Aguilar Hendrickson, 1997, p 530).

[26] It is in the Basque country that we find the highest proportion of households receiving benefit (1.93% in 1993).

[27] In the Basque country, 36.5% of the 1990 recipients were still receiving income support in 1995.

[28] In Barcelona, adult training actions take place in educational centres authorised by the Catalan Government and supervised by the social welfare department, which supports actions to encourage, orientate and train, organised by the labour department with private companies, local and country councils, corporations and NGOs. In Vitoria, the city council has set up a wide network of civic centres to which recipients are directed in order to attend training courses.

[29] However, it should be noted that there is a very low proportion of immigrants among the recipients in both cities.

[30] The pension system has undergone a massive reform in recent years, with pensions becoming less generous, and criteria homogenised across categories.

[31] Since 1997 a child allowance has been introduced for very low income households including at least three under-age children, irrespective of the source of the household income.

[32] Only in October 2000 was a national framework law in this field (no 328/ 2000) approved. Although it mentions the introduction of a nationally regulated minimum income scheme, this is dependent on the approval of another law, still to be prepared.

[33] Thus, for instance in Turin, as in many northern Italian cities, older people receiving a *Pensione Sociale* may have it integrated up to the social security minimum one, if they are below a given income threshold.

[34] In Milan the degree of discretion also depends on the services concerned: it is low in CADA (Home Care Centres for the Elderly), intermediate in SSMI (Mother and Child Social Services), and high in the UAD (Office for Adults at Risk).

[35] Law no 19-A/96 of 29 June 1996. This statute was undergoing a period of experimental application during which several pilot projects were implemented on the basis of the *Portaria* (governmental regulation) no 237-A/96 of 1 July 1996. The model is the French RMI, yet the minimum income benefit granted under this scheme is of a variable amount (although generally very low) and duration. There is thus an ample degree of discretion; moreover, the benefit may be refused, even if eligibility conditions are respected. The insertion programme is composed of actions – negotiated and agreed upon between the local commissions and the persons entitled to the benefit – aiming at the creation of conditions that should facilitate a gradual insertion (or reinsertion) of the recipients and their families.

FOUR

Why some people are more likely to be on social assistance than others[1]

Marisol Garcia and Yuri Kazepov

A medium range approach

Are some categories of people more likely to be on benefits because they are really more needy? Or is it because the entitlement structure privileges them as a group? It is not easy to answer these questions, as it requires a large amount of information and the consideration of many aspects. In order to give a tentative answer, we need to pull together the issues discussed in Chapters Two and Three of this book: the way in which the local context produces vulnerability and poverty, and the way in which the problem is conceived and tackled at the national and local level. We intend to examine in particular the role of the institutional mechanisms: how they work and how they influence the process of becoming a beneficiary of social assistance.

In order to understand this process, we have to consider the main dimensions that influence the experience of poverty and downward social mobility, which are: (a) the socioeconomic context (including demographic changes), (b) the social network of the potential claimant, and (c) his or her personal capabilities. These dimensions, together with the institutional design, interact with one another to define the degrees of social vulnerability and the risk of becoming poor (and hence the risk of being on social assistance). Of course, the same interaction also defines the set of resources and opportunities that people may use to escape poverty. This chapter, however, focuses on the paths into social assistance and highlights how the contextual *driving factors* (described in Chapter Two) are transformed by the institutional setting (described in Chapter Three) into socially defined conditions of need of income support.

Figure 4.1: The dimensions influencing downward mobility

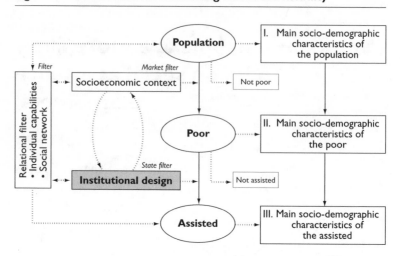

Figure 4.1 shows how the main dimensions interact with one another. We are aware that at this stage the resulting picture is approximate and does not take into account the full range of complex interactions between these dimensions. Nevertheless, it allows us to appreciate that the vulnerable groups 'produced' by the interaction between a given population and its socioeconomic context are not necessarily in a condition of economic need per se. This need emerges through a further selection process involving the institutional dimension, which is at the core of our explanation. The institutional dimension structures people's life course by defining how public (and partly also private) resources are – or should be – allocated in relation to the risks emerging during critical status passages in life[2]. Such passages occur in relation to age-specific phases and specific events (entering the labour market, becoming unemployed, retiring, and so on). The link between the two is self-evident, but it is important to keep them analytically separate, as social policies address them differently.

The ways in which risks are distributed institutionally among social groups become more evident by contrasting different contexts. Unemployed people deal with their vulnerable situation in relation to the labour market in different ways according to the policies that exist in the specific country; their generosity, coverage, accompanying measures, and so forth (Gallie and Paugam, 2000). It is very different having to rely on unemployment benefit of 30% of the last net wage for 180 days (as in Italy)[3] and a benefit of 60-70% for nearly two years with several funded retraining options (as in many other European countries). Of course, specific social-demographic factors, like an unbalanced age structure, can produce more (or fewer) people who find themselves in need of care and support (Micheli, 1997). But how many of these turn into cases of economic need is a matter of institutional intervention and policy design (Goodin, 1996). This implies that, on the one hand, the dimensions identified above produce social groups that are more (or less) vulnerable and, on the other hand, that vulnerability turns into concrete need because social policies, by structuring the flow of resources – both monetary and in kind – redistribute the risks of becoming needy. In other words, living conditions in general, and conditions of economic need in particular, are largely the result of the filtering process occurring at the institutional level. Therefore, different institutional arrangements and configurations produce large variations in the distribution of living conditions.

The literature is not always clear about this process. With few exceptions (for example, Behrens and Voges, 1996; Leisering and Leibfried, 1999), most scholars (for example, Esping-Andersen, 1990, 1999; Ferrera, 1998) tend not to emphasise the relations between the different policies and the related synergy effect in relation to poverty, even though they acknowledge the influence of the welfare state in structuring the social stratification of society.

The interaction among policies and among the dimensions that structure the distribution of risks in society vary according to history and geography, but at a different pace. An increasingly wide range of events can trigger downward mobility by breaking down the equilibrium between available resources and needs. The individualisation of need (Andreß and Schulte, 1998) also implies the individualisation of risks (Beck, 1992). This means that the readjustment of policies is lagging behind social transformations and that their adequacy suffers the burden of de-contextualised solutions. The strategic importance of schemes designed as the last safety net or last resort against poverty, like social assistance, is increasing. The number of claimants is rising (Atkinson, 1998b; Eardley et al, 1996; Mingione, 1996; OECD, 1998b, 1999) and the overall distribution of social expenditure within welfare policies is increasingly shifting people towards social assistance. But the adjustment of the schemes themselves to the new, emerging needs is slow. Their institutional design is often still focused on traditional forms of marginality, which in fact characterise fewer and fewer of the social assistance claimants.

There are other dimensions that play a major role in the process of becoming poor and socially assisted. Taking further the analysis developed in the previous two chapters, we identify (Figure 4.1) a relational filter, including individual competences[4] and the primary social support network, which activates reciprocity resources (Cochran et al, 1990; Gullestad and Segalen, 1997). The two dimensions can play very different roles, depending on the socioeconomic context and institutional arrangements existing in a given country at the specific local level (region, city). We can identify three main patterns (Kazepov, 1999). In the first, the primary social network presents a *complementary* role, as in welfare systems where family and kin support is integrated into the institutional design of social assistance measures (for example, in Germany, France and most Continental European countries). In these systems, the State not only identifies the family as the main source of support, but also assists it with relatively generous transfers and/or services. This is a form of *active subsidiarity*. The second pattern is more *substitutive* and occurs mainly in countries where little or no direct institutional support is given to families (for example, in Southern European countries). Here the family is burdened with many social responsibilities and has to pool and share resources more than elsewhere in order to cope with events which could trigger downward social mobility. This is a form of *passive subsidiarity* that presents problems of sustainability in periods of continuous transformation and hence increased vulnerability, which redefine the conditions of social inclusion and exclusion. The third pattern is characterised by an *additional* role played by reciprocity networks in welfare systems where the State intervenes extensively for all needs that may arise in the population. Here, the family support network is not burdened with social responsibilities, and the individual is the bearer of substantial rights. Family intervention adds resources to the assistance already granted institutionally.

There are different mixes of these three patterns even within single countries, especially where the socioeconomic context and institutional setting vary considerably at the regional level, like in Spain and Italy. Generally speaking, a sort of *functional equilibrium* develops between the form of family support existing in a given context and the institutional design of income support measures. However, the different role assigned to family solidarity affects the outcomes of public intervention in terms of distribution of income inequalities. It is not surprising that the most unequal distribution is to be found in systems where the family plays a strong role, while the least uneven is found where the family plays an additional role[5]. This outcome is the result of a complex interactive process that highlights the difficulty in breaking down the reproduction of inequalities, particularly for vulnerable families and groups, without the intervention of external resources. In substitutive contexts the family, whose role is also the result of a specific ideological and cultural background, is forced to cooperate and pool resources.

In addition to the socioeconomic and demographic filter, individual competencies and social networks also influence the access to resources and therefore the risk of becoming poor (assisted or not). In order to understand this influence, however, we have to consider it together with the institutional dimension, which determines the family's support strategies. In this sense, our focus on the institutional dimension should not be taken to mean that we underestimate the other dimensions influencing poverty, but as an intermediate position between a structural (more socioeconomic) and an individualistic view of the phenomena. Both elements play a fundamental role and the profiles of the socially assisted are the result of the complex process of social construction, which involves all dimensions. Socioeconomic restructuring and market-oriented reorganisation lead to greater vulnerability, while an individual lack of competencies is an obstacle in adequately facing the new context. Yet, their impact on living conditions is mediated by the institutional set-up, which distributes resources (or not) and prevents (or not) people beginning a path of downward social mobility. The institutional dimension acts as a filtering process, which transforms a larger or smaller part of the poor into assisted poor. In this sense, it is clear that in our analysis we are addressing only a subgroup of the poor, that is those covered formally by the measures and – among them – those taking up the available benefits.

The process underlying the transformation of the poor into welfare claimants and beneficiaries can be approximately formalised in a chain of events on which specific measures (or their absence) have a greater or lesser influence, depending on the resources they can make available. Figure 4.2 shows a simplified version of this process, addressing typified events and listing examples of dimensions contributing to the pre-structuring of potential paths of downward (or upward) mobility. The perspective here is slightly different from that in Figure 4.1, as it attempts to give a more concrete insight into the process taking place. Specific events like family disruption, health problems/illness or unemployment may accumulate over time or may suddenly break down the existing balance between resources and needs.

From the analysis of the ESOPO fieldwork material, in particular the interviews with beneficiaries, it emerged that events triggering downward mobility are related to three main spheres: (a) the labour market; (b) the family; (c) health. A fourth sphere, which may interact with the first three and which affects mainly migrants and refugees is that of *forced mobility*, due to wars, major national upheavals, political persecution or serious economic poverty in the countries or regions of origin. Within these spheres, the degree of variation of events is relatively high, even though there are several elements common to the way in which they structure the specific condition of need that allow them to be grouped together. If we consider, for instance, the labour market sphere, a claimant might have become unemployed after a long working career in the formal labour market, or else might have always been working in precarious jobs at the margins of legality, or have been outside the labour market altogether, as in the case of many lone mothers who apply for income support as a consequence of a marriage breakdown. Often events occurring in one sphere also impact on the equilibrium in other spheres. Serious illness can lead to job loss, family problems and a consequent divorce – or the other way around. According to the results of our fieldwork, the chain of events leading to the condition of need can be the result of three main processes: (a) it can be inherited from the family of origin, where it consolidated and has been transmitted from one generation to the next; (b) it can be the result of a major breakdown event, which tipped the existing balance between resources and needs; (c) it can be the result of a series of smaller breakdown events, which cumulate during a period of time bringing about a progressive but steady downward mobility.

It is clear that the impact of these events is manifold and depends on the resources the person can bring to bear. In Figure 4.2, several options are given as possible ways of coping with the 'crisis event'. These range from being embedded in rich and dense reciprocity networks to facilitated access to new job opportunities on the labour market, perhaps after a retraining course funded by a contribution-based scheme, as in many Scandinavian or Continental European countries. Social policies contribute to structure all these events; and even the perception individuals may have of the risks they are experiencing depends partly on the resources available. And individuals and households develop their coping strategies out of these perceptions.

Figure 4.2 does not show all the possible options a person may have in managing conditions of need (*the crisis*) by accessing reciprocity networks and labour market opportunities directly. Again, this does not mean that we do not consider them relevant. On the contrary, they are often crucial. Rather, we consider them through their interaction with social assistance provisions, since the target of our analysis is people entering welfare. Furthermore, the profiles of welfare recipients depend, to a greater degree than might be expected, upon the institutional design of the benefits they can access, and the role played by the other dimensions is filtered through it. A first set of crucial dimensions of this design relates to the

Figure 4.2: Institutional pre-structuring of social assistance patterns

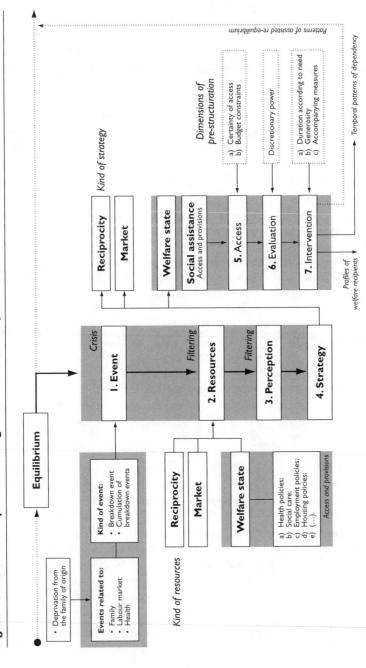

conditions of access (certainty, budgetary constraints, subsidiarity, stigmatisation, and so on), which determine – formally and in practice – the implementation of claimants' entitlements. To these dimensions we must add the degree of discretion social workers have in defining both access and the kind of intervention. The latter is further influenced by a set of crucial dimensions: the adequacy of replacement rates, the duration of payments in relation to the persistence of the condition of need, the existence of accompanying measures, their effectiveness, and so on. Altogether these dimensions – described in detail in Chapter Three – contribute to structure the profile of those who enter social assistance and, as we shall see in Chapter Five, also their patterns of recipiency over time and chances of exiting.

Who is more likely to be on benefits in the ESOPO cities?

It is not our intention to argue that the social and individual characteristics of social assistance recipients[6] depend entirely on the institutional design of social policies. The social assistance archives we have used do not always contain sufficient data to prove such a hypothesis. In addition, the socioeconomic context plays a major role by adding a strong element of variation to the existing diversity in institutional patterns. More modestly, and cautiously, from the vantage point of a comparative perspective, we wish to understand to what extent the over or under representation of some categories is caused by the institutional design of the welfare scheme, and to what extent by the socioeconomic context. Of course, concrete cases are never completely clear-cut, and it is obvious that both dimensions interact strongly.

If the institutional design and pattern of implementation were the same everywhere, the different profiles found in our study could be attributed largely to the effects of the socioeconomic context. In our sample, however, we not only have different national systems, but cases where cities share a common, nationally defined, institutional pattern, and cases where cities, although they belong to the same country and overall welfare system, do not have similar institutional patterns with regard to income support policies. Thus, inter-city differences in social assistance recipients' profiles must be interpreted carefully: they may depend either on inter- or within-country variation in institutional design or implementation patterns, or local social and demographic features. Our study allows us partly to assess the relative weight of these different dimensions, and more precisely, the crucial role of the interaction between the institutional framework of income support policies and the modes of their implementation.

Table 4.1 shows the distribution of first time recipients in the cities examined by selected demographic characteristics at the beginning of the 1990s. Data come from local social assistance records, which in some cases have been specifically reconstructed for this study. Thus, they include only the cities for which such archives were available[7]. Only in the case of the French cities do the data not regard first time recipients, but a sample of the total recipient population. It should be pointed out that the very existence (or lack) of archives – and therefore some form of recording and effort to keep track of beneficiaries, their characteristics and needs – is a significant feature of a policy and its implementation. It points to an attitude and willingness to monitor and be monitored, to be examined from the point of view of implementation and so forth, as well as to evaluate efficacy over time.

The Swedish cities

There are important similarities between the Swedish cities in terms of the characteristics of minimum income recipients entering the measure for the first time, for which there are socioeconomic and institutional explanations. Both cities have a disproportionately high number of immigrants who entered Sweden mainly as refugees, have residence permits and are trying to enter the labour market. These people generally come from a background of civil or ethnic war in their home country. Even though the main crisis event is their forced migration, they often accumulate several conditions of disadvantage. Examples are the lack of knowledge of the language, weak networks in the host country, inappropriate skills considering the conditions of the local labour market. For instance, if an immigrant has worked for 10 years in the public administration of a former communist country, their knowledge and practices are quite different from those common in Sweden. This brings about problems more to do with social integration and stigma than economic integration, which, as in France and partly in Germany, is granted institutionally (see Chapter Three; and Eardly et al, 1996), with benefits for immigrants being the same as for nationals.

In both cities young people are highly over represented, even though they are often quite highly qualified. This may be at least partly explained by the high individualisation of the Swedish welfare state and cultural approach, which does not expect young people to be supported by their parents while looking for a job. At the same time, the comparatively low

Table 4.1: Distribution of first time social assistance recipients and total population within ESOPO cities according to main demographic characteristics (%)

	Milan[a]		Turin[a]		Barcelona[a]		Vitoria[a]		Bremen[a]		Halle[c]	
	Total	Assisted	Total	Assisted	Total	Assisted	Total	Assisted	Total	Assisted	Total	Assisted
Age (18-64)												
18-29	26.0	18.8	27.4	26.0	25.4	15.4	30.5	28.8	26.9	54.4	23.8	na
30-44	30.5	43.3	31.0	36.8	33.1	35.9	36.5	45.2	33.3	33.2	33.4	na
45-64	43.5	37.9	41.6	37.2	41.5	48.7	33.0	26.0	39.8	12.4	42.8	na
Gender (18-64)												
Male	49.3	64.3	49.9	58.8	48.5	46.3	49.5	44.2	50.7	64.3	52.2	48.9
Female	50.7	35.7	50.1	41.2	51.5	53.7	50.5	55.8	49.3	35.7	47.8[5]	51.1
Nationality												
Nationals	95.1	86.9	98.3	84.7	98.0	95.0	98.0	95.5	86.4	74.2	98.6	92.0
Non-nationals	4.9	13.1	1.7	15.3	2.0	5.0	2.0	4.5	13.6	25.8	1.4	8.0
Household size				(1)								
1	32.0	27.3	33.5	27.3	18.1	45.1	37.1	35.1	44.6	42.5	33.9	na
2	28.0	21.2	27.2	17.6	27.8	18.8	28.6	19.1	32.6	19.9	31.2	na
3	21.2	21.4	19.8	14.5	22.0	14.4	15.8	20.4	11.7	18.7	19.7	na
4 or more	18.8	30.1	19.6	15.4	32.1	21.7	18.5	25.4	11.1	18.9	15.2	na
Marital status							(1)					
Unmarried	39.8	31.0	38.0	29.8	41.8	43.8	47.3	35.9	30.2	36.9	38.0	na
Married	47.5	32.6	49.5	26.3	47.9	23.8	46.6	27.4	51.4	40.9	47.0	na
Separated	1.7	21.4	2.5	10.2	1.6	23.8	na	29.4	(2)	12.1	(2)	na
Divorced	1.8	7.6	1.6	4.4	0.9	4.8	na	3.1	7.7	7.9	(2)	na
Widowed	9.2	7.4	8.4	5.4	7.8	3.9	na	4.2	10.7	2.2	15.0	na
Target groups												
Single adults	32.0	27.3	32.3	23.3	18.1	45.3	37.0	35.1	42.8	41.2	33.9	na
Non-nationals	4.9	13.1	1.7	15.3	2.0	5.5	2.0	4.4	13.6	25.8	1.4	na
Lone mothers	7.7	15.4	6.2	8.5	7.3	26.2	7.0	19.7	4.3[3]	10.6	na	24.6
Couples with children	34.4	26.3	36.2	16.6	45.0	14.5	69.0	19.5	14.5	15.7	na	13.6
Number of cases	1,311,979	791	979,839	1,230	1,643,542	585	206,116	385	549,357	849	303,000	652
											(4)	

continued

Table 4.1: Distribution of first time social assistance recipients and total population within ESOPO cities according to main demographic characteristics (%) (contd)

	Gothenburg[a]		Helsingborg[a]		Lisbon[a]		Saint Etienne[b]		Rennes[b]	
	Total	Assisted	Total	Assisted	Total	Assisted	Total	Assisted	Total	Assisted
Age (18-64)										
18-29	31.3	51.1	28.1	59.0	23.4	15.7	32.3	41.8[8]	40.9	43.0[8]
30-44	35.2	35.1	34.1	27.1	30.5	36.4	33.1	39.1	30.1	42.1
45-64	33.5	13.8	37.8	13.9	46.1	48.0	34.6	19.1	29.0	14.9
Gender (18-64)										
Male	50.3	53.2	49.4	53.3	46.6	32.8	48.5	48.0	na	45.7
Female	49.7	47.7	50.6	46.7	53.4	67.2	51.5	52.0	na	54.3
Nationality										
Nationals	89.0	66.7	93.2	78.9	98.2	95.4	89.1	76.3	95.9	91.7
Non-nationals	11.0	33.3	6.8	21.1	1.8	4.6	10.9	23.7	4.1	8.3
Household size										
1	18.2	67.0[6]	13.8	61.5[6]	23.9	23.3	34.6	44.9	37.6	47.5
2	26.6	15.9	27.2	16.4	28.4	20.2	29.7	18.8	29.3	24.2
3	20.6	8.5	21.8	13.5	21.3	24.7	15.3	12.7	15.0	14.7
4 or more	34.6	8.6	37.2	8.6	26.4	31.8	20.4	23.6	18.1	13.6
Marital status										
Unmarried	43.6	na	36.3	na	28.1	27.3	33.2	57.1	45.1	66.1
Married	43.2	19.0	49.8	na	53.3	38.9	52.5	27.2	43.5	13.6
Separated	n.a.	na	na	na	2.6	13.6	(7)	(7)	(7)	(7)
Divorced	11.7	na	12.0	na	4.3	11.6	9.7	11.8	4.7	16.9
Widowed	1.5	na	1.9	na	11.7	8.6	4.6	3.9	6.5	3.4
Target groups										
Single adults	18.2	67.0	13.8	59.8	23.9	23.2	34.7	44.9	37.6	47.4
Non-nationals	11.0	33.3	6.8	20.9	1.8	4.5	10.9	23.7	4.1	8.3
Lone mothers	(6)	13.0	(6)	17.2	1.9	23.7	6.7	na	7.8	na
Couples with children	(6)	12.0	(6)	16.0	50.4	31.8	31.0	na	26.8	na
Number of cases	449,200	2,213	114,000	244	663,394	198	199,464	267	197,494	122

Sources of data

Total population:
If not specified the source is the relevant census of 1990 or 1991.
Germany: Mikrozensus, 1991.
Portugal: Lisbon population, 1992.

Assisted:
(a) ESOPO longitudinal sample on first time recipients.
(b) Oberti (1998)
(c) 10% sample 1991 cohort, Ölk and Rentzsch, 1997.

Notes
(1) Differences to 100% missing data.
(2) Data for separated and divorced included in widowed.
(3) Households on household total.
(4) Year 1994.
(5) 20-64 age bracket.
(6) In Sweden households are defined differently (see text).
(7) Divorced and separated are considered together.
(8) 21-29 age bracket.
Data on target groups do not equal 100% because they do not include all beneficiaries and in some cases overlap. Year of reference when not specified differently is 1991.

stigma attached to receiving income support allows an instrumental or strategic use of the benefit. It is used while looking for an acceptable or interesting job, having a child, and so forth. The existence of training opportunities and various job insertion activities reduces the risk that such strategic use of social assistance may turn into a self-defeating choice.

The disproportionately high incidence of single person households on benefits also requires an institutional-administrative explanation. In Sweden cohabiting adults – if they are not a family (ie, a married couple with children below 18 years of age) – are often considered to be singles from the administrative point of view, even though their income is assessed on a household basis. This is clear from our database on first time recipients, where quite a few 'single' persons received social assistance at the rate that corresponds to half the amount set for two adults on the basis of the equivalence scales (that is, a slightly lower amount than that granted to a person actually living alone). For this reason the resulting number of single person households is slightly overestimated.

Given the remarkable similarity, both in design and implementation of policies, in the two cities (see Chapter Three, as well as the Appendix), cross-city differences must be explained mainly by differences in the demographic and economic context. In particular, the lower incidence of the age 30 to 44 cohort among the socially assisted in Helsingborg is largely due to the lower unemployment rate there, due to its position as a border town with Denmark. Adults in the prime of life succeed more easily there than in Gothenburg in holding an adequately paid job or finding a new one if they lose it.

The French cities

The analysis of recipients in the two French cities included in our study, as well as the impact of the institutional design of the RMI on their profiles and the interaction with other forms of income support provided by the French welfare system, reveals similarities and differences.

Firstly, we look at some similarities. In Rennes, the largest age group of recipients comprised those aged between 21 and 29 (43%), followed by the 30 to 44 cohort (42.1%). The same cohorts also accounted for most claimants in Saint Etienne (41.8% and 39.1% respectively). In both cities single people without children constitute nearly 60% of the recipients, while lone mothers with children represent a mere 20%. The latter fact is due at least partly to the existence of another, more generous, measure targeted at poor lone mothers with children under the age of three. Notwithstanding the exclusion of childless young people living alone from the RMI, the recipient population in both cities seems to be predominantly young, and also relatively well educated. The in-depth interviews confirm this picture, and social workers of both cities emphasised that the share of young people accessing the RMI is increasing more than proportionally compared to other age groups, particularly the long-term unemployed, who are usually in their forties or older. This trend may be related to the joint effects of other measures that help older workers more than the young. The latter are consequently the group with fewer opportunities, in particular when they accumulate several disadvantages (low level of schooling, weak primary social networks, and so on).

Despite these common characteristics and trends, there are also some relevant differences between the two cities. In Saint Etienne, for instance, there is a larger proportion of people with a low level of education. Here the main reason for entering the programmes seems to be either the difficulty in finding a job or family-related events, such as childbirth, divorce or illness, which break down a precarious equilibrium between needs and resources. The small number of cases (according to the interviews) that come from deprived families is concentrated in Saint Etienne and not in Rennes. These are all lone mothers, who have an accumulation of conditions of need. Among the other groups, the presence of families with children and the able-bodied indicate that difficulties in entering the labour market are the main cause for becoming recipients of the RMI.

Institutional practices filter these social assistance claimants in the two cities in a different way. Formal national homogeneity, in fact, does not mean that there are no differences between cities in implementation and synergy with other measures. In fact, in Rennes, three times as many insertion contracts are signed as in Saint Etienne. There are many possible explanations. In socioeconomic terms, it may relate either to the higher education level of claimants in Rennes and thus their higher employability, or the fact that in Saint Etienne nearly a quarter of claimants are of non-French, mostly Maghrebin, ethnic origin (23.7% against 8.3% in Rennes). On the other hand, from a policy perspective the difference could be related to the long-standing interventionist tradition in Rennes. In fact, the municipality has institutionalised a broader network of social partners, developing insertion programmes and job access strategies by actively coordinating the relevant actors in the local welfare system. The interaction between these two possible explanations and the broader institutional framework, explains most of the differences in claimant profiles between the two cities. The result is that the more vulnerable groups of Saint

Etienne are made even more vulnerable, because there is a relatively 'passive insertion policy' with fewer resources invested. In Rennes, on the contrary, a smaller number of recipients can count on a broader and more effective range of active insertion measures.

The German cities

In Germany – as in France and Sweden – immigrants are a particularly weak group that is over represented among the recipients of social assistance. Again, this over representation has various explanations. On the one hand, their over representation points to the higher incidence of need and social disadvantage within the immigrant population. On the other hand, we could say that, given this higher vulnerability, they are over represented because they are entitled to the measure. In this sense, it could be considered an indicator not only of a condition of need, but also of a system that designs entitlements according to need and not nationality. This is truer for Bremen than for Halle, for two reasons. Firstly, as indicated in Chapter Two, the number of foreign immigrants in Halle is very low; secondly, a new ad hoc social assistance programme for refugees was created in Germany in 1991, as their number had been steadily rising throughout West Germany. Before this date, they were treated in the same way as all other needy immigrants and nationals. Since first time recipients in our study in Bremen are those who first entered the programme in 1989, they still include a sizeable number not only of 'economic' immigrants, but also refugees.

Another group that is over represented in both cities is that of lone mothers, but this is for different reasons. In Bremen, lone motherhood bears a specific risk of triggering an impoverishment process because of the prevalent gender and family models. Married women with children, and more generally women with children, are traditionally not expected to work outside the home, although things are changing in the younger generations. Thus, marriage breakdown or widowhood before retirement age, as well as single motherhood, easily bring about lack of access to a male breadwinner income. In Halle, as in all former East Germany, this phenomenon is quite new and not explained by any shared cultural gender and family model, but by the gender-specific effects of reunification and industrial restructuring in the East. German reunification, in fact, brought about a radical transformation both in the labour market and in the regulatory frameworks, which, among other things, discouraged married women's employment (Hanesch et al, 2000; Leisering and Leibfried, 1999). The West German model, based on the subsidiarity principle, has been extended to the eastern *Länder* and support measures for women in the labour market have been reduced. Special leave for working mothers has disappeared in the *Länder* of former East Germany, and there is a drastic reduction in childcare and similar services. The reduction both in the offer of childcare services and the demand for them (due to women's unemployment), have in turn contributed to a reduction in the demand for women's labour, creating a vicious circle. As a result, women's unemployment has risen dramatically, particularly among those with young children and in middle age. Women's employment rates, formerly very high, have also fallen to the West German level. This has made women more dependent on a male breadwinner, and therefore on social assistance when the partnership/marriage breaks down.

In general, however, there are fewer people on social assistance in Halle than in Bremen, which is striking given the high rates of unemployment in the former. This is partly a heritage of the former socialist regime, and the attitudes and values it developed with regard to social assistance and paid work[8]. Partly it is due to the role played until very recently by ad hoc active labour policies set in place after reunification, which keep a substantial part of the otherwise unemployed off the welfare rolls. Since these policies were being substantially downsized in the late 1990s due to budgetary constraints, it is likely that the rates of social assistance recipients will increase in the near future and converge towards those of West German cities.

Given this background, entry into social assistance in the early 1990s in Halle was more likely to be triggered by an accumulation of crisis events than a single event (Leisering and Leibfried, 1999; Olk and Rentzsch, 1997). Compared to Bremen, therefore, social assistance recipients have more characteristics rendering them vulnerable and making it difficult to insert them in the active labour policies (or less attractive for those in charge of these policies), such as lack of skills, age, gender, presence of children, and so forth. They also seem to depend more heavily than their Bremen counterparts on initiatives and suggestions by social workers. Social workers tend to blame this attitude on the cultural heritage of the socialist regime, which 'took care of everything'. Yet, this is a very simplistic way of looking at what actually occurred.

Formerly, in East Germany when a person did not pay their rent they were not evicted, rather the firm took up the payment, reducing their wage. As there were formally no unemployed – even though some people were not working, they were registered on some firm's payroll – this situation was not considered a problem. In the long run, however, it contributed to determining a certain degree of dependence, or lack of initiative, among those who were not able to support themselves or adequately plan their expenses, because there was an institutional solution beforehand. Now this is no longer the case and people at the margins of the labour market or who are experiencing economic hardship are not backed up by any other system than social assistance, to which *they must take the initiative to apply*. Often they do not, however, because of their lack of knowledge of the system and the way it works. As a consequence, they may remain behind in paying their rent or utility bills, which in turn starts a series of administrative actions that bring about a formal eviction order. Up to the mid-1990s, in the cities of the eastern *Länder* the number of homeless increased considerably for this reason (Häußermann and Kazepov, 1996).

In addition, from the point of view of expectations, the passive attitude that social workers accuse beneficiaries of adopting in Halle does not appear to be confirmed in our interviews with beneficiaries themselves. On the contrary, the strong work ethic shared by both men and women in this city, which has its roots in the socialisation of the former socialist regime, prevents them from 'settling in' to receipt of social assistance as an acceptable long-term option. Rather, they tend to see it as a means of bridging a difficult period, or refurbishing their skills in order to be able to re-enter the labour market.

The Italian cities

The Italian cities in our study exemplify well the fragmentation and great local differentiation in the Italian social assistance system, and the profiles of the people cared for by social services reflect this situation. Within this picture there are, however, some similarities. In most Italian municipalities, for instance, entering social assistance is the result of an accumulation of crisis events that have affected peoples' attitudes, making them less active in seeking an end to dependency. From the interviews, it emerged that in several cases people were simply managing their lives from day to day; others were trapped in poverty because the condition of deprivation and need had been transmitted from one generation to the next. This is the result of the institutional design, more than the outcome of specific socioeconomic differences. The restrictive rules only grant access to people accumulating several conditions of need: low qualifications, weak access to the labour market, marginality and weak primary social networks. The resources obtained by the claimants are scant and the activation measures weak and often non-existent, even though something has started to change since early 2000.

At the same time, there is also a substantial degree of variation among the cities. In Turin there are more young people on benefits than in Milan, also slightly more immigrants and more unmarried people. Is this the consequence of a real over representation of these groups among the population in need? Not necessarily. It is also the consequence of more generous and less discretionary practices in Turin than in Milan, where the young in particular are stigmatised and have less access to social assistance. The same occurs with immigrants. They represent a higher proportion of the population in Milan, but access to social assistance for them is stricter than in Turin, where regular residents are not discriminated against on the basis of nationality. The contrary is true for lone mothers and families with children, who are, in relative terms, more numerous among social assistance recipients in Milan than in Turin. The more pronounced categorical organisation of social assistance in Milan considers them more *deserving*, therefore they receive support more easily than other social groups.

The different degrees of discretion and generosity in these two cities also account, partly at least, for differences in the overall size of the populations of beneficiaries: recipients in Milan and Turin are respectively 0.13% and 0.06% of the population. Of course, the socioeconomic context of the two cities contributes to these institutional differences. As we have seen in Chapter Two, the grown-up children of Turin's blue-collar workers are likely to find more difficulty in entering the labour market than their counterparts in Milan, where the transformation to a service sector-based economy has a longer and more developed history. But polarisation in the tertiary sector is increasing in this city and the difference in the numbers of those receiving social assistance cannot be imputed only to a lower incidence of need.

The picture in Cosenza is even more desolate. The lack of data reflects the lack of meaningful measures targeted to the needy. Even lone mothers, who are the beneficiaries of the only measure granted for up to two years, are likely to find themselves among the many who receive the risible once a year payment when entitlement to the former is exhausted. So what does this case demonstrate? Lack of policies does not imply a lack of poor. On the contrary, in Cosenza the high unemployment rates (32.2% for adults and 77.2% for young people in 1998) create a vast area of vulnerability, which particularly affects large families. These may have multiple sources of income, but low pensions and irregular incomes do not allow them to reach the poverty threshold. This situation fosters the reproduction of poverty in a context of high rates of illiteracy and low skills. All those interviewed, who received at least a minimum of income support, not only accumulated conditions of need, but also received no help in getting themselves out of their situation. This is true not only for middle-aged recipients, but also for the younger ones. Thus, while women are left to their identification as full-time homemakers, with no incentive to upgrade their skills, men too are left to the informal economy of casual and unskilled jobs, if not the criminal economy. The boundaries between legal and illegal behaviour seem very slim. Being caught and sentenced to prison does not carry a stigma; rather it evokes the need for solidarity by the kin network. This attitude is reinforced by the working of social assistance itself: not only is it totally inadequate but, as we saw in the previous chapter, it is also highly discretional.

The Spanish cities

Social assistance recipients in Barcelona and Vitoria and have different profiles. In Vitoria there is a heavy preponderance of the 30 to 44 age group (see Table 4.1), while younger and older claimants are clearly under represented. In Barcelona, although the frequency of this same group is slightly above average, it is those aged over 45 that are significantly over represented. These are usually able-bodied single men, who are either long-term unemployed or have had an irregular working history. Usually, they also have competency problems, influenced mainly by weak (physical and psychological) health. In Vitoria, on the contrary, it is the households with three or more members that are over represented. Lone mothers are a very significant group in both cities. The reasons for accessing the measure are seldom limited to a single cause in either city. In fact, a series of crisis events (separation from partner, illness and loss of employment) very often accumulate before people access social services.

From the interviews it became clear that the breakdown of social networks (loss of one's partner, death of a significant family member, and so on) had a strong impact on people who were already in a disadvantaged position on the labour market. Moreover, most of the people interviewed have low levels of formal education – they had rarely finished the upper secondary level and often did not even reach it. They also had low professional skills. In most cases they have been in and out of the labour market; thus irregular forms of employment prevailed – whether in the formal or informal economy. An exception is some lone mothers, who had upper secondary or even university education, and used the measure in an instrumental way to bridge temporary conditions of need. From the interviews, this seems to be more clearly the case in Barcelona than in Vitoria, where we find more cases in which beneficiaries come from deprived families.

Is it possible to explain these differences by looking at the institutional design? The two income support measures were designed independently in the two cities (because of the strong regional autonomy in Spain), but both follow the model of the French RMI (in particular in the Basque country). In this sense, neither of the two regional regulations targets specific groups[9]; they are addressed to all people in a condition of financial need. The profile of beneficiaries should, therefore, reflect the socioeconomic characteristics of the two contexts, since differences should not derive from the institutional design. But this is not the case. Both cities are relatively wealthy and have traditionally been industrial regions; there is no obvious indicator to explain the marked differences in the figures. Thus, despite the overall similarity, we have to consider that the existing relevant differences are due either to differences in implementation practice, or in some dimension of the institutional design, or both.

Looking more closely at the programmes, one notices that although they share a common model and outlook, they have different degrees of generosity and selectivity; therefore, they cater to different populations. In particular, even though the income thresholds are low in both cases, the amounts paid and the equivalence scale used are more generous in Vitoria, where they are also supplemented by other benefits (for example, payment of rent). This may explain the higher incidence of large families compared to Barcelona. But in Vitoria means-testing is also stricter; thus it is more difficult for applicants with informal resources, or with family and kin (such as the very young), to be accepted in the programme. In Barcelona the low benefit is considered an incentive to search for complementary income sources, for example, in the informal economy, which is tolerated by social workers.

With regard to implementation, in Barcelona, households where there are children, especially if headed by a lone mother, are considered a priority by social workers. The same is true for single (usually older) adults with weak networks and capability problems. Thus, the programme here has a strong emphasis on social integration for persons who are either deemed as especially deserving (children, lone mothers), or already socially excluded or on the way to being so. Further, despite the fact that the aim of activating recipients is part of the strategy in both cities, we find that only in Vitoria does the municipality provide welfare recipients directly with low-qualified temporary jobs (for example, cleaning, gardening, and so on). On the other hand, the labour market is more fragile in this city and generates less market employment than in Barcelona. Thus in the two cities the institutional design interacts with the urban context, adapting to the specific economic and social circumstances.

The Portuguese cities

The Portuguese cities were – at the time of the fieldwork – in a period of significant institutional change towards a new social assistance system similar to the French RMI, that is a so-called second generation measure of social assistance, which puts a strong emphasis on activation and re-employment projects accompanying the payment of benefits. Our fieldwork, however, was not able to take the new measure into due consideration because the testing phase was just starting. The results presented here therefore refer to the old measure, and show its strong institutional influence on the profiles of claimants. Unfortunately, as mentioned in Chapter One, data on Porto are less systematic and firmly grounded on quantitative sources than in Lisbon.

In Lisbon data show clearly that there is a considerable over representation of lone mothers among social assistance recipients (23.7%), compared to their incidence in the city's population (1.9%). This is a good example of institutional pre-structuring, because this over representation is mostly explained by the fact that social workers (and the old institutional frame of reference) consider lone mothers a deserving group that needs special attention in order to prevent the reproduction of poverty. Single able-bodied adults on welfare are often lone people over 45 years old, who are suffering from physical illness (AIDS or others) or psychological pathologies, or are at risk of becoming homeless, and sometimes already in a condition of social marginality. However, the most salient group in relative terms – although strongly under represented compared to the overall population – is that of families with children. 'Responsible and honest parents' wanting to overcome their condition of need are considered more deserving than other groups, who on the contrary have to accumulate multiple conditions of deprivation in order to have access to the benefits. In fact, most minimum income claimants have experienced an accumulation of crisis events, are unemployed and in need of both economic and other support. This is not unusual in a city in which 65% of the unemployed have never benefited from any unemployment subsidy and where there has long been a reproduction of poverty associated with bad housing conditions, although only 0.7% of the population have had access to 'social aid'.

Social assistance benefits are often targeted towards paying off a debt or buying medicines, but are so low that, as in Cosenza, they cannot have a significant impact on recipients' lives. Given the competency problems of many recipients, according to social workers, it is a success when they become able to administer their own lives day-to-day. Active attitudes towards life, however, are very rare. What is clear in the two cities is the crucial support role played by social workers in offering opportunities to overcome specific crises. The resources and means at their disposal, however, do not allow incisive social and economic reintegration projects, and the social workers' role was often that of social and psychological support. The very low level of generosity of income support in both cities means that priority was given to those households with multiple problems; and programmes were very selective. In Lisbon the existence of a 'qualified need' (such as family disruption, isolation or illness, in addition to economic need) was considered part of the legal conditions for access.

In Porto claimants were not considered per se bearers of rights, and discretion by social workers in assessing need as well as 'worthiness' plays a strong role in granting or refusing social assistance. As a consequence, only very severe cases of destitution and lack of personal capabilities are found among recipients: middle-aged, and often illiterate, men returned from former colonies who cannot integrate into Portuguese society; middle-aged women with children whose husbands have abandoned them, or are in jail; or households with children where the parents are poorly educated, severely ill, drug addicts, or have had some experience in jail.

In both Portuguese cities deprivation inherited from the family of origin is very common, but more so in Porto, especially in the case of lone mothers. This often involved the recipients having to enter the labour market or to marry at a very early age with only a primary education or even remaining illiterate. As a consequence, their level of skills is very low and the jobs they are likely to find unstable, not offering long-term economic guarantees. The income support they receive from social assistance is not enough to get by, but fills emergencies such as medicine or paying off a debt in order to be able to enter another one (with the backer, the landlord, a relative). Odd jobs, older children and/ or occasional charity may offer additional income.

The highly targeted nature of the measures and the scarce resources they provide, as in Cosenza, severely limit their success, both from the point of view of helping beneficiaries to face their everyday survival problems and supporting longer-term strategies to exit from poverty.

Filtering and streaming the poor

The above analysis of the profile of social assistance claimants in the different cities clearly shows how the interaction between the socioeconomic context, which produces conditions of vulnerability, and the institutional frameworks, which transform some of the poor into the socially assisted, may create its own inclusions and exclusions, as well as forms of welfare dependency. This is more or less specific to the local context, depending on the nature of the national or local policy.

Thus, for example, the percentage of immigrants among social assistance recipients does not depend solely on their overall incidence in the local population or their vulnerability in the different cities. To a large degree it depends on the level of entitlement granted to them by national and local regulations, as indicated clearly by the comparison between Turin and Milan, as well as between these two cities and the Swedish ones[10]. But the issue is – of course – far more complex. Migration flows to these countries have, for example, been different in their timing. In Southern Europe immigration is far more recent – in the 1950s and 1960s, these countries were mainly subject to emigration. Only since the end of the 1970s have the migration flows changed direction. This has influenced the fact that the immigrants' rights were not an issue on the political agenda for a long time. Now, in a context of structural unemployment and welfare retrenchment, it is more difficult to widen access to rights and benefits.

We can argue a similar case for the young, who are over represented in Northern European cities, while virtually absent in Southern Europe. The lack of young people aged under 25 among direct claimants in the French and Spanish cities is clearly a function of the regulations that exclude them, not an indication of lack of need. All the more so in the light of the growing number of young applicants and beneficiaries in Rennes, for example. On the other hand, the very small number of recipients aged under 30 in Southern European cities, even when there are no special rules excluding them, must be read in the light of at least two normative features: the obligation of parents to provide support, and the lack of social security measures tailored to the young[11]. Together with the high occupational precariousness among the young, these two features encourage them to remain at home with their parents much longer than in Central and Northern Europe, so that they can share the household resources and economies of scale, while developing their strategies in the labour market. Functionally speaking, this too may be read as a welfare system (not State) characterised by a high degree of social integration[12]. Yet, as we have already pointed out, this equilibrium has quite a different distributional outcome compared to that of rights-based systems. The pooling of family resources has a very low 'redistributional' impact if it is the main or only source of resources. Families become overloaded with social responsibilities, ending up in a process that reproduces consolidated inequalities (see also Saraceno, 2000).

Paths into assisted poverty

The role of the family is crucial both in shaping patterns of vulnerability and in providing resources for coping with them. Families with young children experience a particular tension between the dual need for income and for care, which is heightened when there is only one adult to cope with both, as in lone-parent households. On the other hand, individuals living alone have only themselves to care about, but this can also mean that they have nobody to make recourse to in case of need. These patterns of specific vulnerability interact with, and are partly shaped by, policies at the local and national level (Saraceno, 1997; Negri and Saraceno, 2000). Generous child benefits can greatly alleviate the otherwise possible imbalance between earnings and care needs. Good quality and affordable childcare services may help parents, and particularly mothers, to conciliate paid work with caring responsibilities. Good and affordable social services and home help may support households with a severely disabled or frail older member, and so forth.

In order to understand better how these interactions are played out in our different cultural and policy contexts, we have analysed in-depth cases exemplifying three different household compositions: (a) single adults living alone, (b) lone mothers, and (c) couples with children. Immigrants have also been taken into account as a fourth category, although they may be found in all others. They, in fact, provide interesting comparative material, given the considerable institutional diversity in the way this category is handled when in a condition of economic need. The choice of cases is the result of the analysis of more than 300 in-depth biographical interviews performed in the 13 cities of the ESOPO sample. We have chosen 18 emblematic cases, highlighting different paths towards social assistance. Each case illustrates the complex interplay between the dimensions identified in the first part of this chapter.

These personal trajectories show the role that events and contexts have played in the path followed by each recipient both before and after entering social assistance. In order to allow a systematic interpretation of the in-depth information provided by these life histories we have constructed two typologies. The first is based on events and contexts, focusing on the 'form' taken by the beneficiaries' trajectory towards reliance on social assistance. The second is based on how the recipients themselves perceive their condition as social assistance recipients and focuses on how they organise their life strategies.

The first typology addresses the form taken by the breakdown of equilibrium between needs and resources. Implicitly, it assumes that the *normal* condition is a dynamic equilibrium that varies from family to family (or from individual to individual), but keeps people away from social assistance. More specifically, the typology derives from the effect specific factors related to the family, health and the labour market (see Figure 4.2) have on the ability of the beneficiary to cope with stressful events. We have distinguished between three different forms: (a) cases in which the condition of need for social assistance is the result of a *single crisis event* that breaks down the equilibrium (for example, unemployment, divorce); (b) cases where there is an *accumulation of crisis events* (for example, unemployment plus separation, together with health problems) breaking down the equilibrium progressively; (c) cases of *early exclusion* (Benassi, 1995), where beneficiaries – due to their socialisation context and lack of resources – have higher chances of experiencing intergenerational deprivation. The form taken by *early exclusion* is, consequently, an accumulation of crisis events that have consolidated over time in the passage from one generation to the other.

The distribution of these cases is not random in our sample of cities and social assistance schemes. Some degree of coherence characterises the beneficiaries' profiles and the institutional design of the measures addressed to them. A more generous welfare state will have – proportionally – fewer cases of early exclusion and accumulation of crisis events. There, people have more opportunities and resources at their disposal to stop their downward mobility at an earlier stage.

With regard to the second typology, we distinguish between people who: (a) make an *instrumental use of the measure*; (b) are *actively organising their lives*[13]; (c) are *managing their life from day-to-day*; (d) have the feeling (experience) of being *trapped in poverty*. Clearly, those with better chances of exiting the condition of need are those who make an instrumental use of the measure and those who are actively organising their own lives. The former are generally people who use social assistance to bridge a specific difficult period within their lifecycle. Here we found many lone mothers with children who were able to separate from their partners (because of difficulties in the relationship) thanks to the support received through social assistance. The latter are people with relatively optimistic approaches to life, who – both in generous (earlier) and selective (later) schemes – find their way out of dependence. 'Administrators of daily life', are those entrenched in a condition of need, who have difficulty in overcoming the causes that keep them financially dependent, yet are usually integrated within meaningful networks and activities that make them feel they have a purposeful life. In the more generous systems, these are candidates for long-term dependency, and in the more selective systems to a further downward slide, as the limited resources available cannot prevent further crises.

Being trapped in poverty (or feeling as if this is so) is common to people on benefits in most cities, in particular to long-term beneficiaries. Their proportion among the population on benefits, however, varies considerably between systems. In the more generous ones there are relatively few, because a wider range of beneficiaries are entitled to income support. In the more selective systems, they represent a higher proportion and contribute to perpetuating the stigmatisation of social assistance schemes. Of course, to feel trapped in poverty implies a limited capacity for choice. It signals real difficulties in using external resources, combined with limitations in personal capabilities.

Both typologies help us to make some cautious suggestions as to the causes of entering social assistance. In the following analysis we examine how the forms of the life trajectories and attitudes of claimants towards the measures crystallise in their biographies. In particular, we attempt to present the crucial structural elements that relate to the institutional design of the social assistance schemes in the cities considered. Of course, we cannot expect a clear-cut deterministic model to emerge. Active organisers of life can experience a period of income constraints (with or without a major reorganisation of life) in both more generous and more selective systems. The point is that in the first case they have better opportunities to exit, even though the feeling of stigmatisation may be the same. In the 18 trajectories presented here we also describe the features of the local economic context. Thus, we can appreciate the substantial, objective and subjective differences between a single man aged 45, who feels trapped in poverty because there are no income opportunities available for him in Gothenburg, and a family of four trapped in poverty in the inner-city of Cosenza.

Single adults

Single adults living alone are over represented in some cities (Barcelona, Bremen, Gothenburg, Helsingborg, Rennes and Saint Etienne), while not in others (Milan, Turin and Vitoria). They are an exception in Cosenza. From the interviews we can see that their profile differs substantially from context to context and that no homogeneous typology emerges. Claimants who experience extreme material need and have difficulty in coping with life exist in all our cities, but in those where thresholds and benefits are higher, social assistance programmes offer support to a both greater and more heterogeneous proportion of single adults in economic need. On average, in the latter cities the socially assisted are – in a way – 'better off'. This is particularly true for single adult beneficiaries in the Swedish cities, compared to those in Southern Europe.

All these able-bodied single adults on social assistance are unemployed. The two main profiles are: (a) long-term unemployed males over the age of 45; (b) young people who have not yet entered the labour market. The first group includes people who, after a relatively stable working career, become long-term unemployed. Their professional skills are usually low, or obsolete, and they often have weak family and informal networks. Their low degree of employability causes them to stay on benefits for long periods of time, not only because of limited job opportunities, but also because they often enter a vicious circle of decreasing motivation and emotional instability. This reduces their chances of getting off the dependency track. They are often so discouraged that they do not even enter insertion contracts or other activation measures, even when these are available, since they do not perceive them as useful for themselves. Mr A in Gothenburg is such a case.

> Mr A lives in Gothenburg. At the time of the interview (1997) he was 45 years old, enjoyed good health and had been on income support for three years. He had applied for social assistance after an *accumulation of crisis events*: his separation from his girlfriend coincided with becoming unemployed in 1992. The experience of unemployment weakened his confidence, although he did some odd jobs paid under the counter during these years, while remaining officially unemployed. He stressed the negative effects of unemployment on his life: "time runs away doing nothing" he said. Good health and solid social networks (many of his friends are in a similar situation) do not prevent him from being pessimistic about the future. He acknowledges the efforts of social workers – "they try to push me, I have all the help I need to apply for jobs" – and yet he cannot believe in a real chance to find a new permanent job and get off social assistance. He finds himself *trapped in poverty* and in a vicious circle that reinforces this feeling.

Long-term unemployment, particularly if coupled with the lack of a personal relationship, renders middle-aged men particularly vulnerable everywhere, since it weakens the basis on which traditional male gender identity is premised. Yet, this is not acknowledged everywhere as a particularly vulnerable situation, as we have seen. Or rather, it is so protected by traditional social security mechanisms that only the most vulnerable cases, usually involving people without regular work and/or with additional health or psychological problems, eventually arrive in the social assistance offices. This is often the case in Southern Europe where the combination of relatively high protection for adult men in the official labour market, a high concentration of young people with badly protected and temporary jobs, and highly selective ungenerous social assistance schemes, means that the system only acknowledges the needs of middle-aged single men who have little chance of ever getting on their feet due to an *accumulation of breakdown events* and irregular employment. The case of Mr B in Turin is a good example of such a biography, which may find analogies in places as distant as Porto or Vitoria.

Mr B lives alone in Turin. At the time of the interview he was 53 years old. He was born in Sicily and migrated first to Switzerland, then to other Northern European countries and then back to Switzerland, where other members of his family lived, finally arriving in Turin in 1980. He has no formal school certificate, although he followed some professional training when he was younger. He acquired his professional skills mostly through work experience. In his job career there is a period of work stability as a carpenter in a Swiss village. After he migrated to Turin, he lived first on his savings and then on income from odd jobs, mostly in the informal economy. At some point he tried to become self-employed but never got off the ground, incurring a small debt with the Chamber of Commerce. He sees his family background as particularly hard: after his father's death (he was 6 years old) he lived in a childcare institution. He was married for a short period, but was left by his wife who was granted custody of their daughter. Several members of his family, especially sisters, helped him in several periods of his life. He entered social assistance because of the *accumulation of breakdown events* and is now dependent on his social assistance income for paying basic expenses (utilities). He eats in soup kitchens and gets a few irregular additional sums of money by repairing abandoned chairs in the streets. He also has drinking as well as psychological problems – depression and strong feelings of failure. Although he still owns his flat, he expects that his accumulating debts will force him to sell it. He *feels trapped in poverty.*

The second group includes younger male and female recipients, who have either left their parents' home to live by themselves or entered an early marriage or cohabitation, which then ended. These recipients often combine social assistance benefits with temporary jobs to bridge what they perceive as a contingent situation in their lives. The possibility of overcoming dependence is linked either to entering a new relationship or finding a regular job. These cases are fairly frequent in the Swedish, French and German cities, the difference being that in France only those aged over 25 may apply for RMI. In all cases we found that low qualifications were part of the problem. Thus, insertion contracts and different kinds of training and activation measures may prove a valuable resource, if adequately tailored to individual capabilities and chances. The case of Ms C shows how this can go beyond mere job insertion support.

Ms C lives in Rennes, and was 26 years old at the time of the interview. She arrived in Rennes from Brest in 1996 to live there with her boyfriend. Before leaving Brest, she had been studying law for three years and had good social networks. Coming to Rennes, however, she left school to look for a job, with no success. This was the main reason for entering the RMI, even though she applied only when she left her boyfriend. Within the programme she signed two insertion contracts aimed at a job search and got a limited-term contract in a public library. The measure helped her to overcome a big change in her life, she said. Having left her boyfriend, the social service provided the support she needed to improve the organisation of her life by developing her own active strategies. She stressed the importance of this help: "I had a bit of trouble getting organised because I had no sense of planning". She developed – with the help of the programme – a more independent existence and an attitude of *active organisation in her life*.

Only the most generous programmes can afford to dedicate considerable resources and time to this group, which is on average perceived as the least needy and deserving, given the young age of claimants and lack of family responsibilities. Yet, as the above example shows, getting help at an early stage may prevent them from entering a dead end or vicious circle. This appears particularly crucial for the young of both genders who choose to leave school in order to get a job, only to find themselves vulnerable in the labour market later on. For women specifically, it may represent an alternative to entering or staying in a partnership just because they cannot envisage a different way of supporting themselves. An example, concerning an older single woman in Vitoria, is that of Ms D.

Ms D lives in Vitoria and was 34 years old at the time of the interview and has no children. She was born in a nearby town, where she lived with her mother after her father died when she was a teenager. She did not finish her vocational training "I preferred to give up studying to be emancipated", she said. She had job experience helping with domestic work. After several jobs, she married at the age of 23. She was married for six years, but at some point she felt mistreated by her husband and left him. The process of separation took three years. The first time she contacted the social service was in 1990 in her hometown and she obtained her formal separation in 1993. This *breakdown event*, the separation from her husband, was the main reason for entering social assistance. However, the event had a positive impact on her life, bringing about an overall reorganisation. Within the support programme she completed vocational training in the field of administration and began actively looking for employment, also taking a course in the Basque language at the time she was interviewed. She became *an active organiser of her life*, who tried to find concrete solutions.

The first two cases (Mr A and Mr B) clearly show how the claimants' profiles have been influenced by the institutional filters of the different urban contexts. In the first case (Mr A), social services in Gothenburg were – and still are – able to afford the cost of maintaining a person who has no income, but otherwise survives with dignity. In the second case (Mr B), the selection was tighter and the claimant supported only when there was an accumulation of crisis events and problems of capability. Despite the fact that, formally speaking, he should not have been entitled to social assistance (he owns a flat), his situation was understood in a flexible manner by social workers. These institutional frameworks interacted with the local socioeconomic contexts in their own specific ways. The situation of full employment that characterised the Swedish economy until the end of the 1980s meant that Mr A was employed in the formal economy for many years before becoming unemployed. Mr B migrated to Turin in a period of de-industrialisation in the early 1980s, when the high unemployment rates, combined with his low formal education and psychological instability, pushed him into more irregular employment. Whereas both men, finding themselves in need of economic support, claimed social assistance, the financial situation of Mr A after entering welfare is much better than that of Mr B, not only because of its generosity, but also its continuity and the existence of accompanying measures. The latter have helped Mr A towards social integration, whereas Mr B suffers partial social isolation. He feels unable to keep up social obligations and is left alone. Despite these large differences, the two men share the subjective feeling of being trapped in poverty, which can be interpreted in terms of feelings of relative deprivation.

In the other cases, (Ms C and Ms D), the institutional design also plays a major role in the structuring process of the claimants' conditions of need. In both cities (Rennes and Vitoria), social assistance helped the beneficiaries to reorganise their lives with the support of social workers, who helped them to develop medium term strategies to reorient their lives. In most other Southern European cities, these cases would have not been considered eligible. Both can be considered examples of temporary dependency in which the accompanying measures, linked to the minimum income programmes, help beneficiaries to find ways out of the previous condition of need, providing opportunities for improving their life conditions. In Vitoria, the woman was able to take a training course that eventually improved her chances in the labour market. In Rennes the institutional framework of RMI, with its well-designed programme of insertion contracts and solidly structured social service network offered the way out of welfare dependence. Also, the age and good condition of health of both women can be considered positive resources.

Altogether, these four cases show how the differences in programmes shape the individual trajectories by providing different sets of opportunities and resources. The resulting profiles reflect the working of these mechanisms, and influence – in turn – the effectiveness of the measure. If a multiple condition of need is the implicit condition to access the benefit (as in the case of Mr B), the opportunities to break a vicious circle are weak. If access conditions are wider, more people are entitled to enter and have the opportunity to break the downward path at an earlier stage (as in the case of Ms D), or to stabilise their lives at a low but decorous level (as in the case of Mr A).

In addition to these two main types, we also have other profiles among the single adults on benefits. They are mostly individuals with health problems and a life history of emotional instability, often caused by the fact that they have a background of deprived families with persisting problems of social integration.

Lone mothers

Lone mothers are a category that is over represented among recipients in almost all the cities studied. Yet the trajectories of women who entered the social assistance schemes in the 13 cities are far from homogeneous. There is a clear difference between the unmarried women (usually younger) who applied for minimum income support because they were pregnant, and those who became lone mothers because of separation, divorce, or desertion by the husband/father of the child/children. In addition to age, the quality of family-kin relations and networks is a crucial variable. Network support proved to be very important for the reorganisation of the lives of these women in general, but more so in the Southern cities, given the lower generosity and often temporary nature of income support. The case of Ms E is an example of this situation.

Ms E is a woman aged 39 living in Turin. She migrated to Turin with her family from Basilicata (a region in the south of Italy) in the 1950s. At the age of 19 she married. She had two children and separated from her husband in 1991. At the time of the interview her children were aged 17 and 14. What brought her onto social assistance? Her long work experience was a mixture of informal economy jobs (odd jobs paid under the counter) and unskilled employment in the low qualified service sector. In 1983, the couple had pooled savings to start their own small food shop. However, both the business and the marriage collapsed in 1990. She experienced an *accumulation of breakdown events* and felt alone without a husband, no income and poor health. In 1992, she became a recipient of social assistance. Within this she found not only some income support, but also moral support and encouragement (from one social worker in particular). In the following five years, she also had the support of her family, friends, church charity and even the ex-husband. She pooled resources, avoiding the extremes of poverty, and when her eldest son started working they exited social assistance.

In cities where the principle of subsidiarity with regard to family solidarity holds – the Italian, Portuguese and Spanish, and partly also German ones – social workers try to involve the family networks in supporting lone mothers. This is not the case in Sweden, France and to some degree also in Germany. In these countries either the programmes are structured around more individual rights (Sweden), or lone mothers with young children are the object of relatively generous, though temporary, support, which is less stigmatising than social assistance as such (France and Germany)[14]. As the stories of Ms F and Ms G exemplify, however, having a supportive network helps in more than a merely financial way, even in the more 'individualistic' contexts.

Ms F lives in Helsingborg and was 25 years old at the time of the interview. She became pregnant at the age of 17 while she was living with her partner. When the baby was about one year old, they separated and she moved with her baby into a flat. She has a secondary school certificate, but her work experience in the service sector as a cleaner and as a shop assistant did not give her particular qualifications. She entered the minimum income scheme partly as a result of the child's birth, making an *instrumental use of the measure*: in order to have both time to care for her child and to look around for convenient job opportunities. Previously she had benefited from other welfare schemes such as unemployment and educational benefits. This woman has strong network support, which helped her considerably when she became a lone mother. At the time of the interview she was off the measure, living with a new boyfriend and working in a part-time job as a cleaner. After separation she *actively reorganised her life*, succeeding in finding help in circumstances of need.

> Ms G was born in Bremen, where she grew up. She became a mother at the age of 37, and with the birth of the child took parental leave from her job. She also separated from the father of the child shortly before the child's birth. As a result, she claimed welfare support for herself, while the baby's father supported the child financially. Her family background helped her indirectly to take these steps, as she had herself been raised by a lone mother with modest financial means. Part of her strength comes from her family and her network relations (including the ex-partner), which are solid and well developed, even if they do not provide income. She lives with her three year old child. As an *active organiser of life*, she used income support pragmatically until the child could attend kindergarten, then she returned to her job. This woman values her free time with the child, as well as her creative capacities and for this reason prefers to work part-time. This choice does not free her from the anxiety of having to fall back onto social assistance and being left with a small pension.

The worst situations are found when neither generous public support nor family-kin support are available. As may happen to unmarried and formerly married lone mothers who live in Southern Europe and who for some reason are cut off from their family-kin networks, or can count only on impoverished and over-stressed networks, as in the case of Ms H.

> Ms H is a 35 year old woman living in Lisbon, who married at the age of 17 and had two daughters (aged 18 and 7 at the time of the interview). She entered social assistance due to an *accumulation of crisis events*. She broke off relations with her family and her husband, who became a drug addict and died. She and her daughters lived with her brother-in-law until he kicked them out of his house. Afterwards she lived in a car for one year. She has very poor social networks and her job experience consists of a series of unskilled and badly paid jobs. The social assistance measure helped her to cover some fixed expenses, such as rent and kindergarten fees, until she could find a new job. She has now proved to be an *active organiser of life*, combining her earnings with social assistance income support and a small widow's pension.

In this story, difficulties in personal relations and the absence of support from kin combine with high vulnerability in the labour market due to lack of skills. The low amount of income support, together with the absence of accompanying measures, left this woman to 'botch together' a mix of resources with little hope of really improving her situation in the long-term. Yet she tries. After the introduction of the new system in Portugal in 1997, this woman would have been entitled to a more generous benefit and structured accompanying measures, helping her to build up her skills and to make it easier to re-enter the labour market on a stable basis, given her relatively young age. A similar story of employment vulnerability is that of Ms I in Halle, but for quite different reasons.

Ms I is aged 55 and mother of five children, living in Halle. She entered the minimum income scheme as a result of an *accumulation of crisis events*, including separation from her second partner and forced exit from work. She had left school at the age of 14, and after a short and unfinished apprenticeship in industry, started to work as a typist. She worked for 18 years in an industrial plant and after that 11 years in a welfare organisation. With the reorganisation of the welfare system following reunification in 1991, she was made redundant. Unemployment and separation occurred within a short period of time. She has been on income support for five years, and claims that social assistance support has made a clear improvement in her life conditions. She is strongly involved in family and neighbourhood networks and enjoys being with two of her children, aged 14 and 16. She *manages her life* from day-to-day with little hope of getting off social assistance given her age and qualifications, but without feeling either isolated or stigmatised because of this.

These two latter cases show contrasting experiences of motherhood and life trajectories in relation to social assistance. Ms I suffered the consequences of the restructuring of Halle's labour market, coinciding with a major transformation in her own household. Within social assistance she has found the support she needed, but little prospect of getting off it due to the triple disadvantage of age, gender and low level of professional skills. In the case of Ms H., given her limited skills, the Lisbon labour market does not offer many chances, except in the informal, ill paid sector. Moreover, her family network has proved to be very weak. The public informal support she receives is not enough for her and her family to rely on, but it is just one piece of a patchy budget she puts together from other sources, including her occasional earnings. Notwithstanding her active attitude, without substantial changes in the opportunities offered, she might pass on this history of precariousness to her daughters as well.

All our sources (vignettes, interviews, social assistance data) confirm that lone mothers constitute a category that is normally considered highly deserving because of the priority given to children. This is particularly true in all Southern European countries. Yet, there is a dual edge to this 'priority', as lone mothers are likely to be subjected to close scrutiny. The more budget constraints there are within a programme, the more access to benefits will depend on the social worker's judgement about the claimant's 'qualified need' and 'how deserving (s)he is'. If the potential recipient is considered untrustworthy, the examination of the case by the social services regarding her own or her family resources may be stricter than usual. In Barcelona, for example, social services carry out a close examination of the marital situation and whether the ex-husband (or the family) provides some support for the lone mother or not. Once the case has been accepted by social services, the main purpose of the intervention is to ensure that children receive proper care. Careful examination of the cases was also reported by social workers in Saint Etienne, and is common in Turin and Milan as well. In Cosenza the situation is more extreme. Lone mothers have access to some sort of temporary institutional support, but they are kept under close scrutiny for their morality and performance as mothers. In the German and Swedish cities, on the contrary, access has less 'interpretative' filters by social workers, and once entitlement is granted, no additional examination is needed, even if supportive services are offered.

Couples with children

Comparing the proportion of recipients who are couples with children to the overall population, we see that this category is under represented in most cities, with the exception of Bremen. However, this does not imply that the number of couples with children receiving crucial income supplements is necessarily low. In the welfare states that provide specific income support targeted at children (allowances, tax deductions, or both), these may be enough to keep families above the minimum income threshold. Among the countries in our study, this is clearly the case in France.

Also, the number of mothers in paid work is a crucial element in reducing the number of dual parent households on social assistance: dual worker families are better protected from economic vulnerability than single worker ones. A telling example is Sweden, whose child allowances are much less generous than in France, but the vast majority of mothers are in paid work and very few dual parent households are on social assistance. Thus, in these countries couples with children receiving income support are either very marginal cases where both parents are out of work, or lifestyle choices, or cases in which earned income plus child benefit is still below the minimum income threshold for the household size and is being topped up. In all these cases there is a high proportion of immigrants, given their difficulties in entering the labour market and accumulating entitlements in social security schemes.

In the southern countries, where children are considered financially dependent well beyond legal age, child benefits are scarce, often targeted[15], and thus do not provide a general safety net for families with children.

At the same time, as we have said previously, in these countries children are considered among the most deserving poor, and local income support policies are often targeted specifically at them. Thus, couples with children are an important proportion of beneficiaries, often representing, as in the Northern cities, very serious situations of need with an accumulation of problems, but for different reasons.

To provide some illustrations of this group of beneficiaries, we have taken cases from the cities where in our sample the proportion of couples with children is highest. We also describe a variety of trajectories that compare families in contrasting social assistance regimes with different levels of generosity. In all cases, the households were receiving support at the time of the interview, with little prospect of getting off social assistance by their own means. This is particularly true for households J and K, in Bremen and Saint Etienne respectively, where they are entitled to stay on social assistance as long as the condition of need persists. In Milan (household L) and Porto (household M), on the contrary, social assistance support will not necessarily be granted for the duration of need. Finally, in the case of Cosenza (household N), income support is so small that it does not make a great difference to the family budget. In these last three cases, particularly in Cosenza, the relationship with social workers, rather than the income provided is the only support available to the family.

Mr and Mrs J, both aged 36 and living in Bremen, entered social assistance during a period of *reorganisation of their lives*. In both cases there is a history of divorce from previous partners resulting in a loss of income. She has been on welfare for six years and he for five. Before entering social assistance he worked as a taxi driver at night, but this did not suit his new family life, and he did not want to pay alimony to his ex-wife and child. Therefore, he gave up his job as a taxi driver and claimed unemployment benefit until he exhausted it. She had become a housewife after the birth of her first child with the first husband, after having previously worked as a clerk. When she divorced, her ex-husband refused to support her and the child financially. She wanted to be with her child at home rather than to work for pay and claimed social assistance. Both have financial debts and seem to lack supportive social networks. Now with three children – aged 2, 4 and 8 – and a fourth coming, they are not making positive steps to get off social assistance. He does not want to work for anybody else, as he is not prepared to comply with authority and discipline. She wants to be at home with their children. They both feel a little like victims of circumstances; however, they receive enough income to get by, *administering their daily life*.

Household K lives in Saint Etienne. Mr K is 42 years old and was born in Tunisia; Mrs K is of French origin, and they have three children. The *breakdown event* that brought them into the measure was the loss of his job in the building industry in 1992. He was a semi-skilled worker and the family breadwinner. After exhausting unemployment benefit, he signed two RMI insertion contracts and undertook some *petit boulots* (odd jobs). He applied for RMI when one of the children fell ill. Although he feels that "the only solution will be a new job", he is rather pessimistic: he thinks that employers prefer younger people. He continues to search for employment *actively organising his family life*, but with limited expectations. He knows about other welfare programmes and counts on friends who give them a hand as well.

These two cases show similar conditions of reliance on welfare in which the breadwinner has the responsibility of finding a new source of income, while the wife takes care of the children. They portray, however, two different attitudes – one more passive and the other more active. In both cases the criteria for keeping the entitlement are not limited by time and budgetary constraints, nor even by conformity to standard behaviour (Mr J is not forced to seek a regular job, both women are not really expected to look for paid work). By contrast, the following two cases involve not only a condition of economic need and serious inability in dealing with the problems of everyday life, but also a restriction of entitlements due to budgetary constraints and discretionary regulations. These two cases will probably not be able to remain in the measure as long as the condition of need persists.

Mr L, 49 years old, was raised in the south of Italy. When he was younger he worked in Puglia (a region of the south of Italy), but after marriage he wanted a better job and moved with his wife to Milan in search of better opportunities. They live in this city with their youngest daughter now aged 25. He is the family breadwinner and assumes that his wife should not work and earn an income. They applied for income support after having *accumulated several breakdown events*. He resigned from his job after 27 years of working in a cooperative as an associate member. Afterwards, he suffered two heart attacks. Leaving the cooperative, where he had worked for so long, destabilised his health as well. The cooperative had not made social security payments for him, so he did not have any entitlement to any kind of pension scheme and he is still much too young to apply for a social pension. For a while he did some odd jobs, but their savings came to an end. His brother and a couple of friends have helped them. However, they have accumulated debts. They live in social housing (on a local council estate) and are temporarily on income support. He suffers psychologically, because he has to rely on other people, 'damaging' his self-image as an independent person able to support his family. At present, with his health problems, he manages to *administer his family's daily life*. When the income support he is now receiving will be curtailed due to time regulations, he and his family will have only their kin and friends network to rely on, or they will have to turn to charities.

Mr and Mrs M live in Porto and are both in their forties. They have six children, two of whom were still living in the household at the time of the interview: an adult son aged 27 and a younger son aged 13, as well as a granddaughter (one of the daughters is a lone mother). They live in social housing (in local council housing). The reason for applying to the measure was an *accumulation of crisis events*. The man had an accident while working in the building industry; afterwards he worked in a manufacturing firm and has been in prison four times accused of drug dealing. He is currently unemployed. The wife worked as a household cleaner until she fell ill in her late thirties. The son had a job at the time of the interview, and was a drug-addict. They had accumulated debts, but received some income support from one of the daughters. They exhibit an active attitude, as they continue the search for income opportunities. The amount of income support they receive from the municipality is very small and they do not know how long they will continue to receive it. Given their family situation, they have little chances of getting employment and are *trapped in poverty*.

Mrs N, aged 37, and her husband, aged 38, have two children aged 14 and 9. They live in the town centre of Cosenza. The man's father was a building labourer who migrated to Germany and sent money to the family, while the mother sold vegetables in the market. As a child, the man used to help his mother, thereby missing school. As a result he is practically illiterate and has no professional skills. Neither has he constructed a regular job career: he works occasionally in the informal economy, mainly in construction work, sometimes receiving payment in kind (food). The wife, also without professional skills, works occasionally as a house cleaner for a few hours a day. She was born in a family of 11 children and never worked before marriage: "that could never happen in Mascali" – her village – she emphatically declared. Both had experienced a kind of *early exclusion* in their childhood: their families could not provide essential resources, including basic schooling. In their present situation, they experience strong community solidarity within the neighbourhood, which provides personal services and even food and other resources. However, what the community is not able to offer them is work. Thus, his odd jobs are often found through contacts outside the neighbourhood. The very small monetary contribution obtained from social assistance does not change their life conditions. *They are trapped in poverty*.

These three cases illustrate well the characteristics of many of the poor families that are selected through the social assistance schemes in Southern European cities. In the first two cases, the financial and social network resources are already very limited. Even if relatives want to help, often the financial resources are not there or are insufficient to provide a decent life. On the other hand, the limited resources provided by the schemes themselves give little room for improvement. Social workers are very supportive from a psychological and moral point of view; they provide encouragement and even help recipients to look for whatever income opportunities may appear available to them. Despite good will, however, often this assistance has a limited impact on the families' prospects of improvement. The Cosenza family is an extreme case in this sense. What sustains this family is neighbourhood solidarity, combined with odd jobs and very little irregular income. Yet, the possibility that the pattern of early exclusion translating into lifelong exclusion will be repeated also in the third generation is all too clear.

Immigrants and members of minorities

The life trajectories of immigrants are even more heterogeneous than those of the other beneficiaries in the cities we have studied. Thus, our analysis of this category of recipients of social assistance will be only very sketchy and partial. Migration flows underwent a fundamental change in the EU countries during the 1980s and 1990s. The Southern European countries (with the exception of Portugal) practically stopped sending workers to the other EU countries and have become host countries themselves. There are now waves of immigration, mainly from North Africa and the Balkans to Italy, to Portugal from their ex-colonies, and to Spain from Latin America. At the same time, the immigration flows to Germany and Sweden now no longer involve people from Southern Europe, but from other parts of the world; and asylum seekers have become a large proportion of the new immigrants, in contrast to the traditional *Gastarbeiter* (immigrant workers) of the postwar period (Block and Levy, 1999).

Our analysis is further complicated by the fact that the six countries we have analysed have very different laws both for granting citizenship and extending social rights to non-nationals. We cannot enter into details here of the distinctions concerning the legal status of immigrants in the different countries, but should point out that the differing proportion of foreigners receiving social assistance is an interesting indicator of 'inclusiveness', not only of the proportion of foreigners in the overall population. The range is quite wide: from about five per cent in the Spanish cities, to one out of three in Gothenburg and one out of four in Bremen.

Immigrants and members of minorities on social assistance in the 13 cities share with more vulnerable nationals the constraints in entering the labour market or building stable working careers; but they also experience specific and additional ones. Although in many cases immigrants have few professional skills, their difficulties in finding a job may occur irrespective of their education, as well as of the professional experience achieved in their countries of origin. And the range of jobs open to them is often quite limited and little linked to their skills. Limited knowledge of the language of the host country and limited (or not sufficiently resourceful) social networks, even though offering strong solidarity, are additional factors that hinder these immigrants' integration in the labour market.

Mr and Mrs O are the parents of two children born in 1986 and 1987. They were respectively 40 and 38 years old at the time of the interview, both well educated and with professional experience. Before leaving their home in former Yugoslavia, he worked as an engineer and she as an office clerk. Due to civil war, their lives changed dramatically and they became refugees, arriving in Gothenburg in 1993. When they arrived in Sweden, because of the major *breakdown event in their country of origin*, they claimed social assistance and began to study the Swedish language. The experience of asking for public support was very hard for them. As they put it, "we are ordinary people who had lived a very good life and then we became social assistance recipients. We could not believe that it would be that hard to find jobs". *Constraints on entering the labour market* were the main cause that kept them on the social assistance programme for three years. Finally, he found a temporary job as an engineer in one of the city's hospitals, which allowed them to come off the measure. However, the insecure nature of his employment and the insufficient income it yields, forces them to apply to other welfare schemes to complement it. They can afford only the rent available in a segregated urban area. But they are *actively organising their life* and are making sacrifices on their personal consumption in order to be able to send their children to a private school in a better off part of the city.

Ms P is a citizen of Costa Rica aged 42 at the time of the interview. She arrived in 1991 in Gothenburg to live with her boyfriend. After they separated, she experienced financial hardship and entered social assistance. The separation, however, encouraged her to *reorganise her life* by entering education during the period 1992-96. She finished her upper secondary education but, notwithstanding some previous work experience, she has not yet been able to find a new job. Her family and kin are all in Costa Rica and she has few friends in Gothenburg. She feels that both her social life and her chances of finding a job are constrained by the limitation of her informal networks. In this sense she is highly dependent on social assistance, with little hope of improving her situation. The measure helps her in *managing her life from day-to-day*.

The comparison between cases O and P offers an illustration of the relevance of personal capabilities and attitudes (and of family structures) within a particular institutional framework and local context. It also stresses the different experience of economic migrants and asylum seekers in the host cities. The Yugoslav family illustrates the case of well-educated Europeans forced to move for political reasons. The educational and professional skills of both adults, and particularly of the man, the responsibility of having a family to support, but also the emotional stability derived from having one's own family together, facilitated the path towards a slow inclusion in the labour market and in the wider community: there are clear long-term strategies involving the children's future. In the case of Ms P, the low level of education, low self-confidence, emotional isolation and poor social networks, possibly also age and gender, are extending the period of time spent on benefits and work against the hope of a better future. The generosity of welfare programmes in Gothenburg offer support to both, but their personal circumstances are responsible for different outcomes. In most Southern European cities (Barcelona and Turin being partial exceptions), neither of these cases would even have been considered for social assistance, and if so, only for short periods of time and/or with very limited resources.

The difficulty of developing adequate employment strategies is often reinforced by cultural models of household and family organisation, according to which women working outside the household are not approved of, even if the husband is unemployed, or if there is no other (male) breadwinner available. This attitude plays against women's employability at all stages: it does not give women an incentive to acquire adequate training; it delays and sometimes hinders their search for a job when this becomes necessary; and puts an additional burden on already overstrained relationships. Notwithstanding this, some women succeed in changing the rules in order to improve their own and their family's economic conditions.

In Barcelona, Mr and Mrs Q from Morocco, live with two adult children aged 19 and 21. They arrived in 1974 shortly after their wedding. The children were born in Barcelona and have Spanish nationality. The husband too is Spanish by birth. As with other immigrants, many of the couple's kin are dispersed over several European cities. His health deteriorated and he could not keep his job any longer, becoming unemployed in 1991. His unemployment benefit finished in 1993 and from that year he started doing odd jobs, which provided him with a small and irregular income. They contacted their relatives and received some income support from them. Although the sums of money coming from England and Morocco were very helpful, they proved to be insufficient for their daily subsistence. In 1994, the wife contacted the social assistance services against the will of her husband, who was the one to suffer most from the consequences of *an accumulation of crisis events*. Through the help of social workers she found a job, having to put up with her husband's resistance, since he did not want her to work outside the home. At the time of the interview she was still working as a cook and he had finally obtained a disability pension. Both events helped them to get out of social assistance. She was able to *actively organise their life* and to mobilise public resources and family networks.

Ms R is a lone mother. She was 41 years old at the time of the interview and was born in Algeria. Her family migrated to Saint Etienne when she was five years old with nine more siblings. She *comes from a deprived family*. However, she sees the main reason for entering social assistance to be her divorce. She married at the age of 27 and had a child, but her husband became an alcoholic and did not support her. As a result she divorced him, taking their daughter who was three years old, back to her parents' home. She stayed with them for four years, while starting to do odd jobs in the informal economy (all paid under the counter). This type of employment has not helped her to obtain qualifications. When she was interviewed her daughter was already 12, and she had very few social contacts outside her family. She has been a recipient of the RMI for eight years and her self-esteem has not risen very much, although she has signed various insertion contracts and worked in firms funded by the State. She remains very pessimistic about her real life chances outside welfare dependence. The divorce from her husband was experienced as a major breakdown event as it changed her life, causing a situation that is difficult to manage. The RMI helps her to *manage her daily life*.

Social workers claim that the cities' programmes do not specifically target – either positively or negatively – non-EU immigrants. However, a stricter selection occurs in Southern European cities, particularly in Italy, due to the scarcity of resources and the high political sensitivity of immigration issues. In Germany a specific programme has existed for this group since 1993. Moreover, social workers acknowledge in general that it has been necessary to introduce changes in their approach, which has meant a certain degree of adaptation to foreign cultures by social services. This is clearly the case in Gothenburg, where the proportion of immigrants (many of them refugees) is relatively high. In this city new rules and practices have been introduced in order to deal with recipients who share neither the language nor the prevalent model of social citizenship with its set of rights and responsibilities. The same occurs in Bremen. In other cities, 'cultural mediators' have been hired in order to communicate with the families and communities of the recipients and to support them in improving their social networks inside and outside their own communities. In Barcelona, for example, a network of immigrants' associations has been asked by the city council to provide support for newcomers, and some social workers are very concerned about the conditions in which women, in particular, live in the city.

Among immigrants, the illegal ones are, of course, most at risk of being excluded from any kind of public support, relying only on charities and their own networks. By definition, their numbers can only be estimated. But it is likely that while there are more regular immigrants in the Central and Northern countries, in the Southern European ones, given the relative accessibility of their coasts, the proportion of illegal immigrants is higher[16]. In most countries and cities, exceptions are made for children, whose illegal status should not bar them from receiving essential resources, such as education and health services. Yet, their families may prefer not to allow them to use these resources, in order not to become conspicuous in the eyes of social workers and the police.

Conclusions

We began by asking why some people are more likely to end up on benefits than others. To explore this question at a time when means-testing and selectivity dominates the discourse and practice of social policy (Gough, 2000) was not easy. Several elements have emerged from the analysis of the complex interplay among the various dimensions influencing the process that leads people to social assistance. We have seen that the socioeconomic context and the specific employment opportunities and unemployment risks present in a given city affect social groups differently and produce distinct forms of vulnerability. This vulnerability is in turn acknowledged and supported in very different ways by the social security and social assistance policies. The result is that not only are there different risks of becoming poor, but the chances of receiving social assistance are also unevenly distributed among the different categories of poor and needy. There are several reasons for this but, as we have seen, most of the differences in terms of figures and profiles of the claimants can be explained ceteris paribus by the institutional design of the social assistance schemes, together with the overall system of social protection.

The cases we have reported show how individual strategies tend to reflect the institutional design. Claimants' profiles are more heterogeneous where the thresholds are more generous and access is granted to a larger share of the population. Profiles characterised by a higher degree of marginality and exclusion result where the selection criteria are tighter. An overview of the complex interplay among the different dimensions and strategies producing these profiles was given in Figures 4.1 and 4.2. Their complexity and dynamic nature, however, demand caution in inferring strong causal links. The high proportion of single male adults on benefits in a Southern European town such as Barcelona might, for instance, coincide with a period of high unemployment occurring within an institutional context of very selective unemployment benefits. So, what is the real meaning of the over representation of this group among the socially assisted? Is it due to the business cycle or are other mechanisms at work? It might indicate that the limited coverage of unemployment indemnity, together with growing joblessness, is forcing an increasing number of adult men to turn to social assistance. Yet, given the low income threshold of income support in Barcelona and its bias against single adults, not all unemployed men will be entitled – only those who have exhausted their resources and have an unfavourable personal situation in addition to 'sole' poverty. Thus the high figure might also indicate a spread of social vulnerability among the population, due in part to growing unemployment, but also other factors, such as the weakening of family and informal networks, the spread of non-standard, risky behaviour and so forth. Only a finer analysis can unravel the various factors lying behind this relatively high incidence of single men among the socially assisted. On the basis of our comparative analysis, however, we are able to argue that the Barcelona figures, although apparently similar to those in the Swedish cities, do not include the same kind of people and needs. Single men receiving social assistance in Barcelona are much farther along the path leading to serious poverty and social exclusion.

Finally, the 18 short stories tell us that people have experienced considerable difficulties in their attempts to find the best way of surviving.

Some had been living on the threshold of poverty for some time, when some event tipped the balance, others made recourse to social assistance as part of a medium term strategy to change their life arrangements, others were trapped in poverty and dependency and were unable to see a way out. The proportions of these groups vary from city to city and from scheme to scheme. Instrumental users are more frequent in generous schemes. People coming from deprived families or with an accumulation of 'crisis events' are relatively frequent in the more selective schemes. These differing patterns influence the potential success of the intervention. In this chapter we have attempted to provide examples of the complex issues at stake when people enter social assistance. Chapter Five will explore in more detail what kind of people remain longer on social assistance, what kind of people exit faster and for what reasons.

Notes

[1] This question evokes the provocative and brilliant analysis by Göran Therborn in his *Why some people are more unemployed than others* (1986).

[2] In addition to Chapter One in this book, see Behrens and Voges, 1996; Berger and Sopp, 1995; Falkingham and Hills, 1995; Leisering and Leibfried, 1999.

[3] A large quota of unemployed people in Italy are covered by other programmes that have replacement rates similar to the German ones. However, the access criteria to these benefits still tend to categorise claimants, impeding overall coverage of all the unemployed.

[4] By competencies we mean here the set of resources available to the individual, including literacy and education, social and relational skills, emotional stability, health, and so on. They are resources that ease access to other kinds of resources (for example, work, income, recognition, and so on). These competencies are fundamental in the process of satisfying basic needs (Doyle and Gough, 1991) and in defining the framework of capabilities of the individual (Sen, 1992) and their chances of choosing among alternative lifestyles.

[5] The Gini index gives a rough but clear picture of this effect. For instance, in the Scandinavian countries that belong to the *additional pattern* the Gini index is around 0.24 (Sweden and Denmark), while in countries where a *substitutive pattern* prevails it reaches 0.35 (Greece and Italy, even though the Italian case has a marked north-south divide). In *complementary* countries the figures are intermediate: 0.28

(Germany and the Netherlands). Data are drawn from the ECHP first wave 1994 (Vogel, 1997).

[6] In our analysis, 'first time recipients' include all persons entering social assistance at a given point in time, have not been on benefits in the previous 12 months. For further details, see Chapter Five.

[7] As indicated in the introductory chapter (see first section), privacy regulations in France do not allow the use of social assistance archives. Instead, we have used retrospective survey data on beneficiaries. Yet, the distinction between first time and ongoing recipients is not possible on the basis of survey data. For this reason these data are not directly comparable with those on the other cities. Cross-sectional data tend to over represent long-term recipients, while longitudinal data over represent short-term recipients. Data for Cosenza are not included, due to the occasional nature of the benefit in that city. Data for Porto and Halle are unfortunately missing too for the reasons explained in the introduction.

[8] Almost everybody had a job and only very few were getting social assistance. In 1989 there were only 5,500 people on benefits in the whole of East Germany, that is 0.03% of the population (see Priller, 1994, p 3).

[9] As in the French cities, there is an age limit, since the programmes are addressed to citizens and residents between 25 and 65 years of age. People below 25 are entitled to the measure only if they have parental responsibilities.

[10] Bauböck (1994) points to the consequences for entitlement to social assistance and of the different rules by which citizenship is granted.

[11] For disabled and older people the situation is different: in most Southern European welfare states, they benefit from ad hoc programmes, often defined at the national level. Moreover, they are considered among the most deserving beneficiaries of social assistance at the local level.

[12] Behrens and Voges (1996) for instance, observe that in Southern European countries families play a crucial role during several phases of the life cycle and in relation to the most critical phases.

[13] Active organisation can also take the form of a major restructuring, even of family relations, so that the person experiences a new start in life. These types have been adapted from – and are coherent with – a wide range of existing

literature on the topic (Kazepov, 1995; Leisering and Leibfried, 1999; Ludwig, 1996; Paugam, 1993).

[14] The French programme is the API; in Germany *Sozialhilfe* is supplemented by a *Mehrbedarf*: an additional sum of money awarded to specific categories of beneficiaries of *Sozialhilfe* including lone mothers.

[15] In Italy they are targeted to low income wage workers, in Spain to the poor.

[16] Many of these illegal immigrants enter a country, such as Italy, as a way of reaching other countries in Central or Northern Europe, rather than to remain.

FIVE

Paths through (and out of) social assistance

Björn Gustafsson, Rolf Müller, Nicola Negri and Wolfgang Voges

Introduction

In this chapter we describe and analyse the dynamic pattern of social assistance support. The analysis is limited to those cities for which quantitative longitudinal data were available in the social assistance archives: Gothenburg and Helsingborg in Sweden, Bremen in Germany, Milan and Turin in Italy, Lisbon in Portugal, Barcelona and Vitoria in Spain. This means that the comparison covers fewer cities than in other chapters.

Building up the database was one of the main tasks of the ESOPO study. The existence of information covering a significant length of time has made it possible to retrace the full sequence of periods during which beneficiaries and their families received economic support. Our intention was to overcome the limits of static analyses of poverty. Although static information is of course useful, it does not permit an understanding of the dynamics of poverty, nor of the social assistance provided, and consequently it does not allow an adequate assessment of the efficacy of policies.

As pointed out in Chapter Four, and underlined in other studies, households receiving social assistance in the same city and at the same time may in fact find themselves in very different situations. While some may be experiencing a lapse into poverty, briefly interrupting a basic situation of economic independence, others may be subject to frequent lapses characterising a highly vulnerable life course, and others again may find themselves in a situation of chronic indigence.

Considering only the first episode of social assistance may therefore be highly misleading[1]. Many people conclude a first period of support only to return later (often several times). An analysis restricted to a single episode does not allow the distinction between situations of occasional temporary economic difficulty and the numerous relapses experienced by those who do not have enough resources to free themselves from long-term reliance on social assistance (Leisering and Leibfried, 1999).

In order to overcome these limitations, we have created a harmonised micro-database that is more coherent with the conception of poverty as a dynamic phenomenon, both at the individual and household level. To our knowledge, this database is unique both for number of archives (and countries/cities) included and for the kind of dynamic analyses it allows. The different situations and dynamics have been observed and analysed by reconstructing 'careers in social assistance'. This has been done by examining all entries to and exits from assistance over a period of 42 months in each of the sample cities. Our analysis has greatly benefited from the approaches taken in recent groundbreaking studies on the dynamics of poverty and social assistance. At the same time, it goes further than most, in so far as we consider the whole welfare career of recipients – or at least a long enough part to be able to identify meaningful interruptions, as distinct from brief spells of being off welfare.

In this chapter we will analyse differences between the cities in our sample in terms of the average length of time beneficiaries remain on social assistance. We also consider the specific features of income support schemes (particularly their universality and generosity). In addition, we investigate whether, and to what extent, specific groups of beneficiaries share a similar pattern of social assistance duration across the various cities. Our comparative analysis of social assistance careers will thus be both cross-city and cross-group. However, before developing the core of this chapter, it is fair to point out some limitations of our data.

The first limitation concerns the fact that in order to harmonise the widely differing data sources, we have been unable to take into account certain important information, since this was available in some archives but not others. For example, information on the individual characteristics of all household members receiving social assistance was available in Turin, but not in Bremen. This forced us to analyse household rather than individual dynamics. Consequently, much useful information on specific household members was lost: for example, we do not have individual information on married women living with their husbands, when the latter claim social assistance, or on adult children living in the household[2]. The latter feature is particularly relevant in the Southern European cities, where adult children are counted as household members.

A second limitation concerns the origin of the data. The decision to rely on administrative records had several implications. The sources did not turn out to be sufficiently reliable in all the cities considered in the ESOPO project; further, in France their utilisation was prevented by restrictions connected with the protection of privacy. This meant that the French cities had to be excluded from the analysis presented in this chapter. Last, but not least, the information available represents the point of view of the administration and/or social workers on the relevant characteristics and events in beneficiaries' lives. This can be very different from the beneficiaries' own perceptions of their reality. We have to some degree integrated the data by using material from in-depth interviews, but the basis of our longitudinal analysis nevertheless remains the administrative records.

Despite the shortcomings mentioned above, at the present state-of-the-art, a research strategy based on administrative records appears to be the most satisfactory strategy. Recourse to direct retrospective longitudinal surveys, by conducting interviews with samples of beneficiaries and/or ex-beneficiaries, may avoid the constraints imposed by non-availability, non-accessibility or unreliability of administrative sources[3]; but it is not advisable to depend exclusively on such information for several reasons.

Firstly, the use of surveys faces the difficulty of administering questionnaires to people who, because of their precarious and marginal life conditions, are unlikely to be available for interviews and, in the case of ex-beneficiaries, are often hard even to track down. Secondly, collecting information by means of retrospective questions poses problems connected with the interviewees' memory, such as recall bias, the telescoping effect or heaping effect. It could be objected that these problems could be avoided by using repeated surveys on panels, but this strategy is not feasible in a research project with limited time and a restricted budget. Furthermore, the problems of attrition typical of panel surveys can become serious in the case of social assistance beneficiaries and ex-beneficiaries, many of whom resist being interviewed.

With all their limitations, administrative data are better able to represent the outcome of the interplay between the local, social and economic conditions and modes of intervention, described in the previous chapters. Furthermore, the knowledge acquired from the analysis of information from administrative sources could help define strategies to mitigate the distortions introduced by the interviewees' memory or phenomena of attrition mentioned above.

We believe that part of the added value of this study lies in having created a sound basis for the development of further research programmes. At the end of our analysis, it will be clear that the ESOPO approach, while not fully exhaustive, allows us to expand our understanding of the workings of social policies in a substantial way. Furthermore, the information collected constitutes an empirical database that can be expanded in many directions by future research on social assistance careers.

What we can comparatively evaluate, and what we cannot

Our comparative approach has rendered us keenly aware of the risk of misleading interpretations that could result from a naive reading of cross-country data on social policies. It is an issue that has recently been highlighted with regard to social security measures concerning unemployment (for example, Gallie and Paugam, 2000). It is even more crucial for social assistance policies, given the variety of conditions involved. This has made us highly cautious about the possibility of making an evaluation of the impact of social assistance income support policies based on a straight comparison of the pattern and length of social assistance careers in the various countries/cities (Holland, 1986). In order to qualify the significance of the results presented in the following paragraphs, a brief preliminary discussion may be useful (see also Bosco et al, 1999).

First of all, let us ask what a 'reasonable' outcome of income support policies could consist of. Certainly, the main aim of these measures is to cover the financial needs of poor families. Therefore, the principal task of evaluation would seem simple. To evaluate if an income support policy gives good coverage, it should be sufficient to verify that: a) no poor persons are excluded from benefits, and that b) beneficiaries are assisted *according to need*, that is while their need for income support lasts. Counterfactual information drawn from reference groups of non-beneficiaries is not always strictly necessary for this kind of assessment, although it can be useful.

However, a major negative consequence of income support (often pointed out by those hostile to such policies, but also by many who support them) is that it can produce dependence, becoming itself the cause of continued economic hardship. The assumption of dependence is based on the idea that living on social assistance affects the behaviour of the recipient. This possibility was first brought up in the debate on the US social assistance system (for example Murray, 1984), but is now a widespread concern in the European policy debate. In the most widely accepted meaning, dependence refers to a situation in which beneficiaries are less able to solve their objective state of need, compared to the non-assisted poor. In this view, the poor would be better off in the long-term if they were not assisted, since social assistance weakens their personal capabilities.

It is obvious that if we wish to examine this risk, we have to refer to a control group of non-assisted poor. Yet, there is a serious ethical problem in making recourse to control groups in matters of social assistance. One cannot easily construct an experiment, granting support to one subgroup of the poor, while withholding it from another with identical needs. This is a common problem in the evaluation of social policies. Moreover, setting up a control group is frequently hindered by the lack of sufficiently detailed information on the poor. The use of a sample control group of non-assisted poor is, besides, almost certainly open to problems of selection bias. There is reason to believe that those excluded from social assistance, notwithstanding their apparent similarity with those included, differ in terms of various behavioural characteristics. In categorical systems, for instance, the presence of certain requirements will increase the 'deservedness' to social assistance support; but there may also be differences in the ability to seek a job or become part of the informal economy.

Finally, a cross-city evaluation exercise using control groups would have to assume that all local systems operate according to the same rules, particularly with regard to the length of period for which assistance is provided. As we know, this presumption is unfounded. Thus, the meaning of duration of support may be quite different in different local or national systems, and therefore ambiguous from a semantic point of view. For instance, in Milan, where beneficiaries are not assisted for the whole duration of their need, the assumption of dependence might be confirmed only in cases where assistance periods were longer than the duration of need for non-recipients belonging to a non-assisted control group. But it may neither be confirmed nor denied in the opposite case.

For all these reasons, straightforward evaluation of the impact of social policies is not always possible on the grounds of our data. At the same time, data on social assistance careers of the type produced by our project are crucial if one wishes to make a 'best practice' assessment.

First of all, such data enable us to verify – in each model of intervention and each socioeconomical context – whether people who are benefiting from some form of income support are progressively losing their capacity to live autonomously without support. A study that aims to verify this effect – which we shall define from now on as the 'chronicisation effect' – is far more circumscribed than a study on dependence. As we have seen, the hypothesis of dependence requires comparison with a reference group of unassisted poor. The hypothesis of chronicisation, on the other hand, requires no such comparison, as it focuses only on the effect of duration of assistance on its beneficiaries, that is, whether the beneficiaries' ability to exit assistance improves or worsens over time.

On the basis of the ESOPO data, we can check for the possible presence of chronicisation by establishing whether the probability of leaving social assistance decreases within the period of income support. If people who have received social assistance for one year have a lower probability of exit during the following month than a household that has received social assistance for only three months, a case of chronicisation may exist.

We have in fact adopted this strategy of analysis. Its implementation, however, requires some explanation in order to avoid misunderstanding. It is necessary to consider that a negative relation between social assistance duration and propensity to exit need not be the outcome of the impact of social assistance itself. It might simply be that long-term and short-term recipients are different kinds of person, as observed for instance by Walker and Shaw (1998) with regard to social assistance beneficiaries in the UK. If there is unobserved heterogeneity, that is if some explanatory variables for duration are neglected or unavailable, the shape of the observed 'hazard function' could be biased towards negative duration dependence (Lancaster, 1990). The bias of this observed hazard function is due to a selection effect, reflecting the fact that as time goes by, other things being equal, the group of survivors will increasingly be composed of people with a lower propensity to exit.

Therefore, if we find a decreasing hazard function, we do not know whether the decrease in exit probability is due to continued welfare dependence or to statistical reasons. From the perspective of evaluation, hypotheses of chronicisation can at most be rejected as not proven. If we find a non-decreasing hazard function, we should conclude that no negative duration dependence applies (Bosco et al, 1999). But if the hazard function is a decreasing one, we cannot be sure that there is a negative relationship between duration and propensity to exit from assistance.

Information on the possible presence of a chronicisation effect is just one of the results that can be obtained from analysis of our data. Regarding the selection of best practices, important indications can be gained if we are able to locate and interpret statistics on the duration of intervention and relapses into social assistance within an analytical framework that enables us to: a) highlight the range of effects varying the patterns of social assistance careers across cities and across categories; and b) clarify the relations between these effects and the local welfare systems. The next section will focus on the analytical framework adopted.

The impact of welfare measures and contexts

Given two local welfare configurations, A and B, let us suppose that the duration of assistance recorded in the latter are shorter and the returns rarer than in the former. It is possible that this indicates that the support measures in system B are able to resolve beneficiaries' problems more rapidly and with more lasting effect than those of system A – that is to say, they are more effective.

However, as indicated in Chapter Four, other elements with no bearing on efficacy may affect the pattern of social assistance careers. These can include the influence of the socioeconomic and institutional environment in which the welfare systems operate, and/or the impact of the rules regulating these systems. In order to avoid misinterpretations, a comparative analysis of social assistance careers must also take into account this type of element. In the following paragraphs we will briefly discuss them.

Measure-specific reasons for variations in efficacy

Policies carried out in system B could be more efficacious than those in system A because of the quality of their 'activation measures' (Bosco and Chassard, 1999; Geldof, 1999). It could thus be an effect of the actions taken, in addition to monetary support, to improve the beneficiaries' situation, helping to integrate them back into the labour market and society (see also the figures in Chapter Three). We could thus speak of 'activation measures effect'.

For instance, an important reason for the relatively low local unemployment rates in the Swedish cities is the existence of active labour market policies. As we shall see, many people are able to exit assistance because they take part in this kind of programme. In Sweden, after a period of unemployment, people are usually enrolled in a temporary employment programme. The same may occur after a period of social assistance. During this time they do not need social assistance and appear neither in unemployment rates nor on welfare rolls. Such measures also exist in other countries, but affect a smaller proportion of both the labour force and social assistance beneficiaries.

Another factor that might explain the greater efficacy of system B could be the higher substitution level offered by income support. Here we are referring to the dimension labelled 'generosity' in the figures in Chapter Three, and therefore refer to the 'generosity effect'. The relationship between the amount of income support received and duration is in fact rather complex. On the one hand, the more generous and attractive the benefit, the longer people can be expected to stay on it. On the other hand, if financial support is not adequate, beneficiaries might resort to the informal economy to solve the problems of subsistence. A lasting, albeit precarious 'assisted equilibrium' could be established, based on a combination of income support and resources derived from the irregular labour market (Gallie, 1999; Leisering and Leibfried, 1999; Paugam, 1993).

Both 'activation measures' and 'generosity effects' require the impact of resources provided by social assistance on beneficiaries' capabilities to be taken into consideration. Inasmuch as the different patterns of careers in assistance reflect effects of this kind, their comparison allows evaluations of efficacy.

Influence of the environment on forms of poverty

We know that episodes of social assistance (entries, exits, returns) tend to be triggered by an event or combination of events provoking impoverishment. For example, the main breadwinner in the household falls seriously ill or loses their job without being able to find a new one, a full-time homemaker divorces or becomes a widow, an unmarried unemployed young single woman becomes pregnant, a person is forced to emigrate without any job prospect in the host country. The latter is a typical situation for refugees, but also many irregular migrants.

The incidence of these specific triggering events, and even more so their relevance, varies substantially across the cities investigated. Unemployment represents a much higher risk where the labour market is static and there are very few job options: for example, separation renders women more vulnerable where employment rates and/or opportunities are low among married women. Furthermore, the joint causes that render unemployment more serious, are not constant. In one situation being a separated or divorced woman can be particularly difficult, in another being over the age of 40, in yet another being an immigrant.

Variability in the joint causes depends on the local combination of population characteristics, and socioeconomic and institutional structures. These include not only the public social assistance system, but also the range of resources provided by formal and informal actors in the private and third sector. As a consequence, both the incidence and the composition of the various causes of poverty can vary substantially from one local society to another, as indicated in Chapter Two. From this follows the possibility of considerable differences regarding the population entering the social assistance system. The qualitative problems that local welfare systems have to face in providing support will vary accordingly.

Such differences are the reasons why social assistance periods can be expected to differ in length across the cities investigated, independently of the characteristics of the social assistance itself, in particular the efficacy and efficiency of the measures. We will call this variation the 'forms of poverty effect'. It does not refer to the *impact of the policies* on beneficiaries' capabilities (Sen, 1992), but to the different *original characteristics* of beneficiaries.

Influence of the environment on patterns of social assistance implementation

There are no deterministic relationships between local forms of poverty and the problems faced by public social assistance systems. Two points are particularly relevant in this connection.

First of all, it is necessary to consider that the characteristics of the socioeconomic and institutional environment do not only influence the resources used to prevent the risk of impoverishment. They also influence the resources that can be activated by beneficiaries themselves once they have fallen into poverty. Some local societies are richer in 'preventive remedies' than others, providing a higher capability of recovery. In some cases, for instance, social security benefits for the unemployed are both generous and long lasting. In others, a more flexible labour market makes it easier for the unemployed to become poor, but also allows them to find a new job more quickly. For this reason, when considering that the main road to economic self-sufficiency for able-bodied adult recipients is through paid employment, one should take into account not only social assistance patterns, but also local labour policies and labour market patterns (Grover and Stewart, 1999; Standing, 1990). The effects of such policies can be very different from one context to another.

Variations in the availability of non-social assistance resources can also produce variations in the kind and seriousness of the problems local welfare systems have to face in dealing with beneficiaries' needs. These differences are another important reason why the pattern of social assistance careers may vary cross-city, independent of the type of social assistance measures, or their efficacy and efficiency. We will call this the 'resources for exit effect'.

Second, it is necessary to consider that persons or families who find themselves in financial difficulty often hesitate before applying for social assistance. The situation varies across households. While some apply right away, others wait until they have exhausted their resources, since they find it 'shameful' to request social assistance and try to manage without. These individual differences may be considerable, even within the same society and the same social assistance system. We call this the 'behaviour effect', but must bear in mind that a longitudinal study of social assistance careers (entries, exits, returns) based on administrative archives, can offer very little information in this connection.

Influence of access rules

We know that entitlement rules vary across countries and cities and may be further mediated by the modes of implementation. For this reason, a person who has become a recipient in one city would not necessarily have been acknowledged as such in another. Therefore, in the comparison of longitudinal data on periods of assistance, it is important to consider the different levels of generosity and other rules that regulate access to assistance.

With reference to the figures presented in Chapter Three, the dimensions of the local assistance configurations that must be considered in this respect are those regarding 'selectivity' and the 'universal versus category-based orientation' axes. In Chapter Three, we saw that access rules can differ first of all in the degree of poverty giving access to support (how poor must one be in order to receive support), and second in the degree of universality (whether or not additional personal or household characteristics are required in order to be entitled to support).

Depending on the degree of selectivity in its access rules, a system can therefore support situations of more or less severe poverty. And depending on the degree of universality of such rules, a system may address any income need within a given threshold, or may link support to conditions that render the case 'deserving'. Because of the filters established by access rules, analysis of social assistance careers often cannot cover all the poverty situations present in a local society. The connection between the forms of economic poverty and the typology of beneficiaries depends on the generosity of the rules in question. Therefore, the qualitative problems that local welfare systems have to face can, in many cases, be considered a consequence of the systems themselves.

We now concentrate on the interesting issue of the relationship between the generosity of the access rules and the duration of support. Let us compare a less generous system with a more generous one. Some people who do not qualify for assistance in the former would be accepted in the latter. Such people are likely to be less marginalised and, compared to other recipients, are therefore at an advantage with regard to finding a job or finding other means to achieve self-sufficiency. Due to this mechanism – which from now on we shall refer to as the 'means-test effect' – it is probable that the duration of support in the more generous system will on average be shorter. Within this same system, a shorter duration may be recorded for categories to whom the right of access is acknowledged in a less restrictive manner. In such cases, the shorter duration of income support does not indicate a greater effectiveness or efficiency of the measure; rather it indicates that on average, beneficiaries or a given subgroup, are characterised by a lower frailty or have more personal resources. In other words, it is once again a question of the original characteristics of those on assistance, rather than the efficacy of a given measure.

Influence of the rules concerning duration

The variability of means-tests is not the only cause of differences in the duration of social assistance. These may stem from still other features of the measure. The effect of constraints imposed by the rules concerning the length of time one is allowed to receive income support is important when these do not follow a need-related logic. We will call this phenomenon the 'time constraints effect'. Clearly, this can occur when the right to income support expires after a predetermined period. It applies to local assistance systems characterised by a low score on the axis 'duration according to need' in the figures in Chapter Three. In these cases, a short duration says nothing about the impact of measures on the beneficiaries' capabilities. The exit speed simply indicates the speed at which it is possible to lose entitlement to support.

However, this is only part of the story. Another, rather less straightforward, aspect relates to actions taken by social workers or administrators to push recipients out of welfare assistance. Such actions too may differ according to the system, as indicated by the scores given to different local assistance systems along the axis 'recipients' duties' in the figures in Chapter Three. Such duties can have a positive effect if they improve a claimant's ability to become self-sufficient. Yet, not all actions taken by social workers aim mainly at increasing the economic self-sufficiency of claimants. There is often an element of control, policing or pressure put on beneficiaries to 'go away' (Standing, 1990; Grover and Stewart, 1999; Hvinden, 1999). In such cases, termination of social assistance does not necessarily mean that the claimant's economic situation has improved because he or she has found alternative resources. On the contrary, it might even represent a worse economic situation.

Analytical steps and structure of empirical data

The discussion up to now has shown that there are many reasons why there may be differences in the duration of income support across the cities investigated. Irrespective of differences in the forms of poverty present, the great cross-city variation in entry conditions, exit conditions, and in the process of receiving social assistance make it very unlikely that the periods of social assistance will be of a similar length in all the cities investigated. The effects discussed in the previous section can combine in different ways for each group of beneficiaries, and these variations can also differ from one city to another. We would therefore expect to find differences in duration across categories and, furthermore, expect these cross-category differences not to be identical in all cities.

Since there are no previous studies addressing these same issues for such a large number of cities and countries, there is no well-founded opinion on whether to expect large or small differences. It was therefore difficult to foresee the result of the complex interactions behind the variations in assistance patterns. For instance, the opposing mechanisms of the level of generosity in relation to entry and exit – that is the combination of the 'means-test effect' and the 'time constraints effect' – make it unclear if we should expect a universalistic assistance system operating on needs-based logic to be positively or negatively related to the duration of income support. Therefore, on the whole, it was difficult to formulate and test hypotheses concerning duration of support in given cities or for given categories of beneficiaries.

Because of this difficulty, the first step in the empirical analysis (see sections on: 'Duration on social assistance', 'In and out of assistance', 'Some cross-category comparisons') involves surveying empirically – probably for the first time in such a systematic way – the actual cross-city and cross-category differences produced by the effects discussed above, that is the 'form of poverty effect', the 'resources for exit effect', the 'behaviour effect', the 'means-test effect', and the 'time constraints effect'. The second step is to check for possible interactions among these effects, so that the comparative analysis of the social assistance careers is not marred by problems of semantic ambiguity. This second analytic goal is approached in two stages. Firstly, in the section on 'Some cross-category comparisons', we try to make any interactions between the above effects more transparent by comparing the careers of two specific categories of beneficiary: single parents and immigrants. The advantages of this comparison, from an explanatory point of view, derive from the fact that these categories are quite typical. In fact, social assistance systems – even those of a categorical orientation – are inclined to act in favour of single parents typically in a universal and generous manner, because of the presence of children. At the same time, the forms of poverty of single mothers and the resources available may be very different in the local societies examined. On the contrary, in the case of immigrants, most systems are moving towards greater control and restriction. Moreover, immigrants experience specific problems of both social integration and labour market insertion. Secondly, in the section on 'Using multivariate analysis to explain differences in exit and re-entry', we will try to isolate the different effects causing variation in social assistance duration utilising multivariate analysis techniques.

Having focused the theoretical-methodological framework and the principal passages of the statistical analysis, we now describe in greater detail the structure of the empirical data utilised.

For the eight cities considered in this chapter, we have access to data on all those who started receiving social assistance. Over a period of 42 months, we know month by month whether the household continued to receive social assistance[4]. In this section, we discuss the analytical choices we made in using these data and their consequences for interpretation.

Possibly the most straightforward initial step is to sum up the number of months a household has received assistance during the observation period. This gives an overall view of the situation across the cities. But simply summing the total number of months in social assistance during the observation period, of course, hides the fact that they may be distributed very differently along the time axis. This is illustrated in Figure 5.1. For example, 12 months of income support during the observation period could represent (a) many very short periods, (b) one period of 12 months, (c) various combinations of long and short periods. To the extent that it is important to distinguish between these situations, there are arguments for working with the concept of *episode* as opposed to total time. The episode is defined as a period during which a household continuously receives social assistance. Advances in statistical methods make multivariate analyses of such episodes feasible.

When applying the concept of episode to our data, we faced an analytical choice. Not infrequently, we find 'holes' in our data, representing periods of non-payment of benefits. It often occurs that a particular household apparently stops receiving income support for one or more months, but

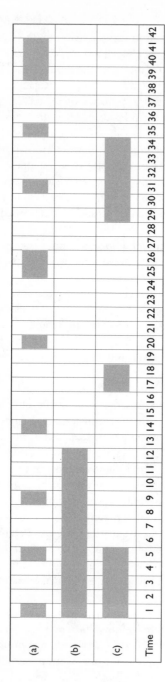

Figure 5.1: Different possibilities to sum up 12 months of recipience

then starts again. How should this be dealt with in the analysis? One possible reason for non-payment during a particular month is purely administrative: in reality, the household did receive income support, but for some reason it was not recorded in the data. This could happen for example because the welfare office was closed for the summer vacation in the month of July and paid income support in advance at the end of June. In this case it would be misleading to state that one episode of social assistance ended in June and another started in August.

Based on this consideration, we 'filled in' all small holes in the histories of income support and worked with the concept of *cash episodes*. One cash episode is separated from another by a period of at least two months in which the household did not receive income support. But this approach can still lead to a large number of short episodes being observed. An alternative is to fill in longer holes too, applying a definition that would lead to longer and fewer episodes.

To investigate to what extent the cross-city comparisons were robust, we applied an alternative definition: the *dependence period*. Two dependence periods are conceived as separate if there are at least 12 months during which the household did not receive income support. These periods are thus generally longer than cash episodes. Comparing the two approaches, it emerged that most of the results based on the definition of a cash episode also apply to dependence period. Thus, we present in our tables and figures only the findings concerning cash episodes. In the text we comment on any cases where the two alternative definitions – cash episode and dependence period – give different views of the situation.

Duration on social assistance

How long do people remain on social assistance?

In Table 5.1 we present the results of the total time on social assistance during the 42 months of observation for the eight cities studied. Let us start by commenting on the proportion of households receiving social assistance for six months or less. Rather large differences are found across the cities investigated. At one extreme are the Swedish cities and Milan, where the majority of households fall in this class; the proportion in Bremen is only slightly lower. At the other extreme are the cities on the Iberian Peninsula, with very low proportions of recipients remaining for a relatively short total time on social assistance.

In all cities a considerable proportion of households received social assistance for between seven and 24 months: from slightly more than one quarter to about one third of all recipients in most cities. Vitoria is the exception with about half the recipients in this group. Finally, we consider the proportion who received social assistance for most of the observation period – that is more than 24 months. Here, Barcelona and Lisbon stand out, both with a majority of the recipients belonging to this group. In the third position comes Vitoria, followed by Turin, the latter with a quarter of the first entrants being long-term recipients. Bremen is ranked number five. The smallest proportion receiving social assistance for more than 24 months is observed in Milan and the two Swedish cities[5].

On the basis of the information on total time on social assistance, the cites can be divided into four groups. The first, where the duration is the longest, consists of Barcelona and Lisbon. Vitoria alone is in the second group. The third group comprises Turin and Bremen. Finally, there are three cities where social assistance receipt is relatively short: the two Swedish cities and Milan.

The analysis of the total time on social assistance confirms that non-negligible variations exist among the cities investigated. This information is of interest for policy makers due to the budgetary consequences of longer versus shorter duration. However, the overall length of time on social assistance may cover differential time patterns. Let us consider recipients A and B, who both received social assistance for 14 months during the observation period. For household A receipt took place during the first 14 months. The support was thus continuous for just over one year; but this was followed by a period of at least 28 months of non-receipt. On the other hand, household B received its overall 14 months

Table 5.1: Total time on social assistance (%) (number of cases in parenthesis)

	1-6 months		7-12 months		13-24 months		25-42 months 1 episode		25-42 months 2 or more episodes	
Barcelona	7.4	(43)	12.3	(72)	19.3	(113)	49.4	(289)	11.6	(66)
Bremen	46.1	(391)	15.7	(133)	18.0	(124)	14.6	(124)	5.7	(48)
Gothenburg	58.8	(1301)	17.8	(395)	15.5	(344)	4.2	(94)	3.6	(79)
Helsingborg	52.0	(127)	14.3	(35)	19.3	(47)	5.3	(13)	9.0	(22)
Lisbon*	14.6	(29)	10.1	(20)	17.2	(34)	58.1	(115)	–	–
Milan	57.3	(453)	19.1	(151)	16.3	(129)	1.4	(11)	5.9	(47)
Turin	38.9	(479)	17.2	(211)	19.2	(236)	10.4	(128)	14.3	(176)
Vitoria	17.9	(69)	21.0	(81)	26.8	(103)	22.3	(86)	6.7	(46)

*In Lisbon there are no further episodes after the first one

of income support distributed throughout the entire period of observation, with occasional interruptions lasting no longer than a few months. These differences are highly relevant both for policy makers, interested in the efficacy of their social expenditure, and for policy analysts, interested in the dynamics of poverty and social assistance. Thus we turn to the analysis of periods (also called spells) on income support.

The first episode (and following ones)

In Figure 5.2 we present a survival curve referring to the first cash episode for each city investigated. The figure shows the proportion of recipients still receiving assistance after a given number of months. It is possible to make a general ranking of the cities according to the length of the first cash episode of social assistance receipt[6]. The result is very similar to that of total time on income support. The survival curves for Lisbon and Barcelona are the highest and cross each other after approximately 12 months of receipt. After this period, a higher proportion remains on social assistance in Lisbon. The survival curve for Vitoria is below that for Barcelona and Lisbon, but higher than those for the other five cities. This is true for the entire observation period.

Figure 5.2: Survival function of first cash episode by cities

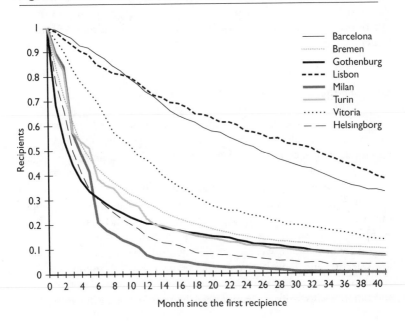

Month since the first recipience

Milan has a survival curve that is rather different from the others and intersects with several other curves. To a lesser extent this also applies to Turin. When we look at the upper left corner of the figure we see that the proportion of recipients remaining on social assistance in Milan after a few months, although smaller than in Lisbon, Barcelona and Vitoria, is not lower than in Bremen, not to mention Gothenburg and Helsingborg. However, after six months the survival curve for Milan is the lowest, with only one fifth of cases still on social assistance. By contrast, not even one fifth of beneficiaries in Barcelona and Lisbon had left continuous social assistance after six months.

We capture the duration of the first cash episode in Table 5.2 in a single number for each city, which is derived from the survival curves. The table shows the median duration for each city investigated, that is, after how many months half of the recipients have terminated receipt. The medians show that half of the people who debut on social assistance in Lisbon remain for almost three years, in Barcelona for more than two years, and in Vitoria almost one year. For Turin and Bremen, the corresponding period is about six months, while in the remaining cities it is even shorter. The median duration for the city with the longest duration, Lisbon, is about ten times as long as for the city with the shortest duration, Gothenburg. This is indeed a very large difference. Table 5.2 also shows the median duration for the second cash episode (or later ones if these exist). Such periods are observed for all cities, except Lisbon. We find that in all cities, the median duration of the second episode is rather similar to that of the first.

Exploring the reasons for the variations in the duration of spells

Both the data on the total period of social assistance and the duration of the various spells already allow us to detect the presence of some of the previously described context effects that explain variations in the pattern of social assistance careers.

If we consider the general features of local social assistance configurations illustrated in Chapter Three, we can observe first of all that the ranking of the cities in terms of social assistance duration (Table 5.1 and Figure 5.2), compares to a certain extent with the ranking of cities according to the generosity of the local welfare systems: duration is shortest in cities with less selective and more universalistic access rules that follow a needs-based logic. From this inverse relation between generosity of the system and duration of receipt, we can detect the importance of the 'means-test

Table 5.2: Median duration of the first four cash episodes by cities (months)

	1. Cash		2. Cash		3. Cash		4. Cash	
	Median	Episodes	Median	Episodes	Median	Episodes	Median	Episodes
Barcelona	26.86	585	25.59	85	15.00	11	(x)	(x)
Bremen	5.57	849	5.58	202	3.18	45	4.10	19
Gothenburg	3.41	2,213	3.27	847	3.49	368	3.22	152
Helsingborg	4.05	244	3.73	115	5.19	40	7.44	16
Lisbon	33.50	198	(x)	(x)	(x)	(x)	(x)	(x)
Milan	4.93	791	5.90	285	5.02	116	5.87	34
Turin	6.09	1,230	6.68	519	6.78	186	6.64	53
Vitoria	11.63	385	9.30	134	12.17	32	(*)	7

(*) >50% censored episodes; no possibility to calculate the median.

(x) No cash episodes.

effect'. In other words, the data seem to show that, overall, the impact of generosity on entry into social assistance is greater than its impact on exit.

Therefore, the four groups constructed on the basis of receipt duration could be partly explained by differences in the beneficiaries' original characteristics, corresponding to differences in the access rules. But this explanation is certainly not exhaustive. For instance, the closeness of Milan to the Swedish cases can certainly not be caused by similar 'means-test effects'. The same thing could be said of the closeness between Turin and Bremen.

In fact, in terms of the characteristics of the local systems, the groups that emerge from Table 5.1 and Figure 5.2 exhibit a high degree of heterogeneity. This is a clear indicator that different mechanisms are producing similar effects on the temporal patterns of social assistance careers in the various cities. Therefore, the reasons both for shorter and longer duration are rather different in the four clusters.

What is the effect then that makes the duration of social assistance in Milan – characterised by a high score on the selectivity axis – as short as that recorded in non-selective systems such as the Swedish one? And what is the effect that locates Turin close to Bremen? The data suggest that, for the Italian cities, the mechanism referred to in the section on 'The impact of welfare measures and contexts' as the 'time constraints effect' must be taken into account. In these cases, therefore, duration is largely determined by the rules of a system that removes people's eligibility after a pre-specified period and/or render recipients' duties highly constraining and subject to close policing by social workers.

The very steepness of the survival curve for Milan (and to a somewhat lesser extent that for Turin) at three and six months show that eligibility rules have been in effect. In Milan, 25% of beneficiaries left social assistance exactly three months after their debut, 21% after a six month period. The corresponding proportions in Turin were 20% and 15%. These are considerably higher than the rates observed for the other cities after the same number of months. They are also higher than those observed one month from their debut. The story behind these findings is that in Milan, and to a lesser degree Turin, a substantial number of new applicants are granted social assistance for a period of three months. Only in the case of certain categories is income support paid for longer periods: for instance, as we shall see, 'deserving' single mothers and, in Turin, individuals whose personal capabilities are seriously impaired.

Before concluding this first exploration of cross-city differences in duration, we should point out that besides the 'means-test effect' and the 'time constraints effect', other effects listed in this section could possibly help explain the data in Table 5.1 and Figure 5.2. Particularly in the Swedish cases, it would seem reductive to assume that short duration is only the expression of original differences in the beneficiaries, selected through particularly generous access regulations. We should also consider that a faster exit speed might be the result of the impact of policies addressing the beneficiaries' human capital, in addition to the workings of a very dynamic labour market. The latter renders the former both more efficacious and more realistic.

Therefore, we cannot exclude the presence of the 'activation measures effect' in the two Swedish cities. In fact, as already pointed out, in these cities many unemployed people exit social assistance because they are recruited into active labour market programmes. However, these programmes are temporary and their termination might trigger a new period of social assistance receipt. In Sweden, the presence of a strong network of activation measures could influence the whole pattern of welfare careers by accelerating the exit speed from assistance, but also multiplying re-entries. Nor can we disregard the 'generosity effect' hypothesis connected to a well-balanced amount of cash support that allows households to keep a reasonably adequate standard of living, without pushing them into a vicious circle of social marginality.

On the other hand, in the case of the Southern cities, including partly Milan and Turin, duration on social assistance could also be the result of the socioeconomic context – that is the 'form of poverty effect' or 'resources for exit effect'. Or, it could be ascribed to an insufficient cash support keeping households in a situation of 'assisted equilibrium', where neither income support nor informal resources are sufficient alone, but must be combined.

None of these additional hypotheses necessarily disqualifies the hypothesis that the pattern of duration across cities is mainly determined by the 'means-test effect' and the 'time constraints effect'. They simply point to the possible presence of mixed effects, difficult to separate empirically.

In and out of assistance

We now examine the proportion of households receiving social assistance after a specific period of time since their debut, and indicate if they are in the first, second, third or higher order cash episode. Then we look explicitly at the process of re-entry into social assistance.

First timers, long timers and in-betweens

The status of recipients is shown in Figure 5.3. At the bottom of the figure is the survival curve for the first cash episode[7]; on top of this, the proportion of households in the second or higher order cash episode are added. We can observe that the longer the time after the debut, the fewer the people receiving social assistance. The figure also shows the proportion of recipients in the position of being between two periods of social assistance at a particular time after their debut. This information should not be misunderstood. In fact, the possibility of observing if a household is between two periods of assistance decreases during the observation period. And at the end of the observation period there is, obviously, no possibility at all of observing if a household is between two periods of receipt. This means that the main use of these curves is in cross-city comparison.

What can be learned from Figure 5.3? One central observation is that the incidence of higher order cash episodes differs quite considerably between the cities investigated. On the one hand, in Lisbon no household is in a second (and therefore also not a higher) period of social assistance. On the other hand, in the Swedish cities many households are observed in higher order periods. As a rule, we notice that much of the clustering of cities presented in the previous section still holds, a partial exception being Turin.

Figure 5.3: Cumulated status distribution of cash recipience

(a) Barcelona

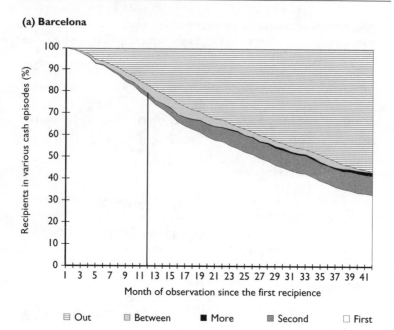

(b) Vitoria

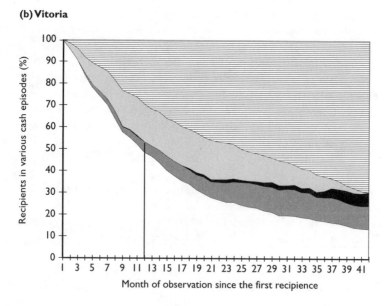

Figure 5.3: Cumulated status distribution of cash recipience (contd)

(c) Gothenburg

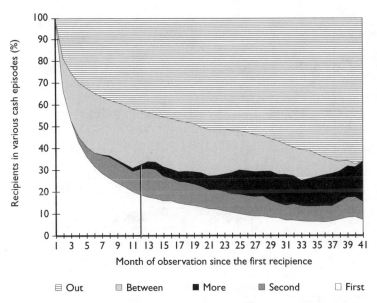

Month of observation since the first recipience

⊟ Out   ▨ Between   ■ More   ▨ Second   ☐ First

(d) Helsingborg

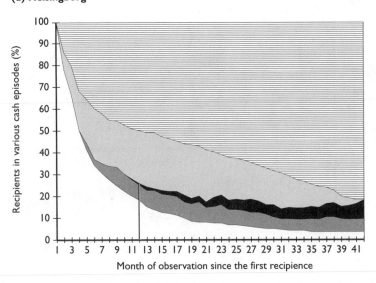

Month of observation since the first recipience

Figure 5.3: Cumulated status distribution of cash recipience (contd)

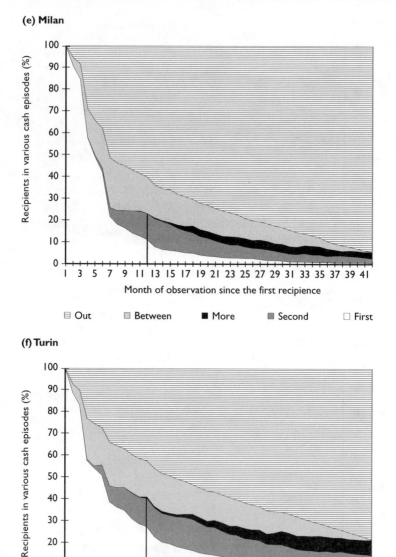

(e) Milan

Recipients in various cash episodes (%)

Month of observation since the first recipience

▤ Out   ▨ Between   ■ More   ▨ Second   ☐ First

(f) Turin

Recipients in various cash episodes (%)

Month of observation since the first recipience

Figure 5.3: Cumulated status distribution of cash recipience (contd)

(g) Bremen

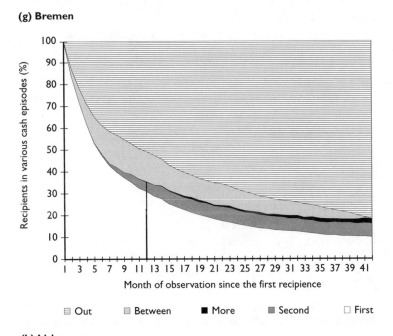

Month of observation since the first recipience

⊟ Out   ▨ Between   ■ More   ▨ Second   ☐ First

(h) Lisbon

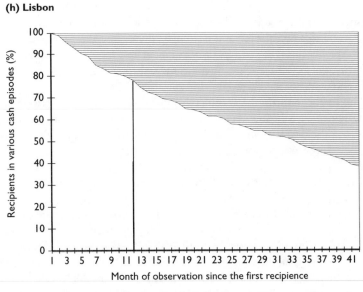

Month of observation since the first recipience

Let us consider, for example, the status 12 months after debut in the various cities (the vertical line in Figure 5.3). In Lisbon and Barcelona three quarters of recipients are still receiving social assistance. Third in this ranking is Vitoria with almost exactly half still receiving social assistance one year after debut. Fourth comes Turin with more than one third in the first episode, and a non-negligible proportion in the second episode. Bremen is ranked fifth, followed by Gothenburg and Helsingborg with about one third, and finally Milan with one fifth of the beginners receiving social assistance a full year after debut.

The data in Figure 5.3 therefore shows that many households have been returning to social assistance in cities where the average length of the first cash episode is short.

Re-entry into assistance

Let us now look more closely at the process of re-entry. It is not surprising to find that cities with the shortest average first cash episode are also those for which we observe the largest proportion of second and high order spells of social assistance. In cities where many have left the first cash episode fairly quickly, there have also been many second episodes. Of course, if most recipients remain in their first case episode, those entering a second episode are less numerous. Therefore, it is more interesting to investigate if there are differences in the propensity to return to social assistance among those who have left the first episode. We investigate this by drawing survival curves that show the proportion of ex-recipients surviving in the non-receipt state. Figure 5.4 shows the information for all the cities investigated except for Lisbon, where no household was observed re-entering social assistance.

This figure confirms the considerable variation across cities. Barcelona and Bremen have the highest proportion of ex-receivers surviving without further assistance. For instance, two years after the end of the first cash episode, three out of four ex-receivers had not yet re-entered social assistance. The other extreme is Gothenburg, where half of the ex-receivers had returned to social assistance 16 months after exiting the first period of receipt.

The finding that the process of re-entry differs from one city to another has consequences when making cross-city comparisons. When basing the comparisons on the entire pattern of assistance careers, the differences with regard to total duration on social assistance are not as large as when basing them on survival curves for the first cash episode only[8]. The clustering of cities based on the first cash episode remains largely the

Figure 5.4: Survival function of those exiting their first cash episode

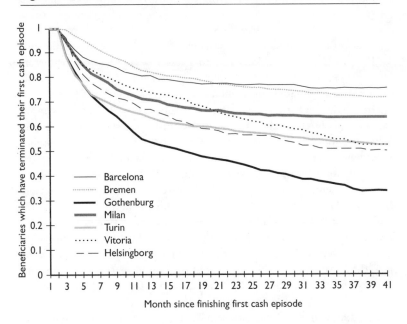

same, but with significant corrections. The largest difference involves Gothenburg: here the first cash episode is shorter than in Helsingborg, Milan and Bremen, but the dependence period (inclusive of the phases in which the beneficiaries temporarily do not receive income support) is no shorter, actually it is longer, than in these three cities[9].

However, the clearest evidence suggested by Figure 5.4, and particularly by Figure 5.3, is that the various clusters are characterised by quite different time patterns of entry and exit from social assistance. This strengthens our hypothesis that the patterns of cash episodes and dependency periods are the result of complex interactions among the context effects concerning the rules governing the local assistance systems described in detail in Chapter Three. These interactions explain the differences among the cities and modifications in their clustering when comparing the first social assistance episode with subsequent ones. They also offer an insight into how these different configurations shape social assistance experiences and career patterns, even when the beneficiaries' needs and capabilities are largely similar.

The impact of 'functioning rules' on the pattern of social assistance careers

The role of functioning rules appears particularly crucial in systems such as those in Lisbon, Barcelona and, to a lesser degree, Vitoria, which are characterised by both high selectivity in access and a needs-based logic with regard to duration of entitlement.

Due to the very strict 'means-test effect', beneficiaries in these systems are particularly vulnerable, with low capabilities and severe difficulties in achieving social and financial autonomy. At the same time, the absence of limitations on the length of entitlement to assistance allows beneficiaries to be supported for as long as they require it. The combination of the two effects tends to produce a social assistance career pattern characterised by a very long first period of assistance. This phenomenon reduces the statistical probability of observing return episodes. But in these cities, returns are also less likely for two other reasons. First of all, as they adopt a needs-based logic, these systems do not expel people who seriously lack the means to be self-supporting. Second, re-entry is hindered, or delayed, by the selectivity of the means-test. Thus, the first assistance episode tends to be the only, but long lasting, one.

An additional effect that can further reinforce the consequences of the interaction between the needs-based logic and selectivity in access rules is the (lack of) 'generosity effect'. In welfare systems such as that operating in Lisbon, the likelihood that social assistance careers crystallise into one long episode of dependence is favoured by the small amount of income support, that increases the beneficiary's efforts to reach some kind of 'assisted equilibrium', either through recourse to the informal economy or other kinds of support from the third sector or charity.

Symmetrically, in Vitoria and (to a lesser degree) Barcelona[10], a relatively high generosity of income support leads to a mitigation of this phenomenon. In these cases, the effects of the interaction between selective means-tests and the absence of duration limits is further mitigated by the presence of 'activation measures effect' (for Barcelona more than for Vitoria), and the fact that the needs-based logic is counterbalanced by the presence of 'recipient duties' (for Vitoria more than for Barcelona).

However, looking at the whole pattern of social assistance careers, the differences between these three cities appear less marked than those relating to the duration of the first cash episode. Substantial affinities (as well as non-negligible internal differences) emerge among these Southern European systems, in that they cater for particularly vulnerable and socially weak beneficiaries supported according to need.

At the opposite extreme from the Spanish and Portuguese systems, but still within the sphere of systems operating in the absence of rules and constraints concerning duration, we find the Swedish cities and Bremen. In these cases, less selective access rules allow support to people with less severe problems of poverty or social integration. Consequently, the duration of the first support period is on average shorter. Also, the presence of 'generosity effects' (relatively high levels of income support) may help to shorten the duration of the first assistance period, while not pushing towards the search for 'assisted equilibrium'.

However, where there are shorter first episodes, there is a higher statistical probability of observing returns. In Sweden, the returns are also counter-intuitively favoured by marked 'activation measures effects'. The same holds for Bremen, where the implementation of rules and practices concerning 'recipients' duties' also contribute to the dynamism of local social assistance careers. In these cities, beneficiaries have a better chance than in Spain or Portugal – both in terms of individual capabilities and structured options – of exiting from social assistance more or less temporarily. But, for at least a certain percentage, this does not necessarily result in stable independence from social assistance in the long run.

Also in the Northern European cases, consideration of the whole pattern of social assistance careers shows the fundamental affinity among social assistance systems characterised by 'stronger' beneficiaries supported while their need persists.

In summary, the data show that in the Spanish and Portuguese systems and also in the Swedish and German ones, affinity and diversity of social assistance patterns are due to 'means-tests effects', which affect the beneficiaries' original characteristics. Further differences are then produced by the impact of the measures on the beneficiaries' capabilities, according to the level of adequacy of the cash benefit and its integration with activation measures. These are the main interactions that shape differences in the careers in systems operating with a needs-based logic. The consequences of these interactions are only marginally modified by the locally specific pattern of implementation of rules concerning recipients' duties, which appear particularly relevant in Bremen and Vitoria.

In Milan and Turin, on the other hand, the pattern of social assistance careers seems to be strongly determined by the 'time constraints effects'. Given the strong selectivity of the means-tests (which helps select the weakest users), the low cash benefits that might encourage resort to informal resources, and their scarce integration with activation measures, we should expect a career pattern not unlike that of Lisbon, and maybe less dynamic than Barcelona and Vitoria. On the contrary, the Italian systems are characterised by career patterns more similar to the Swedish ones and, as we can see from Figure 5.4, faster re-entry speeds than in Bremen.

This similarity is, however, artificial in a certain way. It involves neither the beneficiaries' characteristics nor the impact of support on their capabilities. The similarity – particularly in the case of Milan – is rather the product of formal (or informal) rules and pressure from social workers. Both of these limit the duration of support without always following the needs-based principle. It is obvious that periods of assistance that are too short with respect to need can produce returns to assistance precisely because they do not allow enough time or resources for an individual or household to develop adequate strategies for self-support. At the same time, these periods may actually worsen the beneficiaries' social and human capital, in so far as highly stigmatised support tends to have a negative effect on those receiving it. Thus, in this case too, the dynamic pattern of social assistance is heavily dependent on the specific form of the local welfare systems, although the most relevant features are different to those that explain the Northern European, Spanish and Portuguese patterns. Here the most crucial role is played by rules on duration.

It now remains to investigate whether and how these effects interact with other context effects, in particular those which in the section on 'The impact of welfare measures and contexts', we defined as 'forms of poverty effect' and 'resources for exit effect'. For this purpose it is useful to turn to some cross-category comparisons.

Some cross-category comparisons

In this section we will make two comparisons for each city studied regarding the duration of the first episode of assistance and the first dependency period. In the first case the situation of single parents is contrasted with that of all other beneficiaries. The second one concerns the careers of foreign immigrant beneficiaries with respect to natives.

The questions that this comparison aims to answer are the following: do the careers of these two groups of beneficiaries exhibit specific time patterns and dynamics? To what degree does this specificity (or lack of) reflect differences (or lack of) in the local forms of poverty experienced by these two groups, and the kinds of options and resources available for them? To what degree does the presence (or absence) of cross-category differences indicate 'forms of poverty effects' and 'resources for exit effects'? To what degree do differences depend on the differential impact of social assistance measures on the capabilities of individuals and households belonging to different categories? And, finally, to what degree is the presence (or absence) of differences a consequence of the operating rules of local systems?

Lone mothers on social assistance

Although lone fathers do exist, most lone-parent families consist of a mother and her child(ren). Several processes may lead to the formation of a lone-parent household: in many cases lone parenthood results when the parents separate or divorce (before or after the birth of the child). But also the death of one parent or voluntary single motherhood can lead to a lone-mother family being formed.

Lone parents (lone mothers) can often neither count fully on the other parent's earnings to cushion the lack or inadequacy of personal earnings, nor on sharing responsibilities for care. Lone-parent households, and particularly lone mothers, are exposed to the risk of a double scarcity: of money and time. This vulnerability is particularly evident in countries, and cultural subgroups, in which the male breadwinner/caring wife is the norm, which regulates the gender division of labour within households and the redistributive patterns of the welfare state (for example, Lewis, 1997b; Sainsbury, 1996). Nevertheless, the condition of single parenthood is neither homogeneous nor static. Lone parents often receive some support from the other non-cohabiting partner. If widows, they may receive a pension. They might also receive support from kin. And they may find a new partner. Thus, a lone mother is not necessarily alone in a social sense. In some cases they do not even live alone with their children, but with other adults – often with one or both parents. In fact, statistical definitions of what forms a lone-parent household differ quite substantially across countries (for example, Hantrais and Letablier, 1996) and these differences may also emerge in social assistance records.

Last but not least, many lone mothers obtain their living from paid work. This is one of the features that most differentiates lone mothers, both within-country and cross-country (Bradshaw et al, 1996; Lewis, 1997b). Among the six countries studied in the ESOPO project, the lowest proportions of working lone mothers are found in Italy and Spain, where just over half of the single parents are employed (Vogel, 1997). The other extreme is Sweden, where three out of four single parents have a job[11].

From a legal point of view, lone mothers generally have greater welfare protection than many other social assistance recipients. Transfer payments are typically larger for lone mothers than for couples with children. There may be a court award or an agreement stating that the ex-spouse has to pay alimony. Some countries have introduced systems guaranteeing maintenance payments for children living with a lone parent. Furthermore, when lone motherhood has occurred because of the death of the father, widow's pensions are often paid.

Like other families with children, lone-mother households qualify for child allowances, income-tested transfers such as housing benefits, and benefits replacing income loss due to the care of a newborn baby. These systems vary nationally in the degree of generosity and universality, as does the availability of reliable and inexpensive childcare.

Notwithstanding this, lone mothers in all Western European countries have a higher than average risk of being poor (Daly, 1992; McLanahan et al, 1992). This has been recently documented by studies based on cross-country longitudinal data for Western Europe (for example, Pedersen et al, 2000; Vogel, 1997). At the same time, there is also substantial cross-country variation – the UK having the highest rates and the Scandinavian countries the lowest, while Continental and Southern European countries are somewhere in between.

In all the cities investigated, lone-mother families make up a considerable proportion of recipients. The proportion is the highest in Barcelona, where one out of four claimants is a lone-mother household. In Vitoria this proportion is one out of five. The lowest proportion is in Turin, where only one out of twelve recipients is a lone-mother household.

Do single parents exit social assistance at a different pace from other recipients? Figure 5.5, which illustrates survival curves for lone mothers as well as for all other recipients, indicates that in most cases the survival curves are higher for lone parents than for other households. The difference is greatest in Bremen. In this city, one year after debut, almost half of lone parents remain on social assistance, compared to less than a third of all other recipients. Also in Milan there is a noticeable difference between lone parents and other recipients.

Figure 5.5: Survival function receiving cash benefits for lone mothers and all other recipients

(a) Barcelona

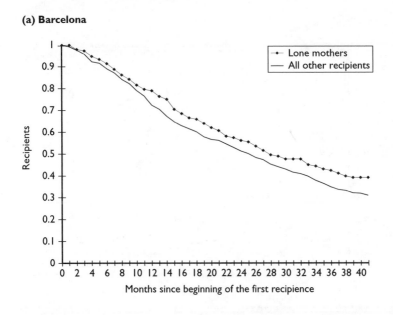

Months since beginning of the first recipience

(b) Vitoria

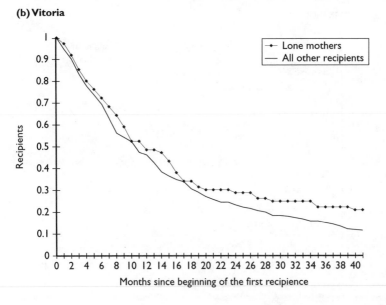

Months since beginning of the first recipience

Figure 5.5: Survival function receiving cash benefits for lone mothers and all other recipients (contd)

(c) Gothenburg

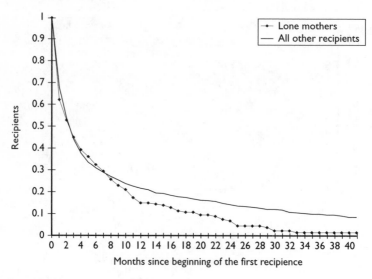

Months since beginning of the first recipience

(d) Helsingborg

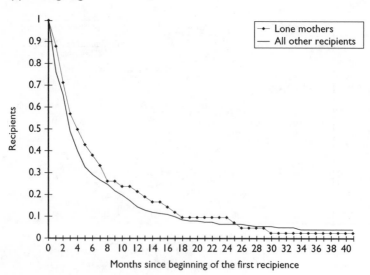

Months since beginning of the first recipience

Figure 5.5: Survival function receiving cash benefits for lone mothers and all other recipients (contd)

(e) Milan

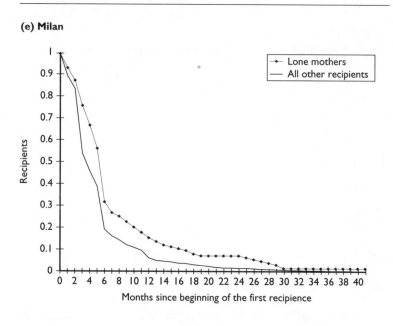

Months since beginning of the first recipience

(f) Turin

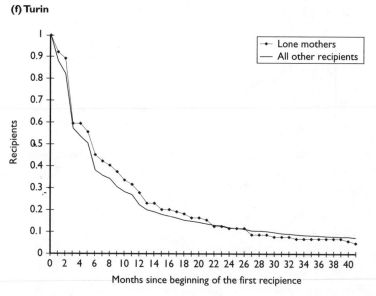

Months since beginning of the first recipience

Figure 5.5: Survival function receiving cash benefits for lone mothers and all other recipients (contd)

(g) Bremen

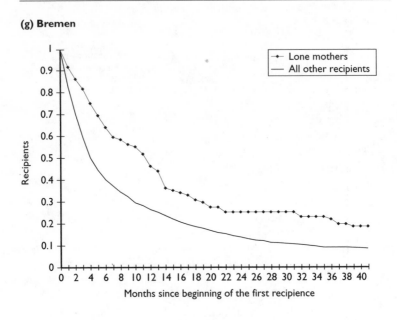

(h) Lisbon

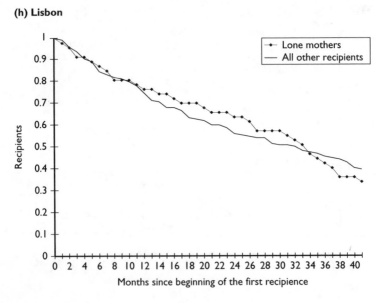

Looking at the medians reported in Table 5.3, we find no example of a lower median for lone parents than for other households. On the contrary, there are some examples of medians for lone parents that are statistically significantly higher than for other recipients. The largest difference again is in Bremen, where single parents stay on social assistance two and a half times as long as other recipients. Similar results are found when analysing both cash episodes and dependence episodes[12].

As a whole the data seems to confirm that lone mothers have greater difficulty than other recipients in entering the labour market and obtaining an adequate wage, due partly to their previous history of non-employment, or interrupted work experience, and partly to their caring responsibilities. Thus, the specific features of their social assistance career pattern is largely due to a 'resources for exit effect'.

This also explains why in the case of Gothenburg there are almost no differences between lone parents and other categories, and in Helsingborg very few. In these two cities, the local and national welfare systems and cultural patterns encourage and support participation in the labour market by women in general, and mothers in particular. On the other hand, the absence of significant differences between lone parents and other categories in Lisbon can be explained by the fact that other beneficiaries share with lone mothers similar, though not identical, difficulties in establishing themselves in the labour market. It is a city with a high rate of poverty and access rules that lead to the selection of beneficiaries among the

Table 5.3: Median duration of first cash episode for lone mothers and all other recipients

	Lone mothers			Non-lone mothers			
		Cases			Cases		
							csf
	Median	Absolute	Weighted	Median	Absolute	Weighted	Sign
Barcelona	28.83	153	130.99	26.12	432	369.86	
Bremen	12.40	90	53.00	5.10	759	447.00	***
Gothenburg	3.37	287	64.84	3.41	1926	435.16	
Helsingborg	5.00	42	86.07	3.94	202	413.93	*
Lisbon	34.25	47	118.69	33.17	151	381.31	
Milan	6.27	122	77.12	4.54	669	422.88	***
Turin	6.55	104	42.28	6.05	1126	457.72	
Vitoria	12.67	76	98.70	11.50	309	401.30	

csf: comparison of survivor function; significance: Wilcoxon (Breslow);

***: $p < 0.01$; **: $p < 0.05$; *: $p < 0.1$

socially weakest. Also in this case, the lack of difference involves the effects of (scarce) availability of resources for exit. Similar effects could be present also in Barcelona and Vitoria. In addition, particularly in Barcelona, the large number of irregular, easily accessible, but badly paid jobs within the informal economy, together with meagre assistance subsidies and badly balanced equivalence scales for large families, tend to create a constellation of resources and constraints which produce patterns of 'assisted equilibrium', rather than full dependence. This in turn may be better suited to dual-parent households than lone-parent ones, given the constraints the latter experience with regard to time and personnel.

But not all the cross-category relationships that emerge from Table 5.3 and Figure 5.5 point only to the 'resources for exit effect'. In the Swedish cities, the lack of significant differences between lone parents and other categories could also be ascribed to an 'activation measures effect', in so far as lone mothers might receive particular support in their efforts to enter the labour market. But even this is insufficient to explain all the cases.

Availability of resources for exit and activation measures cannot, for instance, explain the scarce differentiation between lone parents and other categories of beneficiaries in Turin. Although women's (and mothers') activity rates in this city are higher than the Italian average, and lone mothers' children are given priority in childcare services, there is very little systematic support in terms of job insertion measures. In Turin, the 'means-test effect' has a more important role in explaining the lack of cross-category differences than in most cities. Given the lower selectivity of the system where lone mothers are involved, this group is more heterogeneous than others in terms of life stories and individual capability. There is therefore a lower percentage of cases of severe vulnerability. The same may hold true in part for Vitoria and Barcelona. In both of these cities, in fact, due to the priority given to children, the selective access rules, as well as the requirements involving recipients' duties, are relaxed in the case of lone mothers.

The much longer duration of social assistance for lone parents in Bremen cannot be explained solely through the resources for exit effect, nor the activation measures effect. Certainly, there is a lack of childcare services and relatively few activation measures compared to those available in the Swedish cities. However, interviews with social workers have indicated that lone parents in Bremen are expected to fulfil 'recipients' duties' to a lesser degree than other beneficiaries, and that caring for their children is the main duty expected of them. Consequently, they are less subjected to nagging and cajoling by social workers to 'be active' and 'on the move'.

This attitude is certainly coherent with the widely shared model of gender and mother's obligations in this city, which is also responsible for the scarcity of childcare services for very young children.

A similar attitude by social workers is responsible, possibly to a greater degree given the high selectivity of the system, for the longer duration of social assistance for lone mothers in Milan. Although this city has the strictest rules concerning duration, they are relatively relaxed in the case of lone mothers, because of the concern for children.

On the whole, the cross-city comparison between lone parents and other categories shows that the rules governing local assistance systems can affect cross-category differences – sometimes reinforcing them, sometimes weakening them – as these are determined by the socioeconomic and institutional context.

Immigrants on social assistance

The cities investigated have very different histories in relation to their experience of international migration, as indicated in Chapter Two. This has produced immigrant populations with differing size, origin and duration of stay. During the 1950s, 1960s and at the beginning of the 1970s, many workers and their families moved from the Mediterranean countries to Northern Europe. Italy, Portugal and Spain were countries of international emigration, receiving very few immigrants. In West Germany, efforts were made to recruit workers from abroad. Sweden also experienced a substantial influx of worker immigrants. In this case, however, the most important sender country was Finland; this occurred within a context of free mobility between the Scandinavian countries, and was motivated by differences in per capita GDP. During the 1980s and 1990s, out-migration from Italy, Portugal and Spain became substantially less than in-migration, the latter mostly from Eastern Europe and developing countries (for example, North Africa). All three, however, continue to have smaller proportions of foreign-born population than Germany, Sweden or France. At the same time, the immigration flows to Germany and Sweden have changed in many respects. Asylum seekers and their relatives, rather than work immigrants, have become the majority of new immigrants. Many recent immigrants to Germany and Sweden originate from distant non-European and non-industrialised countries. Since they face difficulties in finding employment, many rely on social assistance for their maintenance.

In the cities examined in our study, some immigrants are not entitled to social assistance income support. One example is asylum seekers waiting for a residence permit, who are entitled to assistance from other programmes specifically targeted to them. Another group is illegal immigrants, without a residence permit, who make up a substantial proportion of all immigrants, even if the number can only be estimated. Additionally, legal immigrants who have not yet completed a given period of residence and do not have a long-term residence permit are usually not entitled to social assistance[13], although they may receive some kind of occasional, temporary support. Once they fulfil the entitlement criteria, however, non-nationals and non-EU citizens are not treated as a specific category in the systems we have investigated.

In our data we can identify beneficiaries who are foreign citizens. These make up different proportions of the beneficiaries in the various cities. For instance, they represent only about one in twenty in Lisbon and the Spanish cities, while at the other extreme in Gothenburg one in three recipients is foreign. Bremen too has many foreign recipients (one out of four) and in Helsingborg one out of five recipients is foreign.

In Table 5.4, we report medians for foreigners and natives. In the case of Bremen there is also a specific curve for immigrants of German descent. It emerges that all three possible situations are present: that is cases where foreigners have longer, similar and shorter periods on social assistance than natives.

The median periods are significantly longer for foreigners than for natives in Bremen and the Swedish cities. The difference is quite large in Sweden – the median for foreigners is about three times as long as for natives. The long duration of social assistance among immigrants in the three Northern European cities is without question due to specific difficulties in finding a job. No statistical difference in medians is found for Barcelona and Vitoria. Medians are statistically shorter for foreigners than for natives in Lisbon, Milan and Turin. Basing the comparison on the first dependence period gives a very similar picture. The main exception is Milan, which shows no significant differences between natives and foreigners.

On the whole, the cross-category differences seem to point to effects relating to the availability of resources for exit, with particular reference to the possibility of finding employment. Two patterns of differentiation between the careers of foreign immigrants and natives emerge. The first is found in the Northern European cities, where the labour market is characterised by many jobs in the regular, formal economy. Immigrants, however, penalised by a lower degree of social integration, have difficulty in obtaining them.

The second pattern is found in the Southern European cities. These

Table 5.4: Median duration of first cash episode by nationality

| | Non-nationals | | | Re-settlers | | | Nationals | | | csf |
| | Cases | | | Cases | | | Cases | | | |
	Median	Absolute	Weighted	Median	Absolute	Weighted	Median	Absolute	Weighted	Sign
Barcelona	35.00	32	27.40	–	–	–	26.65	553	473.46	***
Bremen	7.36	219	128.98	5.80	136	80.09	4.78	494	290.93	***
Gothenburg	7.62	737	166.52	–	–	–	2.74	1476	333.48	***
Helsingborg	10.17	51	104.51	–	–	–	3.68	193	395.49	**
Lisbon	23.50	9	22.73	–	–	–	34.17	189	477.27	**
Milan	3.94	104	65.74	–	–	–	5.01	687	434.26	*
Turin	3.99	188	76.42	–	–	–	6.28	1042	423.58	**
Vitoria	14.50	17	22.08	–	–	–	11.53	368	477.92	

csf: comparison of survivor function; significance: Wilcoxon (Breslow); ***: $p < 0.01$; **: $p < 0.05$; *: $p < 0.1$

are characterised by a large number of paid jobs in the informal economy that facilitates the possibility of the economic (though not social and cultural) integration of immigrants (Dubet, 1989; Garonna, 1992; Piore, 1979; Reyneri, 1996). Given the availability of jobs and lower expectations of immigrants in terms of pay and social security, in cities like Lisbon, Turin or Milan immigrants remain on social assistance for less time than natives, and in Barcelona and Vitoria the period is not significantly different. This does not imply that *regular* immigrants exit social assistance more quickly because they compete successfully with natives in the informal labour market. Labour demand in the low paid, low-skilled informal economy is in fact addressed primarily to illegal immigrants, who can be paid less. In addition, employing them irregularly in most countries is less risky than employing regular immigrants or natives, as they are less likely to report their employers to the employment or tax offices (Reyneri, 1996). Yet, the informal and irregular labour market also facilitates the employment of regular, legal immigrants, in so far as it offers ill-paid jobs in manufacturing and personal social services. Such jobs pay too little and their conditions are often too substandard to be reasonably acceptable to natives. If cheap immigrant labour were not available, these jobs would remain unfilled. Despite the unpleasant conditions and even health hazards, they are more acceptable to immigrants, at least for a while, because they are perceived as a necessary step in a process of social insertion, and also because they are compared with expectations and the standard of living in the countries of origin (Reyneri, 1996).

Immigrants receiving social assistance tend to be subjected to closer scrutiny by social assistance services, even if they are in the host country legally, particularly in countries and cities where social assistance is highly selective and categorical. Thus, they will avoid the risk of being found cheating the system by combining social assistance and income from the informal economy – a risk that is more easily taken by natives. Finally, if they remain too long on social assistance, foreigners may risk losing their residence permit.

Figure 5.6 shows survival curves for foreigners and natives in the various cities[14]. These confirm the presence of distinct patterns of differentiation between natives and foreigners in the north European cities and the south European ones. The south European pattern seems to manifest itself in a typical manner in the curves for Turin. During the first few months, there is no difference between natives and foreigners in survival on social assistance; but after approximately four months foreigners begin to leave social assistance faster than natives.

This figure also helps us to understand differences among the three

Figure 5.6: Survival function receiving cash benefits for natives and non-nationals

(a) Barcelona

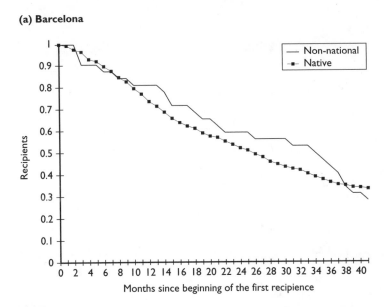

Months since beginning of the first recipience

(b) Vitoria

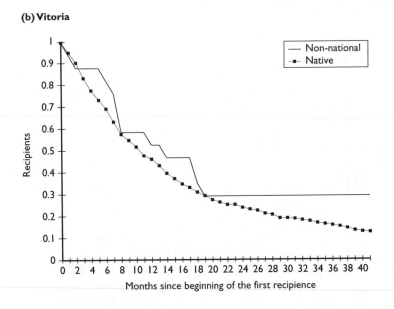

Months since beginning of the first recipience

Figure 5.6: Survival function receiving cash benefits for natives and non-nationals (contd)

(c) Gothenburg

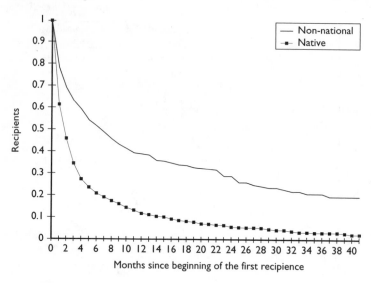

Months since beginning of the first recipience

(d) Helsingborg

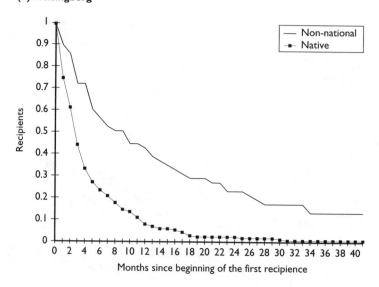

Months since beginning of the first recipience

Figure 5.6: Survival function receiving cash benefits for natives and non-nationals (contd)

(e) Milan

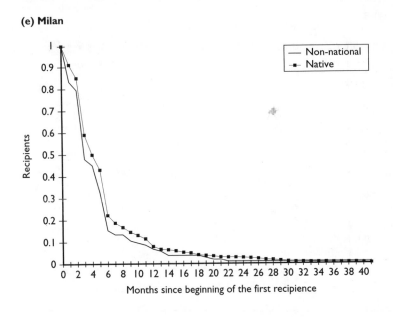

Months since beginning of the first recipience

(f) Turin

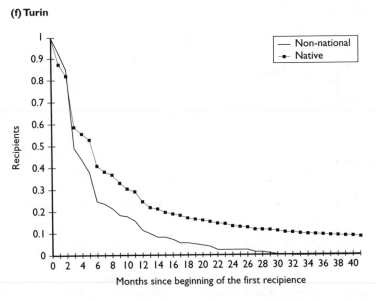

Months since beginning of the first recipience

Figure 5.6: Survival function receiving cash benefits for natives and non-nationals (contd)

(g) Bremen

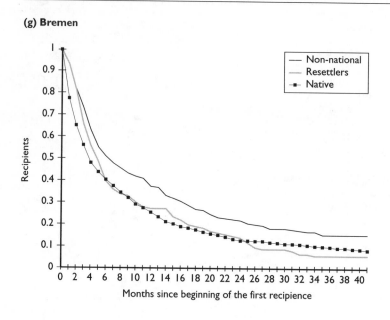

Months since beginning of the first recipience

(h) Lisbon

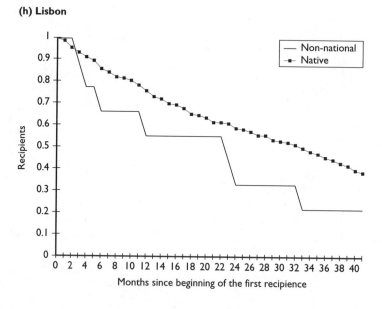

Months since beginning of the first recipience

categories of recipients considered in Bremen (natives, German re-settlers and other immigrants). During the first months of social assistance, re-settlers resemble other immigrants, but after three to six months, they leave social assistance at a faster rate than other foreigners and also faster than natives. After six months, the survival curve for re-settlers and natives is fairly similar. This points to the efficacy of programmes aimed specifically at re-settlers.

Using multivariate analysis to explain differences in exit and re-entry

We now try to assess the weight of the factors in explaining duration and patterns of social assistance careers. We present estimates of different multivariate models, using the 'hazard rate model'.

The hazard rate is the propensity to leave a given original state: in this case the status of receiving cash benefits and of being dependent on them. The hazard rate is an estimation of the probability per time. Just like a survival curve, the hazard rate model shows whether there is a difference between specific groups[15].

One can use many different hazard rate models. Usually, the different models describe specific 'shapes' of transition rates over time. These shapes may decrease monotonously, be constant, increase then decrease, and so on. For the best modelling of the rate, one should use a model with a shape very close to the empirical shape. The shapes we found in the different cities in the explorative analysis were very different. For this reason, models with a specific shape – like the sickle-model or exponential-model – could not be used. We therefore decided to use a piecewise constant model. This model has a constant baseline rate for defined time segments.

The tables below show the results of the estimation in different hazard rate models. A high value of coefficients in the model represents a high rate of leaving social assistance. The difference from the reference category, in this case the natives, is shown by 1/0 coded dummy variables. The 1/-1 coded dummy variables (lone mothers, couples with children, single adults, non-target group, age groups, and cities) show the difference from a central value (centred effects).

Models of exit from the first episode of social assistance

We start by analysing the first cash episode on social assistance. To do this, we have estimated one model for each city. Independent variables in

Table 5.5: Determinants of the rate leaving first cash episode: separate models for different cities

	Barcelona	Bremen	Gothenburg	Helsingborg	Lisbon	Milan	Turin	Vitoria
Month 1-3	-4.94 ***	-2.24 ***	-1.34 ***	-2.02 ***	-4.31 ***	-3.04 ***	-2.94 ***	-3.49 ***
Month 4-6	-3.95 ***	-1.86 ***	-1.41 ***	-1.23 ***	-3.75 ***	-1.34 ***	-1.74 ***	-2.73 ***
Month 7-42	-3.53 ***	-2.85 ***	-2.45 ***	-1.96 ***	-3.76 ***	-1.38 ***	-2.53 ***	-2.89 ***
Lone mothers	-0.21 **	-0.46 ***	0.00	-0.20 **	0.02	-0.49 ***	-0.06	-0.30 ***
Couples with children	0.19	0.15	-0.05	0.09	-0.12	-0.03	0.10	0.19 **
Single adults	0.20 **	0.20 ***	-0.03	0.14 *	0.17 *	0.59 ***	-0.27 ***	-0.09
Non-target group	-0.18	0.11	0.09	-0.03	-0.07	-0.07	0.23 ***	0.21 ***
Non-national	-0.04	-0.43 ***	-0.84 ***	-1.12 ***	0.55 **	0.39 ***	0.39 ***	-0.38
Re-settlers	–	-0.13	–	–	–	–	–	–
Age 18-29	-0.04	-0.03	0.06	0.30 ***	0.01	0.01	0.20 ***	0.13 *
Age 30-44	0.30 ***	0.22 ***	0.04	-0.33 ***	0.12	0.05	0.09	0.18 ***
Age 45-64	-0.26 ***	-0.18 *	-0.11	0.03	-0.13	-0.06	-0.29 ***	-0.31 ***
Log likelihood								
Starting values	-1554.43	-1583.16	-1159.32	-1453.35	-1478.02	-1386.78	-1565.30	-1697.42
Final estimates	-1523.84	-1522.46	-1072.97	-1339.81	-1469.62	-1251.65	-1487.67	-1671.06

Significance: ***: p < 0.01; **: p< 0.05; *: p < 0.1

the specification indicate: (a) the type of household, using a string of dummy variables (indicating if the applicant is a lone mother, a couple with children, a single adult or in a different condition); (b) citizenship of the household head (foreign or native); and finally (c) age of the household head (by age classes 18-29, 30-44, 45-64 years). The estimates are reported in Table 5.5.

Beginning with the variable referring to lone mothers, we find that there are four examples of negative coefficients with a high degree of statistical significance, indicating cases where single-parent families leave the status of social assistance recipients more slowly than others. In fact, we find indications that lone mothers are likely to experience longer episodes of social assistance in more than half the cities investigated. These are, in the order of size of the parameter estimate, Milan, Bremen, Vitoria, Barcelona and Helsingborg. In the remaining group of cities (Gothenburg, Lisbon and Turin), the estimate of the coefficients for this category has a low degree of statistical significance[16].

The coefficients of the multivariate model stress what was highlighted previously. In other words, they show that the presence, absence and depth of the differences between the group of lone mothers and the other groups of beneficiaries are the product not only of differences in efficacy of the policy measures, but also a mix of context effects that vary from one local system to another.

A first confirmation comes from the fact that in cities such as Gothenburg or Helsingborg, lone mothers have statistically non-significant or negative coefficients with a low value, and single adults with no children have non-significant or positive coefficients, also with a low value. These values clearly indicate that in cities where there is a positive attitude, and supporting services, with regard to working mothers and more generally working women, the differences between those who have to deal alone with childcare demands and those who do not are non-significant or very small.

Symmetrically, we can assume that the significant negative differences found in the other cities can be ascribed – at least partially – to the greater difficulties that lone mothers face in becoming financially self-sufficient. These are caused by the structure of the local welfare systems and the labour markets as a whole – the effect we have defined 'resources for exit'. The coefficients for Lisbon also confirm the presence of a 'resources for exit effect'. The non-significance of the coefficient for lone mothers (and also couples with children), and the positive but rather low and not very significant coefficient for single adults, show that the household structure does not make a big difference in terms of chances of achieving financial independence when resources for exit are generally limited.

Second, the model underlines that the differences between lone mothers and other beneficiaries are greater in local systems that either impose higher constraints on the latter concerning the period of assistance – such as Milan – or make their provision conditional to specific duties – such as in Bremen. This effect is confirmed by the coefficients for lone mothers and single adults. For the former, the high absolute value of the negative coefficient reflects the relaxing of constraints on duration and pressure to exit social assistance, since lone mothers are considered 'deserving'. Likewise, the high value positive coefficients for single adults without children show that this group, traditionally regarded as 'undeserving', is subjected to more rigid time limits and more intense pressures to get off assistance.

Furthermore, the model clearly shows the levelling effect – seen typically in Turin – caused by means-tests that vary in generosity according to the kind of beneficiary. The fact that in Turin the coefficient does not indicate slower exit for lone mothers is coherent with the presence of more generous access regulations for this category. Moreover, the high negative coefficient recorded for single adults without children reflects the fact that the means-test excludes all but the most serious cases of vulnerability among single adults.

Traces of the 'means-test effect' can also be found in Vitoria, although in a less evident way than in Turin. In fact, single adults do not leave assistance significantly faster than lone mothers, even though they do not have the additional difficulties of childcare demands. In the case of Vitoria, however, the multivariate model reveals the specific difficulty in becoming financially autonomous for lone mothers in comparison with dual-parent families.

As in Bremen, in Barcelona single adults leave social assistance much faster than lone parents. Differently from the other Southern European cities, the data shows no evidence of 'means-test effects'. It should also be noted that the theoretical possibility that dual-parent households may be more efficient in integrating resources is not borne out by reality, since they do not exit social assistance significantly faster than lone mothers. We can thus confirm the hypothesis that in the social, economic and institutional context of Barcelona, such households can settle into situations of 'assisted equilibrium': a mixed use of resources triggered by insufficient income support as well as equivalence scales that penalise large households and income earned in the irregular labour market.

Turning to the effects of foreign citizenship, we can see that negative coefficients, indicating a slower termination of social assistance, have a high degree of statistical significance in the Swedish cities and Bremen. In contrast, positive coefficients are observed for some other cities, as in the case of the Italian cities and Lisbon[17]. However, in the case of Milan, a similar statistically significant positive effect is not observed in further analysis, which have taken into account the first dependence period. As a whole, the multivariate model confirms that the careers of foreign immigrants follow the two models discussed above: one of difficult integration, typical of the formal economy of Northern Europe, and the other of easier economic integration, typical of Southern Europe, facilitated by insertion in the informal economy.

In Vitoria, Turin and Bremen there are negative parameter estimates for the 45-64 age bracket, estimated with a high degree of statistical significance. The opposite sign, thus indicating a faster termination, is found for the age group 30-44 in Barcelona and Bremen. Results indicating that people aged 18-29 exit social assistance faster than others are obtained in Helsingborg and Turin. Therefore, there is some evidence that the age of the household head has a negative effect on social assistance termination, although this result is not observed in every city.

What does the model say about the probability of leaving social assistance on the basis of length of receipt? There is not much evidence indicating that leaving social assistance receipt becomes more difficult as the period of receipt increases. Confirming the results of other studies (for example, Walker and Ashworth, 1998; Walker and Shaw, 1998), there is no clear evidence of the phenomenon that was previously defined as the 'chronicisation effect'. The clearest exception is perhaps Gothenburg, where the probability of leaving assistance for households who have received social assistance for more than six months is considerably lower than that of households who have been receiving assistance for less time. Yet, even in this case, we cannot confirm the presence of chronicisation effects. As we argued in the section 'What we can comparatively evaluate, and what we cannot', a negative relationship between social assistance duration and propensity to leave social assistance is not necessarily a consequence of income support measures. It may be the outcome of unobserved original differences among the beneficiaries. Thus, as time goes by, the group of survivors on social assistance is increasingly composed of people with characteristics that render them less capable of benefiting from employment opportunities and even from targeted activation measures. A similar observation was made by Walker and Ashworth (1998) in the conclusions of their study of social assistance dynamics in Great

Britain during the recession of the early 1990s and shortly afterwards. They comment that,

> ... during the recession of the early 1990s, the people who moved on to benefits were almost a cross section of the British population. However, while the young, the better educated and those unencumbered by children rapidly returned to employment, the most disadvantaged remained behind, spending long periods on benefit. (p 219)

It is possible that the effects of unobserved heterogeneity emerge more clearly in local social assistance configurations that, as in Gothenburg, are characterised by the kind of activation measures that render the pattern of social assistance careers highly dynamic for most beneficiaries.

Effects of the context and categorical problems

As a whole, the analysis carried out in this chapter shows that, although there are some similarities in the pattern of speed with which social assistance receipt terminates, these similarities are not very great. Interactions among a multiplicity of context effects do not allow the identification of a single general mechanism influencing the timing of entry into and exit from social assistance in all the cities studied. Thus, simply on the basis of a comparison of social assistance career patterns, we cannot ascertain whether cross-city differences in average duration of income support depend on differences in the distribution of categories of beneficiaries.

Nevertheless, if we control for the effects – whatever they might be – of each local context on entry and exit patterns, we may obtain some indications of the impact on social assistance careers of the characteristics of specific categories of beneficiaries. In order to develop this last step of our analysis, we have pooled all the data sets from the cities investigated (see Table 5.6). For this new data set we have estimated different models. The first has explanatory dummy variables that indicate the city only. In the second specification, we have added variables indicating the type of household, and finally, in the third model, variables indicating the age of the household head are added. We are primarily interested in verifying whether parameter estimates for the variables indicating the city change when more variables are added to the estimated model.

By analysing the parameter estimates in the first column, a now familiar ranking of cities emerges. Social assistance terminates most slowly in Lisbon, closely followed by Barcelona. Then comes Vitoria, followed by

Table 5.6: Determinants of the rate leaving first cash episode: integrated models for pooled cities

	Model 1		Model 2		Model 3	
Month 1-3	-2.80	***	-2.76	***	-2.79	***
Month 4-6	-2.14	***	-2.08	***	-2.10	***
Month 7-42	-2.74	***	-2.66	***	-2.67	***
Barcelona	-0.99	***	-1.04	***	-0.98	***
Bremen	0.13	***	0.17	***	0.10	**
Gothenburg	0.63	***	0.75	***	0.68	***
Helsingborg	0.61	***	0.71	***	0.65	***
Lisbon	-1.13	***	-1.19	***	-1.13	***
Milan	0.79	***	0.77	***	0.79	***
Turin	0.26	***	0.19	***	0.24	***
Vitoria	-0.29	***	-0.35	***	-0.35	***
Lone mothers	–		-0.15	***	-0.19	***
Couples with children	–		0.04		0.01	
Single adults	–		0.06	**	0.11	***
Non-target group	–		0.05	*	0.07	**
Non-nationals	–		-0.50	***	-0.52	***
Age 18-29	–		–		0.13	***
Age 30-44	–		–		0.07	***
Age 45-64	–		–		-0.21	***
Log likelihood						
Starting values	-12721.10		-12721.10		-12721.10	
Final estimates	-11764.90		-11708.94		-11681.27	

Significance: ***: $p < 0.01$; **: $p < 0.05$; *: $p < 0.1$

Bremen, Turin, Helsingborg, Gothenburg and finally Milan[18]. We wish to stress once again that this ranking, which is preserved in the second model, as well as the third, is composed of very different factors. The parameter estimates for the variables indicating the city are, in fact, more or less the same in all the specifications.

If we now examine the beneficiaries' characteristics, an interesting piece of information emerges in Table 5.6. There are negative effects, with a high degree of statistical significance, for three dummy variables. These indicate that single (female) parenthood, foreign nationality and an age of 45-64 all lead to slower exit from social assistance receipt.

Finally, we report the estimated models relating to the first re-entry into social assistance. Table 5.7 shows the multivariate models for re-entry for each city. Table 5.8 shows the results when we analyse the observations for all pooled cities (except Lisbon). The same explanatory variables used for the models analysing the duration of the first cash

Table 5.7: Determinants of the rate of first re-entry into cash episode: separate models for different cities

	Barcelona	Bremen	Gothenburg	Helsingborg	Milan	Turin	Vitoria
Month 1	-18.54	-15.69	-15.46	-16.9	-16.01	-15.49	-15.88
Month 2-4	-3.6 ***	-4.85 ***	-2.97 ***	-3.67 ***	-3.76 ***	-2.76 ***	-3.25 ***
Month 5-7	-3.87 ***	-3.95 ***	-3.02 ***	-3.63 ***	-3.35 ***	-3.19 ***	-3.43 ***
Month 8-end	-5.16 ***	-4.8 ***	-3.74 ***	-4.69 ***	-4.94 ***	-4.63 ***	-4.16 ***
Duration first cash	0.01	0.03 **	0.03 **	0.06 ***	0.03 **	0.01	0
Lone mothers	-0.2	0.15	0.07	0.2	0.65 ***	0.02	0.34 **
Couples with children	0	0.04	0	0	0.48 ***	0.05	0.13
Single adults	-0.1	-0.09	0.06	0.16	-1.03 ***	0.07	-0.01
Non-target group	0.31	-0.1	-0.13	-0.35 *	-0.09	-0.13	-0.46 ***
Non-national	0.02	-0.94 ***	0.02	0.09	0.13	0.13	-0.57
Re-settlers	–	-0.04	–	–	–	–	–
Age 18-29	0.15	0.27 *	0.07	0.05	0.23 *	-0.01	0.19
Age 30-44	0.21	-0.07	0.07	-0.11	0.02	0.01	-0.03
Age 45-64	-0.36 *	-0.2	-0.15	0.06	-0.26 **	-0.01	-0.16
Log likelihood							
Starting values	-397.25	-674.69	-814.88	-1154.83	-951.73	-1033.37	-866.55
Final estimates	-370.44	-652.61	-781.29	-1080.5	-848.2	-942.5	-832.29

Significance: ***: $p < 0.01$; **: $p < 0.05$; *: $p < 0.1$

Table 5.8: Determinants of the rate of first re-entry into cash episode: integrated models for pooled cities

	Model 1		Model 2		Model 3	
Month 1	−15.23		−15.17		−15.21	
Month 2-4	−3.5	***	−3.45	***	−3.5	***
Month 5-7	−3.52	***	−3.47	***	−3.51	***
Month 8-end	−4.65	***	−4.6	***	−4.64	***
Duration first cash	0.02	***	0.02	***	0.03	***
Barcelona	−0.68	***	−0.71	***	−0.65	***
Bremen	−0.53	***	−0.51	***	−0.56	***
Gothenburg	0.78	***	0.78	***	0.74	***
Helsingborg	0.28	***	0.25	***	0.2	***
Milan	−0.1		−0.11		−0.05	
Turin	0.23	***	0.27	***	0.3	***
Vitoria	0.02		0.01		0.01	
Lone mothers	−		0.21	***	0.18	***
Couples with children	−		0.13	**	0.12	**
Single adults	−		−0.13	***	−0.11	**
Non-target group	−		−0.2	***	−0.19	***
Non-nationals	−		0.04		0	
Age 18-29	−		−		0.16	***
Age 30-44	−		−		0.04	
Age 45-64	−		−		−0.21	***
Log likelihood						
Starting values	−5988.67		−5988.67		−5988.67	
Final estimates	−5619.55		−5604.97		−5595.24	

Significance: ***: $p < 0.01$; **: $p < 0.05$; *: $p < 0.1$

episode are now used in both tables, with the addition of the length of the first episode of assistance.

Estimates in column one of Table 5.8 show that the cities can be ranked on the basis of how quickly re-entry occurs. Re-entry is fastest in Gothenburg, followed by Helsingborg and Turin, then come Vitoria, Milan, Barcelona and Bremen. This ranking is basically the same when more variables are added to the specification. It is interesting to note that a significantly higher re-entry risk corresponds, ceteris paribus, to a longer first welfare episode, even when the coefficient has a low value. Table 5.7 shows that this relationship applies to Bremen, Milan and the Swedish cities.

In situations like those in Sweden and Bremen, where there are activation measures that speed up exit from social assistance for the majority of beneficiaries, this could be an indication that people with more (unobserved) difficulty in leaving social assistance are also less likely to be able to move from a protected job to a regular one. A pattern of longer duration combined with return may also involve people who have greater difficulty (once more unobserved) in remaining self-sufficient. Having few skills, they lack a cushion of protective resources, and are thus easily tipped into poverty by a minor crisis, while at the same time taking longer to exit once they have entered it. Leisering and Leibfried (1999, p 247) indicate this group as being "people with permanent low incomes" that are sometimes just above, sometimes below the income threshold entitling them to income support. Or they may belong to the category (mostly young men), whom the same authors (p 248) define as people with unsettled modes of existence – those who deliberately use social assistance over a lengthy period, with some intermissions, intentionally 'commuting' between different lifestyles and social status.

The meaning of the data for Milan is more ambiguous, given the unclear and more discretionary access and duration rules. It might involve the same two groups as in Sweden and Bremen. Or it might involve other kinds of people with whom the local system has, for some reason, been more generous, both in terms of duration of the first period of benefit and the criteria for being accepted back. This second explanation seems to be confirmed by the fact that lone mothers in Milan have a higher risk of re-entering social assistance than other groups (Table 5.7). This is a finding that must, in fact, be interpreted in the light of the lower stringency of the system in Milan in dealing with this group of beneficiaries.

Generally, while lone parents in all cities return to social assistance receipt faster than other categories, native citizenship statistically has no significant impact (Table 5.8, column 2). We also see that young recipients re-enter more quickly than older ones (Table 5.8, column 3). These differences, however, cannot always be imputed linearly to the recipients' characteristics. Only in the most generous and universalistic systems, which cater to a more heterogeneous population, does this relationship hold to a reasonable degree.

Conclusions

People who become social assistance recipients in Barcelona and Lisbon remain recipients longer than in any other city. Half of the beneficiaries in these cities go on to receive social assistance continuously for more than two years (but less than three) after their debut. Vitoria ranks third, as half the recipients have a period of continuous assistance that lasts for over a year. In the remaining five cities the period is shorter. Among these, Turin and Bremen often seem to have longer durations than Gothenburg, Helsingborg and Milan.

Termination of receipt cannot be ascribed to a single general mechanism. For this reason, the above ranking is ambiguous from a semantic point of view. In particular, it would be incorrect to base our evaluations of minimum income policies in the various cities, in terms of efficacy and efficiency, on this ordering criterion only. However, bearing these difficulties in mind, it is possible to obtain some useful suggestions from such a ranking, particularly in view of the design of policies.

As a whole, the ranking seems to be mainly determined by the generosity of the rules regulating access, that is to the so-called 'means-test effect', as well as to the rules governing entitlement over time, that is the 'time constraints effect'. Both effects, separately and through their interaction, affect duration of social assistance, independently of the effect of policies on beneficiaries' capabilities.

In explaining cross-city differences in the length of social assistance recipiency, the 'means-test effect' highlights the crucial role of the original characteristics of the people selected. In cities where entry into social assistance is limited to those with very low income and suffering from severe deprivation, beneficiaries are on average more marginalised than elsewhere. For this reason, in systems where means-tests are less generous, but there is no time limit, the duration in assistance can actually be longer. It has also been noted that, in the categorical systems where access rules are differentiated according to the claimants' category, the 'means-test effect' can level the differences found between categories in less categorical systems.

However, our finding that periods of benefit are shortest in cities where access rules are most generous should not be taken too far. In the systems where there are time constraints, all relationships between persistence of need and duration of intervention disappear.

Further, in the categorical systems, a differentiated implementation of time constraints can increase the differences between categories of clients: the opposite of what happens with the just mentioned 'means-test effect'. Once again, the data referring to the cross-category differences between lone mothers and single adults in relation to the duration of the first episode of social assistance reveal this kind of amplification effect in Milan. Similar effects can also be caused by differential enforcement of recipients' duties by social workers. Again, by comparing the situation of lone mothers to other categories, some signs of such an effect have been noted in Bremen, though not as marked as in Milan.

From all this, it follows that short periods on social assistance are not necessarily desirable from the beneficiaries' perspective, nor from the perspective of achieving lasting financial autonomy. The analysis has also highlighted that besides the 'means-test' and 'time constraints' effects, there are a number of other possible reasons for differences in the length of receipt in the cities. These too are connected with features of the socioeconomic and institutional context, and do not imply any effect on the capabilities of beneficiaries.

We focused in particular on a possible 'form of poverty effect' and a possible 'behaviour effect'. Analysis of the empirical data has stressed the importance of the 'resources for exit effect', where the dynamics of social assistance careers is strongly influenced by the resources available to beneficiaries outside the action of welfare systems. From this point of view, the conditions of the labour market have proven crucial.

Considering the importance of the 'resources for exit effect', we feel that, to a large degree, the variations in welfare career patterns depend on whether or not income support programmes are combined with more ambitious public policies in other spheres. The most important of such spheres is the labour market, which influences the propensity to become financially self-sufficient through paid work. According to this interpretation, the fact that the periods of social assistance in Lisbon and Barcelona are the longest is at least partly due to the lack of active labour market policies in those cities. The relevance of labour market resources and active labour market policies for social assistance duration is supported by the finding that periods on social assistance are shorter in the Swedish cities, although benefits are more generous than elsewhere. This argument must be further specified in the case of women, and particularly lone mothers, in so far as the likelihood of their being integrated in the labour market depends on prevalent gender and family models, as well as the availability of good quality and affordable childcare.

The results of the multivariate analysis indicate that, owing to the complex interactions among all these effects, the observed differences in age, type of family and citizenship cannot fully explain the observed difference in length of duration across cities. However, the analysis suggests that, despite the great variation among the cities investigated in terms of their social assistance systems as well as other relevant policies and circumstances, lone parenthood on average leads to longer periods on social assistance. The gender division of labour in marriage and the family, with its impact for women's labour market participation, together with limited access to low cost and reliable childcare are among the main reasons for this. The exception of Sweden is in fact a confirmation, in so far as policies supporting a conciliation of work and caring responsibilities are more developed there, and paid work is perceived as a normal, if not prescribed dimension of an adult woman's life.

Furthermore, it has been noted that foreign citizens exit social assistance at a different speed than natives in some of the cities, but not all of them. Most notable is the slower speed in the Swedish cities and in Bremen. Many refugees and their families have immigrated to these cities and have great difficulty in finding a job. On the other hand, immigrants to Turin who rely on social assistance seem to have a better possibility of supporting themselves than the natives. These differences seem to depend mainly on the exit resources available in the different labour markets. From this point of view, it is important to distinguish a north European model, characterised mainly by the availability of formal resources, and a south European model, characterised by the availability of informal jobs, which render immigrants' economic integration easier.

Finally, in some cases we have been able to explain cross-city variation in the duration of social assistance on the basis of specific effects of income support measures on the beneficiaries' capabilities. In these cases, and only in these, the efficacy of such policies may be assessed as such.

In particular, the importance of providing an adequate amount of income support has been underlined – referred to as the 'generosity effect'. In fact, where the amount of the benefits is insufficient, as in Lisbon, beneficiaries have to seek to integrate the amount, by making a mixed use of welfare resources and informal jobs. This situation tends to persist over time once it has been established. On the other hand, in the cases of Bremen and the Swedish cities, a more dynamic welfare career pattern corresponds to more generous cash receipts. As a consequence, it has been noted that in general the cities with less generous levels of social assistance are those where the duration of receipt is the longest. Obviously, this does not mean that simply increasing the generosity of income support will shorten the period of social assistance, particularly if labour market opportunities remain scarce and/or activation measures do not exist.

Our analysis has also highlighted the relevance of activation measures, particularly in the case of the two Swedish cities, Bremen and to a lesser extent Vitoria. What has been defined as an 'activation measures effect' contributes in these cases to make career patterns far more dynamic. Periods on social assistance tend to be shorter, as people are either able to find a job on the labour market, or are moved to publicly funded job programmes. In the latter case, some may return to social assistance once the programme is terminated, thus indicating that there may be a revolving door effect and that dependence on social assistance is longer than it appears just by looking at the length of each episode. Yet, these programmes do offer the opportunity to enrich or maintain skills, to experiment with different possibilities, and avoid settling into 'assisted equilibrium' solutions.

A final observation on the results of the analysis carried out in this chapter concerns the issue of 'chronicisation' – the likelihood that coming off social assistance becomes more difficult as time goes on. The widespread assumption that this phenomenon is dependent on the generosity of the income support scheme (in terms of amount and duration) is not confirmed by the analysis. In practically none of our cities did indications of a 'chronicisation effect' emerge. The only case that might be compatible with this hypothesis was Gothenburg, where the length of the first period of assistance was linked to a lower probability of leaving assistance. Moreover, in Gothenburg, as well as in Helsingborg and Bremen, the length of the first assistance period was also associated with a higher risk of returning later. Both relationships might indicate that the capacity of beneficiaries to become and remain self-supporting decreases with the length of time they remain on social assistance. Yet, the very fact that these linkages appear in the most dynamic contexts undermine the hypothesis of chronic dependence. It is more likely that we are dealing with an unobserved heterogeneity among claimants, which tends to be greatest in the most universalistic and generous systems.

Notes

[1] Such as Blank (1989), for instance. For a review of the large US literature, see Moffit (1992). As is well known, the choice of the first episode is linked to the need of avoiding left-censoring problems.

[2] Only the professional condition and age of the household head are in fact recorded.

[3] This has been the option chosen in the French cities of this study, after the use of archives was revealed to be impossible.

[4] Depending on the social assistance archives, the 42 months cover slightly different years: they start in 1993 in Lisbon; in 1991-92 in Barcelona, Milan, Turin and Vitoria; in 1990-91 in Helsingborg; in 1989 in Bremen. In Gothenburg, the observation window of 42 months (from 1991-94) is fixed, therefore it includes cases observed for one month only until cases observed for 42 months. With the exception of Bremen and Helsingborg , where data refer to a sample of starting beneficiaries, in all other cases they refer to the universe of starting beneficiaries. In most data sets, we cannot observe the small number of out-migrants.

[5] The proportion of recipients receiving social assistance for a long time would be higher in Gothenburg, if the data were prepared under the same conditions as the other data. Additionally, the proportion of those receiving social assistance for a very short period would be lower than that shown here.

[6] In this kind of description the limitations of the Gothenburg data have no effect, because this method gives a solution to handle the cases with missing information at the end of the observation window (right-censored cases).

[7] Only for Gothenburg do we find a little difference, because, as we have said, data include cases that are observed for less than 42 months. The status distribution for Gothenburg is therefore a corrected plot that shows the proportion of cases at a certain point of time, but only related to the number of cases that are still observed until that point in time.

[8] We may compare these data with those concerning RMI beneficiaries in France (as a whole). According to estimates by the CNAF – the institute responsible for its payment – the duration pattern is somewhat intermediate between that typical of the north European cities, as well as Milan and Turin, and that in the Spanish and Portuguese cities (see Oberti, 1998, p 4). Among all those who started receiving RMI between January 1991 and December 1992, 27.4% had terminated within the following year, sometimes after one or more relapses. But if we compare the French case only with the social assistance systems that do not impose time constraints, the similarity between the outcomes of RMI and the north European systems is clearly evident. Among those who entered between January 1988 and December 1989, the rate of termination was 19.9%; while for those who entered between January and December 1995 the exit rate was 32.2%. These data indicate that, although in recent years RMI has provided long-term support for many beneficiaries facing exclusion from the labour market (Oberti, 1998, p 5), the rate of exit within the first twelve months has almost doubled seven years after the introduction of this measure. Part of this improvement derives from a better pattern of implementation. But it should also be taken into account that when a measure such as this is first introduced, it is likely that the most difficult cases are over represented. Over time, as the new measure becomes known, a larger part of the population may apply: the proportion of 'new entrants', with a more recent history of vulnerability and possibly less serious capability impairments is likely to increase. From this point of view, it should be mentioned that between 1988 and 1995 the number of RMI beneficiaries in France increased by a rate oscillating between 15% and 20%. This process of extension may well have contributed to the increase in yearly exit rates. Further, comparing the exit rates estimated by CNAF and those in our study, we should note that the former do not allow us to

satisfactorily calculate the number of people entering the measure more than once: entrants in a given year do not all represent first time entrants. A number may be returning after an interruption. Thus the cohorts of beneficiaries in the CNAF sample are not fully comparable to those in our study – they may over represent difficult cases, that is those without enough resources to remain off social assistance. It is likely that data without these censoring problems would indicate an even higher similarity to those of the north European cities.

[9] The medians of the first dependence period read: Barcelona 34.4 months, Bremen 8.1 months, Gothenburg 10 months, Helsingborg 6.4 months, Lisbon 33.5 months, Milan 6.5 months, Turin 10.7 months and Vitoria 15.4 months.

[10] In Barcelona the amount of income support is lower than in Vitoria.

[11] It should be pointed out, however, that at least in Italy separated and divorced (not widowed) lone mothers have on average higher labour market participation and employment rates than married ones.

[12] The median for the cash episode among single parents is significantly higher than for other recipients in Helsingborg, while the corresponding is not found when analysing dependence periods. The reverse (statistically significant longer dependence episode, but not cash episode) applies to Vitoria.

[13] This rule may also be applied to EU citizens.

[14] There are very few foreigners in the samples for Lisbon and Vitoria.

[15] The greatest advantage of this model, in comparison with the survivor function, is the possibility to consider many different co-variables and estimate their effects on the rate. Besides, we can see the significance of the effects on the rate. The significance depends on the number of events (transitions out of social assistance) and the distance in the calculated rate. Therefore, the cities whose data shows a higher number of cases would structurally reach a higher significance. To avoid this problem, we have weighed the cases so as to get a total of 500 cases for every city.

[16] These results on significant coefficients for variables measuring type of household are confirmed when models explaining the first dependence period are estimated.

[17] The estimate for Lisbon is based on a small number of observations.

[18] However, when analysing dependence periods the ranking is slightly different, that is: Barcelona, Lisbon, Vitoria, Turin, Gothenburg, Bremen, Helsingborg and Milan.

SIX

Deconstructing the myth of welfare dependence

Chiara Saraceno

Social assistance in the face of changing demands for support

Long-term unemployment among adults, delays and constraints in entering the labour market among the young, impoverishment of women and children due to the gender division of labour, as well as growing marital instability and the weakening of father–child ties[1], are all phenomena that challenge the traditional solutions offered by social assistance. In countries where income support measures in the form of a basic or minimum living allowance have been developed as a temporary stopgap for those who have lost the social security protection linked to their status as workers, changes in the labour market conditions and in life course patterns are transforming both the type of beneficiary and their experience. Together with the growing number of unemployed people who now have less opportunity of finding a new job due to age or lack of required skills, and the growing number of young people who have difficulty even entering the social security protected labour market, there is also a growing number of people who find themselves with little or no income or social security protection for reasons not directly linked to the labour market. Among these are unmarried, separated or divorced women with small children who invested in raising a family rather than in paid work, young people who have adopted self-destructive behaviour, families who are over-strained by the long illness of one of their members, and immigrants who encounter obstacles in their efforts at social integration and social mobility.

Income support may thus be received by populations who are dis-homogeneous not only with regard to their life course, needs and personal resources, but also with regard to the perception of their situation, as well as the strategies developed[2]. There may be individuals and groups who are ashamed to resort to social assistance and who ask for help only when they have exhausted or severely weakened their own and their social network's resources. In contrast, other individuals and groups develop great skill and ingenuity in trying to get hold of some kind of entitlement to social assistance. Together with those who mix dependency on social assistance with more or less formal work activities and income, and those who use social assistance as a temporary measure while they look for a job, there are those who use social assistance as a substitute for searching for a low paid job. The proportion in which these different groups may be found in social assistance schemes, however, does not depend solely on their incidence in the population in a given country or city. It depends also on the working of the social assistance schemes themselves: their filtering mechanisms, time rules and so forth. Thus, social and political awareness of the heterogeneity of the potential claimants for some kind of support may differ cross-country and cross-city, depending on the country and city-specific institutional definitions of who is entitled to support.

For the same reason – the impact of institutional definitions – changes both in labour market opportunities and in social security regulations may increase this heterogeneity of social assistance recipients, thus also of trajectories within it. Individuals and families who in the past would have received non-means-tested unemployment benefit or a disability pension, may now have to rely on social assistance for shorter periods, due to changes in the criteria governing the entitlement to social security provisions. Furthermore, the growing number of non-standard labour contracts that, particularly in Southern Europe, are mainly concentrated among adult women and the young of both genders, is creating a subgroup of workers who by definition are less protected by social security measures. This is a particular risk in those countries in Continental and Southern Europe where social security is highly categorical and linked to the workers' status and seniority. Not being entitled to unemployment indemnity, these people may have to make recourse to means-tested income support as a last resort. But in some countries, particularly in the Southern European ones, they may not even be entitled to that, unless they are very poor, isolated, or suffer from some severe additional personal or social disability.

Further, in the redrawing of boundaries between social security and social assistance, two, somewhat contradictory, processes seem to be going on. On the one hand, there is some kind of reshuffling or redistribution between categories of welfare state recipients, particularly between social security and social assistance. On the other hand, there is a refocusing of social assistance towards measures that are explicitly work-insertion oriented. The former process, due to the pressure on social security budgets caused by high rates of unemployment, tends to reduce social security coverage, particularly in the case of long-term unemployment (and also invalidity), moving people more quickly to means-tested measures. Moreover, the boundaries between social assistance and social security are becoming blurred. The most explicit move in this direction occurred in the UK when the Jobseeker's Allowance replaced both Unemployment Benefit and Income Support for working age applicants. The result was a blurring of the boundaries between the two groups of beneficiaries, submitting both to the same kind of close monitoring. Also, the requirement to undertake some kind of work in exchange for benefits – or *workfare* – is increasingly being attached not only to social assistance, but also to social security benefits in many countries. This goes well beyond the traditional expectation that unemployed people, especially able-bodied social assistance beneficiaries, accept reasonable job offers[3]. We will return to this in the section on 'Explicit and implicit assumptions in social integration discourses'.

The potential and constraints of comparing social assistance policies

The growing heterogeneity of those requiring some kind of income support, as well as their number, is occurring in a policy context marked by an increasing demand for the evaluation of social policies. Two distinct objectives spur this demand: the control of public social expenditure and the improvement of efficacy. The evaluation of income support policies shares this concern for accountability. Comparative cross-country evaluation is perceived as a useful tool in the sense of 'learning from other countries' and looking at 'best practices'. Yet, it encounters specific and serious difficulties that should be clearly spelled out. This is not to deny the possibility of comparative evaluation, but to clarify the boundaries and limits of such an endeavour, as well as the kind of data needed.

A first difficulty concerns the objectives themselves, both at the institutional level (as defined in laws and regulations) and the implementation level (as defined and perceived by social workers and potential beneficiaries). Bouget and Nogues (1993) claim that the sheer multiplicity of goals in national social policies in the field of income support makes it virtually impossible to identify any common trends, priorities or even philosophies. This is possibly an exaggeration. Yet, as we have seen throughout this book, countries differ considerably in their definition of the 'deserving' and the 'undeserving' poor, their definition of need and the risks of social exclusion, as well as their definition of what is necessary to achieve social integration, and even the meaning of social integration. We have seen that in some countries (for example, Portugal, Italy, and to some extent Spain) only those who are perceived as being at high risk of social exclusion, in that they are extremely poor and/or thought to be unable to take care of themselves, are entitled to income support. In other countries (Sweden and Germany), the mere lack of income entitles one to income support, without any judgement being made on the risk of social exclusion.

A second difficulty concerns the plurality of institutional actors involved in this kind of policy: from the State to regional and municipal institutions, administrators and social workers, as well as public, non-profit and sometimes also market institutions. Each may have a different perception or definition not only of the goal of the social assistance measure in which they are involved, but also of the beneficiaries. And they may combine and interact differently cross-country as well as cross-city, producing distinct patterns of implementation and different definitions of poverty and social exclusion. Evaluation, and the evaluators themselves, including the European Union[4], are becoming institutional actors in so far as their requests (for data and information) and the results of their exercises influence the institutional setting, the self-perception of the actors and, more generally, the perception of the policy in question by the public. From this point of view, it is correct to say that evaluation is never a neutral process, however objective it may try to be (see also Bouget and Nogues, 1993; Rossi and Freeman, 1993).

A third difficulty concerns the various 'policy packages' (of which income support policies are usually part) being developed to combat, directly or indirectly, poverty and social exclusion. The combination of specific access rules, coverage, duration and generosity of unemployment indemnity lead to considerable differences in the timing of entry into social assistance, as well as in the characteristics of its beneficiaries. The generosity of child allowances in one country may keep families with children off social assistance. In another, the existence of specific assistance for lone mothers may help remove the need for this category to resort to general social assistance for some period. The rules in other parts of the policy package therefore have the effect of selecting demographic or other features (for example, age of child) of beneficiaries differently from one country to another, even before the specific filtering mechanisms of the measures analysed and compared operate their own selection.

As a result of these three difficulties, a fourth arises. A cross-country and sometimes even cross-city differentiation in the definition of eligibility for social assistance resulting from the variety of goals, policies and patterns of implementation, produces fundamental differences in the population of beneficiaries. This in turn has consequences for the performance of the social assistance measures themselves. Our research clearly shows that legal and/or de facto eligibility filters have a far more important impact than any other dimension. They affect not only the demographic and social characteristics of beneficiaries, but also the average duration of welfare dependence, the risk of recurrence, the chance of successfully exiting, and so forth.

To these methodological and conceptual difficulties we should add another, more technical one. Cross-country and cross-city comparisons and evaluations can be performed only if there exist good longitudinal local data, collected and recorded according to standard methods. This is an almost trivial observation and is of course valid for any evaluation or comparison, but it has specific importance in the case of social assistance and should not be underestimated. Within a social assistance system, the collection of data on beneficiaries is part of the process of policy implementation itself. Social workers and administrations routinely record a variety of biographical data on beneficiaries. These, however, are not always suitable for monitoring, reviewing, evaluating or comparing purposes. This may be for three distinct reasons. First, the data are rarely standardised. Second, even when they are, they respond more to the needs of accounting (how many interventions and for what cost), than the needs of monitoring or evaluating the impact and outcome of the policy (how many individuals or households are affected, for how long and to what effect on their living conditions). Within-city and within-country monitoring and evaluation, as well as cross-city and cross-country comparison and evaluation, rely on having access to standardised long-term data, which allow the possibility of following the history of individual social assistance recipients. They also require accurate data on policy implementation. The lack of the former sort of data is why we were unable to compare social assistance 'careers' in all the cities involved in this study. Not all cities possessed such information, even in an elementary form, while in other (French) cities they existed, but were unavailable to outside researchers. As for the data on patterns of policy implementation, they must be carefully constructed through a variety of means and sources.

The third reason is of a different kind, as it involves an ethical issue. The need to keep individual data over time and to follow-up beneficiaries after they have left social assistance, in order to monitor and evaluate the performance of social assistance, is to some degree in contrast with the right to privacy. And this is a right that should be particularly protected in the case of those who are already highly vulnerable socially. This is precisely the reason why social assistance records data have not been available for the French cities. While the solution to the first two problems, though often complicated, is basically a matter of administrative culture and choices, the third problem is one that is likely to become more serious in the future. Awareness of the importance of monitoring and evaluation for social policy making and awareness of the inviolability of individual rights – including that of privacy – are both growing, but pulling in two different directions. Possibly the EU is the level at which this apparently intractable contradiction should be addressed, not so much for the sake of research as for well informed and self-critical social policy making.

The recognition of these constraints and difficulties has enriched the framework of our evaluation and also our methodological approach. We have not simply considered and compared the performance of different income support measures in terms of statistical output (how many people, with what characteristics, and for how long). We have tried to reconstruct and compare the overall mechanisms, as well as the sets of actors involved, looking at the whole context within which and through which income measures are constructed and implemented. We have therefore used a local, multiple and integrated perspective, also considering how social assistance is experienced by beneficiaries. The countries have not been compared on the basis of aggregate data, but in terms of the local systems, the workings of which we have, at least partially, attempted to reconstruct.

In the following sections, we briefly summarise our main findings, which we feel are relevant both from a policy and a methodological point of view.

Local contexts, welfare mixes and the diversity of the third sector

The ESOPO research findings allow us to appreciate to what degree it is important when analysing poverty and policies to combat poverty and social exclusion, to not only grasp the relationships between family, State, market and third sector but, even more, to understand and distinguish the forms and dynamics of each of these four dimensions as well as their interaction.

In the first place, our study has confirmed the crucial role of the family in the national and local welfare mixes. Legal and de facto expectations concerning family and kin solidarity, that is the degree of familisation or vice versa de-familisation (Esping-Andersen, 1999; Gallie and Paugam, 2000; Saraceno, 1997), of rights and of access to resources vary greatly across our cities, contributing to the diversification both of the structure of the support package and of the selection mechanisms. At the same time, within the same formal social assistance system, the presence of supportive family and kin may make a huge difference for the well being of an individual and household.

In the second place, our research shows that the usual distinction between State, market and third sector is over simplistic. First, the State itself must be considered in its various forms, as well as its different levels. These have varying importance and degrees of autonomy in different countries. Public institutions – whether State, regional or municipal – have a life and logic of their own, with specific professional as well as institutional interests and cultures. Coordination of different institutional levels and actors of the public administration may be as difficult as that between public and private ones. From this point of view, the different pattern of collaboration between State and municipal institutions in Saint Etienne and Rennes is a particularly telling example. Of course, the market too has its plurality of actors, which may vary considerably from one place to another. This is particularly so for the unofficial, informal market economy, as indicated by the comparison between the Portuguese cities and the Swedish ones, as well as between Barcelona and Vitoria in Spain.

But, second, possibly one of the most interesting findings of our study at this level concerns the crucial and diversified role of the third sector. The third sector is usually understood as being comprised of such diverse actors and agencies as churches, voluntary associations, non-profit organisations, and so forth. And equally simplistically, it is often assumed to be, together with family and kin, the privileged arena of social integration. Yet we have found that both the specific third sector actors present in a given context and the way that they are mobilised may have a very different impact on social integration. Even less does the third sector automatically make up for the lack of a well-developed public one. Thus in Cosenza, the city in the ESOPO sample where the public sector is least developed, the presence and role of the third sector is negligible and overall integration in and of the local community is weak. Although it may happen that a strong public sector monopolises all the collective resources for solidarity existing within given national and local cultures, it seems more difficult for the reverse to occur, at least in our sample cities: where the public sector is weak, the third sector develops and organises with difficulty.

Moreover, there are great differences not only in the role and resources of third sector actors, but also in their social status. We find differences in the human and financial resources they dispose of, as well as in their social or political standing. Highly organised institutions such as Caritas in Italy (or La Misericordia in Lisbon) have very little in common with small groups of dedicated volunteers who, relying on their own resources, go out at night in search of the homeless.

The differentiation within the third sector has been increasing in recent years (Gidron et al, 1992). This is partly because new actors have entered the fight against poverty and social exclusion, often catering for particular categories (for instance, Third World immigrants, children, drug addicts, HIV bearers and AIDS sufferers), partly because public institutions have called on them as the most adequate partners for dealing with poverty and social exclusion, particularly with regard to social insertion programmes. In all cities we found a multiplicity of intermediary structures which are crucial in anti-poverty policies, sometimes in formal collaboration with public structures, sometimes operating in relative autonomy, and sometimes in competition. Though not part of the public system, they are often formally integrated into it. Further, they are being increasingly acknowledged as full partners in policy making, both at the national and at the EU level. Actually the EU has given a strong impulse to the institutionalisation of social partnership – including not only trades and enterprise unions, but also NGOs – not only at the EU, but also at the national level, requiring that they be involved in the open coordination process. Yet, as we have pointed out in Chapter Two, this increasing role of third sector institutions and actors is developing within nation and even local specific traditions, range and type of actors and so forth. This in turn makes for quite different kinds of welfare mixes and more generally of national and local patterns of governance. It makes also for different patterns and understanding of social citizenship, at least from the point of view of beneficiaries. The greater attention for the relational dimension of support, together with the higher flexibility and diversification of provisions, which are usually associated with the action of third sector agencies compared to public ones, are often premised on specific values that identify a given group and associations. This is particularly, but by no means exclusively, the case for religious (as well as for ethnic) associations. These values and shared identity constitute a crucial motivational background for these associations and their social workers; they may also be an integrating resource for beneficiaries. But they may also be perceived by the latter as an additional burden: an obligation or price they have to pay in order to be supported. Further, particularly in places where the public sector does not play an important role in defining criteria for entitlement and provision, the distinction between charity and citizenship rights may be further blurred by the intermediating role of particularistic value laden agencies and actors.

In our sample, the Swedish and French cities are those with by far the most regulation by the public system and the weakest involvement of intermediate structures – both family-kin and third sector agencies – in providing social assistance. This is, of course, premised on a greater individualisation of entitlements. But it may also produce, or ignore as a specific need and lack of personal resources, social isolation when an individual or household for some reason is cut off from family and community ties. At the same level of poverty, this may lead to greater and more rapid isolation and alienation of those who may not count on an informal network of relationships and support, even if they do receive income support.

Despite reunification, the two halves of Germany still display considerable differences in their conception and organisation of policies for dealing with poverty, and there are important local variations even within what used to be the German Federal Republic. Bremen corresponds to a model in which a wide network of local intermediate organisations – trades unions, professional or religious associations – is strongly coordinated to public welfare. Halle still shows signs of the old socialist system, which tended to marginalise volunteer, self-help, non-profit and religious associations. Even if the web of charitable organisations in the city is extending and intervention growing, it has not yet reached the density and diversity of the network in Bremen (where more public resources are also available).

In Italy and Spain, the greater autonomy of the third sector is related to a process of institutionalisation, where great efforts are made to involve non-profit institutions and even to support their development. In Turin and Vitoria, both the secular and religious third sector agencies are being increasingly integrated into the institutional arena of social policies. This pattern is present also in Milan, where, however, collaboration between the public and third sector seems to occur more through an implicit and explicit delegation of responsibilities by the former to the latter, than through coordinated planning. The Italian case demonstrates not only the different patterns of collaboration between the public and private sector that may develop on the basis of the features and history of both sectors. It also demonstrates how interdependent these two, apparently separate, histories are.

As for Portugal, it is undergoing a process of profound modernisation that should lead the country to break with the traditional model where assistance for the poor was closely linked to the notion of charity and private aid. There are, however, different paths to institutionalisation even here. In Lisbon, social assistance policies are run by a non-profit body of charitable origin that is legally controlled by the State, but organisationally and financially very independent. In Porto, policies are run by a public regional social services centre, with no cooperation with other public or non-profit bodies.

Finally, it should be pointed out that the third sector may play a twofold role in combating, or preventing, poverty and social exclusion. On the one hand, it may substitute or integrate public support policies, either through the provision of resources or through the provision of services. On the other hand, it can provide jobs, and thus a way out of economic poverty, particularly for those who suffer from temporary or permanent vulnerabilities in the main labour market[5]. This latter role is increasingly being focused on both in European Union policy documents and by national and local regulations.

Social assistance careers as the outcome of biographical and institutional constraints

Our study has demonstrated that both the demographic and social profiles of income support beneficiaries and the form of their 'social assistance career' is highly dependent on the way conditions for entitlement are institutionally defined and practically implemented. As a consequence, cross-country and cross-city variation cannot be easily and unambiguously interpreted in terms of the greater or lesser efficacy of the welfare assistance provided. Conversely, similar outcomes do not automatically have the same meaning. This apparently negative finding (with regard to the possibility of performing a comparative evaluation) has prompted us to look deeper at the differences and their consequences, allowing us to understand better the workings of a given measure in a given context, as well as to dissolve long-held stereotypes.

Our data offer sufficient grounds to disprove two of the most common critiques addressed to income support measures. Firstly, that they create long-term dependency and secondly, that the more universal and generous the support, the more likely it is that people remain on social assistance for a long time, becoming dependent on it. We found, in fact, that only a minority of beneficiaries in all cities remain for a long period on social assistance, irrespective of its characteristics and the rules for entitlement. Of course, this is not a univocal indicator of success. It might even be suggested that longer periods on social assistance could, in some cases, be more efficacious than forced short periods, in so far as they would allow the investment of time and energy in building up personal resources and assessing possible opportunities. Yet our findings show that the widespread idea that most social assistance recipients are long-term ones simply does not correspond to reality.

Previous studies that were geographically and, to some extent, also methodologically more limited than ours (for example, Duncan, 1984; Paugam, 1993; Walker and Shaw, 1998; Leisering and Leibfried, 1999) have already indicated that there is no evidence that social assistance per se creates dependence. Our study confirms this finding on the basis of a much larger comparative sample, while at the same time qualifying it. On the one hand, it supports the thesis that long-term dependence, when it occurs, is less a consequence of the 'corrupting' impact of social assistance – particularly its generosity or lack of rigid constraints – than of the 'original' features of the beneficiaries. Those who remain for long periods on social assistance, or have recurrent relapses, are likely to have some specific disadvantage, such as being of a mature age, in bad health, female, with heavy family demands, low education and skills, and so forth. Thus, the more common these features in the population receiving income support, the more likely are long careers in social assistance, when these are not deterred by a time limit imposed by regulations.

The concentration of specific vulnerabilities and weaknesses in the population receiving social assistance is, in turn, a result of the interplay between the social, economic and demographic features of the national and local context, as well as the rules governing income support schemes, particularly those pertaining to generosity and universalism. There is a higher concentration where national and/or local economies are weaker and social assistance supports only the very poor, or those who, in addition to being poor, have some specific kind of individual or social vulnerability. This combination holds for all our Southern European cities, where social assistance beneficiaries tend to suffer not only from income poverty, but also a more general situation of social and biographical deprivation. Only in Milan, and to a lesser degree Turin, does this combination not give rise to long social assistance careers, either continuous or with interruptions. But, as we have indicated, this is no proof of the efficiency and efficacy of the system of support in these cities, rather of the rules and constraints applied. With the exception of given categories (for example, lone mothers, people with special needs), income support in these two cities, and particularly in Milan, is interrupted after an allotted time has expired; beneficiaries may not return within a predetermined time limit, irrespective of need. Thus, they often turn to the voluntary and charity sector.

The highest dependence rate was found in Barcelona and Lisbon, where the combination of close targeting of beneficiaries (which restricts entitlement to the extremely poor and vulnerable), the small amount of benefit, and the absence of a time rule, led to longer than average periods of social assistance. In this case, although beneficiaries include a large percentage of people with great difficulty in becoming self-supporting, the benefit is too low to give them a chance to make a fresh start. They are hence compelled to find ways of integrating this benefit with other resources, often in the informal economy, where it is easier for people with low skills or personal difficulty to find an odd job. However, this does not offer them the chance to become self-supporting. From this point of view, the expression 'social assistance dependence' is only partially correct, in so far as social assistance alone does not give these individuals or households sufficient means to survive.

One of the main findings of our study is that close targeting and low benefits create a population of beneficiaries characterised by a high degree of vulnerability and difficulty in becoming completely autonomous from social assistance. This kind of population is of course present everywhere and needs special attention. But when it comprises the majority of social assistance beneficiaries due to strict selection rules, it becomes part of the definition of social assistance itself. The lack of efficacy of welfare measures in rendering this kind of beneficiary autonomous sets up a vicious circle, reinforcing a negative pessimistic view of both policies and beneficiaries. It also de-motivates social workers, increasing their own vulnerability to professional burn out. It therefore constitutes in itself a path to marginality and social exclusion. This may cause different reactions, according to the local political culture and economic resources. Thus, indefinite (partial) dependence may be accepted by some social workers and administrators without prompting any effort to redefine the approach. Alternatively, a revolving door or shifting mechanism (from public to private social assistance) may develop, again without prompting policy innovation, even with regard to this particularly vulnerable population. In contrast, where benefits are relatively generous, beneficiaries more 'mixed' and the chances of success higher, it is less likely that the presence of a certain proportion of 'difficult' beneficiaries will have a strong stigmatising effect on the whole population of recipients, and on the institution of social assistance itself.

Universalism and generosity would therefore appear not only more appropriate to a citizenship culture, since they lead to better social integration, but also more effective in the medium-long term: in so far as they prevent people from exhausting their resources and starting social assistance too late to be successfully supported. This finding, however, needs to be qualified. It is certainly true that within these systems we find a substantial quota of so-called 'bridgers', that is people who use income support as a 'bridge' between periods in which they are working: in other words to fill the gap when they are temporarily out of work and not covered by social security. Social assistance acts for them as a temporary cushion while they look for a new job. However, among these, some people may be subject to some kind of 'revolving door' mechanism, albeit in a highly structured and protected way. Given the interplay between regulations concerning unemployment indemnity, socially useful jobs and income support, in Sweden and Germany, but also Vitoria, one may go through (or be pushed through) the whole system – from work to unemployment indemnity to social assistance – and then start again[6]. It is worth noticing, however, that within this system, and particularly in Sweden, social assistance does not keep beneficiaries off the labour market. Rather it tries to maintain continuity between being in work and being out of work, as well as between being on social assistance and on social security.

This said, both in the less generous and the more generous systems, the presence of a group of beneficiaries with a higher risk of long-term dependence on social assistance cannot easily be dismissed, and is not susceptible to a single solution. It points to a series of different problems that have differing weight in the various national and local contexts: labour market restructuring and high unemployment rates, lack of skills, low paid jobs, the inadequacy of support for families with children, the gender division of labour within the family and its consequences for women's labour market participation. No single policy can of course address all of these. To some degree, measures for dealing with the poor are really trying to cope with failures in other systems: the labour market, social security, the family and school. Thus, it is empirically unfounded to base any request for social assistance restructuring on the assumption that it produces dependence and that most beneficiaries would remain on social assistance if not adequately monitored and pushed out; yet social assistance systems must also deal with the presence of a group who either needs it for a long time, or who cannot be moved out of it without requiring both additional investment in accompanying measures and some change in other areas.

Explicit and implicit assumptions in social integration discourses

The last observation points both to the crucial role of differentiated, accompanying measures in facilitating the social integration of the poor and to the implicit, and sometimes conflicting, assumptions concerning what social integration, or social inclusion, is about, at least with regard to socially vulnerable groups.

We could say that while the countries of Southern Europe tend to emphasise the role of families and communities in providing social integration, even in conditions of long-term unemployment and poverty, the more universalistic systems share an idea of inclusive citizenship mainly based on participation in paid work, for both genders. In the Swedish cities, social integration is in fact easily translated into 'having a job and becoming financially self-sufficient'. Although the UK was not part of our study, the most recent developments in the British welfare system make this idea of social inclusion through inclusion into the labour market most explicit. Yet, this form of social inclusion is only apparently simple to achieve. First, it suggests that jobs – and more so adequately paid ones – are available, and that the problem lies entirely with beneficiaries: either their lack of willingness to work or their lack of skills. Second, it tends to underestimate the amount and value of the unpaid work that is mostly performed by women. Finally, it presupposes that work cultures and willingness to work for wages (and stigmatisation of social assistance) are the same across social and ethnic groups, and are, to some degree, 'found in nature'. Many experiences testify to the contrary.

The 'work ethic' that is part of the tradition of the industrialised world has been constructed through a long and often hotly contested process, in which different work cultures and different ideas of social obligation have competed. We can find traces of this in the unresolved conflict between the needs and ethic of care, and the ethic of *paid* work, which underlies gender conflicts. It also lies behind the increasingly fragile balance in the family's division of labour and the concept of obligations of family and kin. The very different way in which lone mothers with small children are regarded in Sweden and Germany or France for income support purposes, reflects different views of the social obligations of this group of beneficiaries, involving the balance between caring and working for pay. The UK itself, in its move towards redefining lone mothers as breadwinners rather than carers, is using the carrot of improved benefits (including money to pay for childcare), rather than the stick of enforced obligation to be available for work, indicating that social inclusion involves something more than simply being moved into paid work (for this group at least).

Thus, in order to give people an incentive to work, it is not always sufficient to offer them jobs (assuming there are jobs to be offered). These must be perceived by the beneficiaries as providing a good opportunity for their life and family. This in turn presupposes not only a specific cultural outlook and perspective, but also three other things: that the person offered the job has enough training to keep it, that caring obligations and needs are adequately taken care of, and that the job pays enough and offers enough security to be worth taking. The last aspect is particularly relevant in contexts, such as Southern Europe, where the offer of poorly paid and temporary jobs in the official labour market may be in competition with extended family solidarity, and also work in the informal economy. Since time spent in unemployment increases entitlement to social assistance benefits and to being hired in the public sector, taking a poorly paid and insecure job may appear a move that is too risky and costly[7]. In this case, it may seem more rational to remain in the informal economy, with or without social assistance.

As for the idea that any job is better than no job, our data offer some support to Atkinson's (1998b) and Paugam's (1997a) argument that this is a very simplistic view, and that some jobs might lead to greater social and professional exclusion than social assistance itself. Forcing a person to take any job may have negative effects upon their skills, and hence the ability to stay in the labour market. This is particularly true when the unskilled job is not protected by social security. Of course, this general argument must be qualified with regard to specific individual circumstances. Yet it appears that the risk of the revolving door mechanism is greater when the 'any job' rule is strictly enforced. It can make a great difference when, as in the Swedish and German cities, even temporary jobs offered to social assistance beneficiaries give the same entitlements to social security – in terms of pension contributions and unemployment indemnity – as 'normal' jobs. By offering an individual the real status of worker, he or she is at least temporarily reinserted in the circuit of social security. Paugam (1997a) defines this as a form of 'disqualified integration' (if the job is unskilled), in contrast to the 'compromised integration' offered by unskilled jobs in the informal economy where there is no social security coverage.

It should be added that integration achieved by accepting any job (with social security) may work better in places and within social groups who share a strong work ethic. From this point of view, it is interesting that notwithstanding the generosity of the system, Swedish beneficiaries tend to spend less time on social assistance precisely because they have the view that it is one's responsibility, as well as one's right, to work. In Sweden, unlike many other countries, this attitude is shared by lone mothers of small children, who are not covered by special provisions nor temporarily exempted from the requirement to work. The combination of widespread childcare services and a widely shared gender model in which motherhood and paid work are not in contradiction, renders this group less vulnerable than in other countries (where lone mothers tend to become poor because of lone motherhood, not because of loss of a job); but it also puts pressure on women to exit welfare quickly by finding paid work, irrespective of their mothering obligations and desires.

Interestingly enough, the same attitude can be found among lone mothers in Halle, who grew up with the same gender model as their Swedish counterparts, but now find it in contradiction to prevalent models in the reunified Germany where they are incorporated into a system with a very different set of implicit and explicit expectations about gender, social assistance and the labour market. It is much more difficult for lone mothers in Halle to exit welfare than in Sweden, although they share the same expectations and values. At the same time, it is likely to be more difficult for lone mothers in Halle than in Bremen to accept their experience of receiving social assistance as justified by their caring obligations, rather than by their joblessness. Thus, the interplay between local and individual cultures concerning work and family obligations and local opportunities must be taken into account when defining options and projects for social assistance beneficiaries. It is important to help them orient their expectations and to develop strategies so as to avoid social assistance clashing with their personal and social identity, further contributing to a feeling of social exclusion.

The concept of a 'contract' as opposed to a one-sided obligation has been developed precisely to avoid these rigidities and risks. It has been introduced as a policy instrument, particularly in France, to express the mutual commitment of the community and the beneficiary towards achieving social integration and an improvement in the beneficiary's situation. In the British system, it has been phrased in a slightly different way, as a 'new deal'. But in both cases, the responsibility of the parties – the beneficiaries and the State or community – are stressed. Yet, even this idea of striking some sort of contract, making some kind of deal with those receiving social assistance is not without problems.

First, it implies that there really are alternatives or options, which again is not always the case, due not only to the history of the individual, but also to socially structured constraints. Second, it implies a symmetry between the contracting parties. This presumes, on the one hand, a capacity for care and attention in social workers, as well as cooperation between the various local actors in developing specific opportunities. On the other hand, it presumes that the beneficiaries themselves have sufficient human capital to develop projects and to negotiate with social workers. In its actual implementation, this policy can easily be transformed either into a routine procedure, or a form of social control on recipients, or even a new instrument of discretionary treatment, where the 'best contracts' are reserved for the nicest or easiest recipients. In other words, the passage from theory to practice in the implementation of a 'contract' approach to social insertion requires a great deal of innovation, both in the social workers' profession (which was the underlying goal in France) and in the functioning of the local welfare system. At the same time, it is highly vulnerable to disappointment – among beneficiaries, as well as the community and policy makers – if contracts are not available or are not implemented.

Open debates in social assistance discourses

Income support measures for the poor have been under scrutiny in most countries for some time. Different issues are at stake, not only those concerning 'active' versus 'passive' measures. We point out three crucial sets of problems[8].

The first concerns the criteria for defining the groups entitled to income support: to what degree should universalism be corrected through some form of selectivity based on age, residence, family responsibility, family dependence, and so forth? This involves several different problems. One concerns the degree to which family and kin solidarity should be enforced, particularly with regard to parent-children obligations. Another concerns the social and moral acceptability, or opportunity, of giving income support to the young. These two questions are linked, but also distinct. The latter implies not only moral judgements on family obligations, but also on the status of the young as citizens, on what society owes them and their specific vulnerability not only to poverty, but to dependence and passivity. In this respect, it is interesting to consider the rules under which some countries – for example, France, Luxembourg, Spain and Denmark – exclude young people below a certain age from minimum income schemes. It would be too simplistic to interpret it solely in terms of a denial of rights. This choice points to a view of the specific moral vulnerability of the young, and also to the definition of what should be offered to them as an alternative: training, work experience, and so forth[9]. On the other hand, in Denmark (and Sweden since January 1998), young people (18–24 years old) applying for income support have been obliged since 1990 not only to register at the unemployment office, but to accept any training or job offered to them by the municipality, under penalty of losing the unemployment benefit. Although this system may appear strongly compulsive, it still grants the young more resources than in France or Spain (not to mention Italy), where a young person may or may not be offered a training programme, or job experience, while being excluded from the minimum income scheme.

Yet another problem concerns the entitlement of non-nationals, and particularly Third World immigrants. To what degree and under what conditions (duration and legality of residence, past contributory or tax paying history), should they be entitled to sharing the national or local welfare resources?

One way of addressing (or solving) the issue of entitlement is that of prioritisation (and/or categorisation), which is also a way of defining the deserving or undeserving poor. Extreme categorisation, both at the national and local level, occurs in countries such as Italy where there is no nationally regulated income support scheme. But also in countries where there is a national scheme, as in France, Portugal, Spain, it may be added to other existing categorical schemes (for older people, people with disabilities, lone mothers, widows, or poor working adults) as a last resort. In any case, the issue of who deserves or is entitled to social assistance tends to be periodically reformulated according to criteria that may also be dictated by political cultures and expediency. A case in point is the different way of framing the needs and characteristics of lone mothers in different countries: while in some they may be considered the most deserving category (together with older people), in others they are perceived as socially irresponsible users of the system, to be controlled and kept in check.

A particular problem that arises within the issue of entitlement is that of the possible negative effects, particularly with regards to women, set in motion by means-testing of households. Not only is there a risk that the poverty of financially dependent women is not acknowledged through this approach, but their attempts to become financially autonomous may be thwarted. This is a particularly difficult, if not intractable problem, in so far as all countries, even the most individualistic in their approach to social protection, assume for social assistance purposes that spouses and cohabitant couples share their income.

The second set of problems concerns whether income support should be seen primarily as a preventive or as a curative measure. In other words, should social assistance act as a sort of launch pad, that is an incentive structure to prevent the socially vulnerable becoming poor or socially excluded, or as a last resort or 'safety net' for those who cannot help themselves. Though conceptually clear, this issue is easily confused at the policy level – not only because the same measure might be used in a preventive rather than curative (or even exclusionary) way, but because the time-horizon of preventive measures may be out of scale with that perceived and experienced by the poor themselves. Thus, work requirements or incentives may be empowering opportunities, pushing an individual towards adequate job insertion or, on the contrary, they may be used as a means of social insertion for individuals who are not (or no longer) employable, simply helping them to feel useful. At the same time, the timing of programmes – duration of benefits, training courses, work experience and so forth – may be out of step with the subjective perceptions of beneficiaries and with their personal and family circumstances.

It should be added that the focus on labour market participation and paid work as the main route out of poverty, is highlighting not only the hypothetical disincentive effects of social assistance, but also the plight of the working poor. Thus, in a few countries policies are being developed specifically for this population, and particularly families with children (see also OECD, 1999). Once again, following and improving on the US experience with the Earned Income Tax Credit, the UK has been the first European country to develop such an approach, through the Working Families' Tax Credit. It is now being followed in France with a similar measure, and also has an equivalent in Ireland.

Debate on how to support poor working families is going on in many countries. To be more precise, there are two debates, which should not be confused: one concerns income support for families who are below a given earnings' ceiling, the other concerns the subsidy of low productivity jobs. While the former involves integrating the inadequate income of a household, the latter involves subsidising (for example, by reducing the cost of labour) labour market demands for unskilled, or labour intensive jobs. The idea is that these provide employment for those actual or potential social assistance beneficiaries who have the most difficulty in becoming financially independent because of their low skills or other shortcomings.

This is not the place to address the latter issue. As for the former, we should like to point out that, important as it is to acknowledge that efforts must be made 'to make work pay', the mechanisms involved in means-testing on a household basis risks creating further vicious circles, particularly for women. It can make it no longer worthwhile to work extra hours or to have an additional worker/earner in the household. This negative incentive affects in particular two-parent households, rendering them (and especially women) more, not less vulnerable to poverty and social exclusion should something happen to the couple's relationship[10]. Paradoxically, this occurs in the same country, the UK, in which the New Deal for Lone Parents strongly encourages lone mothers to take up paid work as a way of better protecting themselves and their children financially, and being better integrated socially.

In any case, we might suggest that 'making work pay' policies represent an institutionalisation – with all the advantages not only of higher generosity, but of legality and of some degree of social security – of the kind of 'assisted equilibrium' achieved in some of the Southern European cities through the combination of inadequate income support and recourse to the informal labour market. Further, in the case of institutionalised making work pay policies, beneficiaries holding a job are not perceived as cheaters who might or might not be condoned on the basis of social workers' leniency or understanding. On the contrary, they are perceived as better citizens because they are less dependent on public assistance.

The focus on 'active' policies also reformulates the issue of the balance struck between universalism and individually adapted measures. Special incentives (or disincentives), insertion programmes, requirements and 'contracts', cannot be overly standardised if they are to serve their purpose, as they must match the circumstances of beneficiaries. This opens up the whole question of the kind of obligations (both for the social services and for recipients) that means-tested income support for the able-bodied should involve, and represents the third issue in the current policy debate.

What balance should there be between the respect of individual choice and personal freedom, and an authoritative approach that predefines the range of options and imposes a set behaviour? For example, the requirement of willingness to actively search for a job, which is imposed on able-bodied income support recipients in all countries, can represent a positive incentive – a means of achieving social integration and developing personal skills. Vice versa, it may also be a constraint that prevents recipients from developing alternative strategies and ways out of poverty. It can be used as an empowering device or as a constraint, aimed at getting people off the welfare rolls, at stigmatising them or even making it difficult for people to receive social assistance. Moreover, it can easily become an enforced obligation to work, turning social assistance beneficiaries into forced labour, in a contemporary reinvention of the workhouse[11]. It is not at all easy to judge beforehand how this requirement will be implemented and with what consequences. There is a fine dividing line between the two approaches – a line that is often crossed in both directions (more in the actual implementation of policies at the everyday level, than in formal rules and principles of law).

Moreover, the risk of the avoidance of responsibility by social services in the name of freedom for the recipients is as great as that of over control and authoritarianism. It is interesting, from the point of view of the history of ideas and policy models, to view the different status of the term 'workfare' in the past three decades. It was developed in the US in the 1970s in criticism of work requirements introduced as a form of social control of the poor; thus it represented diminished citizenship rights. It has become the catchword of 'progressive' social assistance policy both in the US and in Europe in the mid-1990s, though with a slight linguistic variation in the new UK New Labour vocabulary: 'welfare to work'[12]. This radical shift in usage and meaning certainly presents the risk of being translated into forms of stigmatisation of social assistance recipients, if not forced labour. Yet it should not be interpreted merely as a form of political cynicism. Rather, it points on the one hand to the, largely unfounded, but still quite widespread fear of long-term dependence on social assistance. In some Southern European countries, with large informal economy sectors, this fear may be compounded by that of condoning and even encouraging both fraudulence in obtaining benefits and participation in the illegal (and in the case of Italy, sometimes even criminal) economy. On the other hand, that language shift points to the awareness that inclusion must also address issues of empowerment, acknowledgement and strengthening of individual capabilities.

Whatever the implicit and explicit goals, the stress on active measures also points to new roles and responsibilities for local actors, and particularly for local communities. These can no longer be perceived simply as a passive context in which the events of economic and social history have led to various forms of poverty and social exclusion being experienced. The community also consists of actors responsible for implementing policies – not only applying rules and regulations, but providing insertion programmes, developing 'contracts', forming partnerships, and so forth. The new active policies against poverty and social exclusion imply the existence of a local community: as a place in which poverty and/or exclusion arise, but also one in which forms of social integration are developed. From this point of view, specific sets of local actors can encourage both diversity and a degree of discretion in implementing policies. They can be the instruments for (re-)creating or (re-)structuring local communities, and thus possibly reinforcing diversity and inequality between communities, especially when available resources are limited. Consequently, diversity with regard to measures to combat poverty and social exclusion is likely to increase not only between but also within countries.

This process of policy re-evaluation is going on with varying intensity in all European countries, as well as in other OECD states. Thus it includes countries that already have an established and well defined policy against poverty and some kind of minimum guarantee of resources, as well as countries that do not – at least not as an institutional part of the social rights package or of society's obligations and responsibilities in defining citizenship within the national (central or federal) community. From this point of view, comparative research allows us to understand how different systems define and deal with these and related issues, and what the results are.

At the same time, comparative research can contribute both empirically and methodologically to the process of European policy making. Social exclusion/inclusion is one of the areas in which a common approach is being developed through the method of open coordination. In fact, in order to develop a common understanding of the goals of social policy and to benefit from mutual learning and best practice, it is important to have a clear understanding of the complex network of established practices and institutions, of specific cultural meanings and the patterns of sociability that underlie given policies. Policy transfer between countries is not easy. This is not only because individual policies are usually part of a far more complex package, but also because they reflect nation-specific ways of understanding reality. The opening of a European discourse, with a set of common goals and indicators, is an ambitious attempt to develop shared understandings – requiring more or less radical change in existing nation-specific and local patterns of discourse and policy. Careful testing of stereotypical views and nation-specific experience, contrasting modes of interpretations and patterns of intervention, is needed in order for this effort to be successful in terms of efficacious policy decisions.

Notes

[1] Literature on this phenomenon is substantial. See for example, Barbagli and Saraceno, 1998; Garfinkel and McLanahan, 1990; Marsiglio, 1995; Martin, 1997; OECD, 1990; Seltzer, 1994.

[2] In the new edition of his retrospective longitudinal research on social assistance recipients in a small French town, Paugam (1997b) stresses that different groups

might also represent different stages in the life course of social recipients, although not all recipients go through all phases.

[3] See for example, Grover and Stewart, 1999; Jessop, 1993; Standing, 1990. The studies collected in the European Foundation for the Improvement of Living and Working Conditions, 1999; Lødemel and Trickey, 2000.

[4] As a consequence of the Lisbon and Nice summits in 2000, social exclusion has entered the European policy agenda and countries are requested to prepare two year National Action Plans on the basis of common objectives. Analogous to the National Action Plans on employment, they will be assessed through a peer review process.

[5] The role of the third sector has been one of the focuses of a TSER funded project on the 'Evaluation of local socio-economic strategies in disadvantaged urban areas', ELSES (project 3047, coordinators S. Weck and R. Zimmer Hegman). See ELSES, 2000.

[6] Abrahmson (2000) advances this observation for the Danish case, pointing out that jobs or training courses offered through the social assistance channel are less likely to lead to regular jobs than temporary jobs or training experience offered by the non-protected labour market and training system, since the former are stigmatised.

[7] Jordan (1996, p 36) argues that for people trapped in deprived 'communities of fate', illegality may be a more secure source of income for survival than the new flexible labour market, where extremely irregular employment for below subsistence wages does not provide the basis for a sustainable way of life.

[8] See also Leisering and Walker (1998b), whose list is slightly different, and more articulated, than ours.

[9] In France, the *Emploi Jeunes* programme – a voluntary scheme, launched in 1997 – was the alternative answer to the request that the age threshold for obtaining the RMI be lifted.

[10] We are not denying that the Working Families' Tax Credit is an improvement compared to the previous limitation in working hours allowed, in so far as it addresses the plight of poor dual-parent working households (see for example, Piachaud and Sutherland, 2000). Yet, the effects on the behaviour of all household members in the way this support is given, and its implicit assumptions concerning

the gender division of labour, should not be underestimated. Further, a more generous acknowledgement of the cost of raising children by providing increased child benefits and/or tax allowances could possibly have the same protective effect without creating disincentives.

[11] See for instance, Sunesson et al (1998), who argue that this is presently a risk in Sweden. See also Becker, 1997.

[12] There is not a general consensus on what workfare includes and the use of the term varies over time and across countries (Peck, 1998), besides being a highly charged political term. A restricted definition, used also in a recent comparative study of workfare policies in six European countries, defines it as "policies which require people to work in exchange for, or instead of, social assistance benefits". See Lødemel and Trickey, 2000. For an overview of debates and experiences, see European Foundation for the Improvement of Living and Working Conditions, 1999. See also Barbier, 1998; Standing, 1990.

References

Abrahmson, P. (2000) 'L'activation des politiques sociales scandinaves: le cas du Danemark', in C. Daniel, and B. Palier (eds) *La protection sociale en Europe*, Paris: Ministère de l'Emploi et de la solidarité, Mission recherche-DREES, pp 123-40.

Alber, J. (1995) 'A framework for the comparative study of social services', *Journal of European Social Policy*, vol 5, no 2, pp 131-49.

Allmendinger, J., Brückner, H. and Brückner, E. (1993) 'The production of gender disparities over the life course and their effects in old age: results from the West German Life History Study', in A.B. Atkinson and M. Rein (eds) *Age, work and social security*, New York, NY: St Martin Press, pp 188-223.

Amrouni, I. and Math, A. (1997/98) 'Une part importante des bénéficiaires de minima sociaux les perçoit à un taux réduit', *Recherches et Prévisions*, no 50/51, pp 49-67.

Andreß, H.J. (ed) (1998) *Empirical poverty research in a comparative perspective*, Aldershot: Ashgate.

Andreß, H.J. and Schultz, K. (1998) 'Poverty risks and the life cycle: the individualization thesis reconsidered', in H.J. Andreß (ed) *Empirical poverty research in comparative perspective*, Aldershot: Ashgate, pp 331-56.

Ashworth, K., Hill, M. and Walker, R. (1992) *Patterns of childhood poverty: New challenges for policy*, Working Paper no 169, Loughborough: Centre for Research in Social Policy, University of Technology.

Astier, I. (1997) *Revenu minimum et souci d'insertion*, Paris: Desclée de Brouwer.

Atkinson, A.B. (1998a) *Poverty in Europe*, Oxford: Basil Blackwell.

Atkinson, A.B. (1998b) 'Social exclusion, poverty and unemployment', in A.B. Atkinson. and J. Hills (eds) *Exclusion, employment and opportunity*, CASE Paper 4, London: London School of Economics, pp 1-20.

Aubert, B. (1997/98) 'Seuils de pauvreté et montants des minima sociaux. Remarques sur les usages et les discours', *Recherches et Prévisions*, no 50/51, pp 69-80.

Bagnasco, A. (1977) *Tre Italie: La problematica territoriale dello sviluppo italiano*, Bologna: Il Mulino.

Bagnasco, A. (1986) *Torino: Un profilo sociologico*, Torino: Einaudi.

Bagnasco, A. and Le Galès, P. (eds) (2000) *Cities in contemporary Europe*, Cambridge: Cambridge University Press.

Bane, M.J. and Ellwood, D.T. (1986) 'Slipping into and out of poverty: the dynamics of spells', *The Journal of Human Resources*, vol 12, pp 1-23.

Bane, M.J. and Ellwood, D.T. (1994) *Welfare realities: From rhetoric to reform*, Cambridge, MA: Harvard University Press.

Barbagli, M. and Saraceno, C. (1998) *Separarsi in Italia*, Bologna: Il Mulino.

Barbier, J.C. (1998) 'La logica del workfare in Europa e negli Stati Uniti: i limiti delle analisi globali', *Assistenza Sociale*, no 1, gennaio-marzo, pp 15-40.

Bauböck, R. (ed) (1994) *From aliens to citizens: Redefining the status of immigrants in Europe*, Avebury: Aldershot.

Becattini, G. (1989) 'Riflessioni sul distretto industriale marshalliano come concetto socio-economico', *Stato e Mercato*, no 25, pp 111-29.

Beck, M. and Seewald, H. (1994) 'Zur Reform der amtlichen Sozialhilfestatistik', *Nachrichtendienst des Deutschen Vereins für öffentliche und private Fürsorge*, no 74, pp 27-31.

Beck, U. (1992) *Risk society: Towards a new modernity*, London: Sage Publications.

Becker, S. (1997) *Responding to poverty: The politics of cash and care*, London: Longman.

Behrens, J. and Voges, W. (eds) (1996) *Kritische Übergänge Lebenslaute im Sozialstaat: Statuspassegen und Sozialpolitische Institutio-nalisiezung*, Frankfurt am Main/New York, NY: Campus.

Benassi, D. (1995) 'I percorsi di formazione del bisogno', in Y. Kazepov (ed) *I nuovi poveri in Lombardia. Sistemi di welfare e traiettorie di esclusione sociale*, Quaderni Regionali di Ricerca, no 1, Milano: Regione Lombardia.

Benassi, D., Kazepov, Y. and Zajczyk, F. (1999) 'Politiche sociali e metodi d'indagine: la povertà a Milano', in E. Mingione (ed) *Le sfide dell'Esclusione: metodi, luoghi, soggetti*, Bologna: Il Mulino, pp 83-111.

Berger, P. and Sopp, P. (eds) (1995) *Sozialstrukur und Lebenslauf*, Opladen: Leske & Budrich.

Blank, R. (1989) 'Analysing the length of welfare spells', *Journal of Public Economics*, no 39, pp 245-73.

Block, A. and Levy, C. (eds) (1999) *Refugees, citizenship and social policy in Europe*, London: Macmillan.

Blossfeld, H.P. and Rohwer, G. (1996) *Event history techniques*, Hillsdale, NJ: Erlbaum.

Bonß, W. and Plum, W. (1990) 'Gesellschaftliche Differenzierng und sozialpolitische Normalitätsfiktion', *Zetischrift für Sozialreform*, no 36, pp 692-715.

Bosco, A. and Chassard, Y. (1999) 'A shift in paradigm: surveying the European Union discourse on welfare and work', in European Foundation for the Improvement of Living and Working Conditions, *Linking welfare to work*, Luxembourg: OOPEC, pp 42-58.

Bosco, N., Contini, D. and Negri, N. (1999) 'Out of welfare: functioning of income support in Torino', *Quality & Quantity*, no 33, pp 243-60.

Bouget, D. and Nogues, H. (1993) *Evaluation des resultats des politiques sociales: Experiences internationales. Politiques contre l'exclusion sociale*, Paper presented at the International Seminar on 'Evaluation of social policies: experiences and perspectives', Pavia, 12-18 March.

Bradshaw, J., Ditch, J., Holmes, H. and Whiteford, P. (1993) *Support for children: A comparison of arrangements in fifteen countries*, London: HMSO.

Bradshaw, J., Kennedy, S., Kilkey, M., Hutton, S., Cordon, A., Eardley, T., Holmes, H. and Neale, J. (1996) *The employment of lone parents: A comparison of policy in 20 countries*, London: Family Policy Studies Centre.

Brusco, S. (1986) 'Small firms and industrial districts: the experience of Italy', in D. Keeble and E. Weler (eds) *New firms and regional development*, London: Croom Helm, pp 184-202.

Brusco, S. (1991) 'La genesi dell'idea del distretto industriale', in F. Pyke, G. Becattini and W. Sengerberger, *Distretti industriali e cooperazione fra imprese in Italia*, Firenze: Banca Toscana, pp 25-35.

Buhr, P. and Weber, A. (1998) 'Social assistance and social change in Germany', in L. Leisering and R. Walker (eds) *The dynamics of modern society: Poverty, policy and welfare*, Bristol: The Policy Press, pp 183-98.

Buhr, P., Leibfried, S., Ludwig, M. and Voges, W. (1989) *Passages through welfare: The Bremen approach to the analysis of claimants' careers in 'Publicly Administered Poverty'*, Bremen: Bremen University, Mimeo.

Bulpitt, J. (1986) 'Continuity, autonomy and peripheralisation: the autonomy of the centre's race statecraft in England', in Z. Layton-Henry and P. Rich, *Race, government and politics*, London: Macmillan, pp 17-44.

Cardoso, A. (1993) *A outra face da cidade: pobreza em bairros degradados de Lisboa*, Lisboa: Camara Municipal de Lisboa.

Castel, R. (1991) 'De l'indigence à l'exclusion, la désaffiliation', in J. Donzelot (ed) *Face à l'exclusion. Le modèle Français*, Paris: Editions Esprit, pp 137-68.

Castel, R. (1995) *Les métamorphoses de la question sociale. Une chronique du salariat*, Paris: Fayard.

Castel, R. and Laé, J.F. (1992) *Le revenu minimum d'insertion: une dette sociale*, Paris: L'Harmattan.

Charbonneau, B. and Landais, F. (1996) 'L'insertion professionnelle des allocataires du RMI de 1989 à 1995', *Les dossiers de la DARES*, no 8-9, November.

Cochran, M., Larner, M., Riley, D., Gunnarsson, L. and Henderson, Jr, (eds) (1990*) Extending families: The social networks of parents and their children*, Cambridge: Cambridge University Press.

Coleman, J.S. (1990) *Foundations of social theory*, Cambridge, MA: Cambridge University Press.

Comissão Nacional do Rendimento Mínimo (1999) *Relatório anual de avaliação das Comissões locais de acompanhamento RMG*, Lisboa: Comissão Nacional do Rendimento Mínimo.

Commission of the European Communities (1993a) *Towards a Europe of solidarity: Intensifying the fight against social exclusion, fostering integration*, Communication from the Commission of 23 December, Brussels: DG V.

Commission of the European Communities (1993b) *The future of social policy: Options for the Union. A Green paper*, Brussels: DG V.

Commission of the European Communities (1993c) *Social protection in Europe*, Brussels: DG V.

Commission of the European Communities (1997) *European Employment Observatory. Trends 28, Activation of labour market policy in Europe*, summer, Brussels: DG V.

Commissione di Indagine sulla Povertà (1985) *La povertà in Italia*, Roma: Poligrafico dello Stato.

Commissione di Indagine sulla Povertà (1995) *La povertà in Italia*, Roma: Poligrafico dello Stato.

Commissione di Indagine sulla Esclusione Sociale (2000) *Rapporto sulla povertà e l'esclusione sociale*, Roma: Poligrafico dello Stato.

Cousins, M. (1997) *New directions in social welfare*, Report of a Conference of the Irish Presidency of the European Union, 16-18 November 1996, Dublin, European Foundation for the Improvement of Living and Working Conditions, Luxembourg: OOPEC.

Crouch, C. (1999) *Social change in Western Europe*, Oxford: Oxford University Press.

Dahrendorf, R. (1995) *Economic opportunity, civil society, and political liberty*, Paper presented at the UNRISD conference, Copenaghen 11-12 March.

Daly, M. (1992) 'Europe's poor women? Gender in research on poverty', *European Sociological Review*, no 1, pp 1-12.

Daly, M. and Lewis, J.(1998) 'Introduction: conceptualising social care in the context of welfare state restructuring', in J. Lewis (ed) *Gender, social care and welfare state restructuring in Europe*, Aldershot: Ashgate, pp 1-24.

Dixon, J. and Macarov, D. (1999) *Poverty: A persistent global reality*, London: Routledge.

Donzelot, J. and Roman, J. (1991) 'Le deplacement de la question sociale', in J. Donzelot (ed) *Face à l'exclusion. Le modèle français*, Paris: Editions Esprit.

Doyal, L.and Gough, I. (1991) *The theory of human need*, London: Macmillan.

Dubet, F. (1989) *Immigrations: q'en savons-nous? Un bilan des connaissances*, Paris: La documentation Française.

Duncan, G.J. (1984), *Years of poverty, years of plenty: The changing economic fortunes of American workers and families*, Ann Arbor, MA: Institute for Social Research, University of Michigan.

Duncan, G.J., Gustafsson, B., Hauser, R., Schmaus, G., Jenkins, S., Messinger H., Muffels, R., Nolan, B., Ray, J.C. and Voges, W. (1995) 'Poverty and social assistance dynamics in the United States, Canada and Europe', in K. McFate, R. Lawson and W.J. Wilson (eds) *Poverty, inequality and the future of social policy*, New York, NY: Russel Sage Foundation, pp 67-108.

Duncan, G.J., Voges, W., Hauser, R., Gustafsson, B., Jenkins, S., Messinger, H., Nolan, B., Ray, J.-C. and Schmaus, G. (1993) 'Poverty dynamics in eight countries', *Journal of Population Economics*, no 6, pp 215-34.

Duncan, G.J. and Voges, W. (1993) *Do generous social assistance programs lead to dependence? A comparative study of lone-parent families in Germany and the United States*, Working Paper No 11, Bremen: Centre for Social Policy Research, University of Bremen.

Eardley, T., Bradshaw, J., Ditch, J., Gough, J. and Witheford, P. (1996) *Social assistance in OECD countries, synthesis report*, Department of Social Security, Research Report No 46, London: The Stationery Office.

ELSES (Evaluation of Local Socio-Economic Strategies in Disadvantaged Urban Areas) (2000) *Routes into jobs and the society: Good practice guide*, ELSES.

Esping-Andersen, G. (1990) *The three worlds of welfare capitalism*, Cambridge, MA: Harvard University Press.

Esping-Andersen, G. (ed) (1993) *Changing classes: Post-industrial mobility regimes*, London: Sage Publications.

Esping-Andersen, G. (1995) 'Il welfare state senza il lavoro. L'ascesa del familismo nelle politiche sociali dell'Europa continentale', *Stato e Mercato*, no 45, pp 347-80.

Esping-Andersen, G. (1999) *Social foundations of post-industrial economies*, Oxford: Oxford University Press.

European Foundation for the Improvement of Living and Working Conditions (eds) (1999) *Linking welfare to work*, Luxembourg: OOPEC

EUROSTAT (2000) *Statistics in focus*, Theme 3 - February.

Evers, A. and Svetlick, I. (eds) (1993) *Balancing pluralism: New welfare mixes in the care for the elderly*, Aldershot: Avebury.

Fargion, V. (1997) *La geografia della cittadinanza sociale*, Bologna: Il Mulino.

Fassin, D. (1996) 'Exclusion, underclass, marginalidad. Figures contemporaines de la pauvreté urbaine en France, aux Etats-Unis et en Amérique latine', *Revue Française de Sociologie*, vol 37, no 1, pp 37-75.

Falkingham, J. and Hills, J. (eds) (1995) *The dynamic of welfare: The welfare state and the life cycle*, Hemel Hempstead: Harvester Wheatsheaf.

Ferrera, M. (1984) *Il welfare state in Italia*, Bologna: Il Mulino.

Ferrera, M. (1993) *Modelli di solidarietà*, Bologna: Il Mulino.

Ferrera, M. (1998) *Le trappole del welfare*, Bologne: Il Mulino.

Finch, J. (1987) 'The vignette technique in social research', *Sociology*, vol 21, no 1, pp 105-14.

Flora, P. and Heidenheimer, A. (eds) (1981) *The development of welfare states in Europe and America*, New Brunswick, NJ: Transaction Press.

Fridberg, T. (ed) (1993) *On social assistance in the Nordic capitals*, Copenaghen: Socialforskningsinstituttet.

Gallie, D. (1999) 'Unemployment and social exclusion in the European Union', *European Societies*, vol I, no 2, pp 139-67.

Gallie, D. (2000) 'Unemployment, work and welfare', Paper presented at the conference 'Towards a learning society', Quinte ole Marinha, Lisbon, 28-30 May.

Gallie, D. and Paugam, S. (eds) (2000) *Welfare regimes and the experience of unemployment in Europe*, Oxford: Oxford University Press.

Garfinkel, I. and McLanahan, S. (1990) *Single mothers and their children: A new American dilemma*, Washington DC: Urban Institute Press.

Garonna, P. (1992) 'I processi migratori nell'analisi degli economisti', in A.A.V.V: *Il governo dei movimenti migratori in Europa: cooperazione o conflitto*, Napoli: Jovene editore, pp 35-54.

Gauchet, M. (1991) 'La société d'insécurité', in J. Donzelot (ed) *Face à l'exclusion. Le modèle français*, Paris: Editions Esprit.

Geldof, D. (1999) 'New activation policies: promises and risks', European Foundation for the Improvement of Living and Working Conditions, *Linking welfare to work*, Luxembourg: OOPEC, pp 13-26.

Giddens, A. (1983) *The constitution of society*, Cambridge: Polity Press.

Gidron, B., Kramer, R.M. and Salamon, L.S. (eds) (1992) *Government and third sector: Emerging relationships in welfare states*, San Francisco, CA: Jossey Bass.

Glatzer, W. and Krupp, H.J. (1975) 'Soziale Indikatoren des Einkommens und seiner Verteilung in der Bundesrepublik Deutschland', in W. Zapft (ed) *Soziale Indikatoren. Konzepte und Forschungsansätze III*, Frankfurt am Main/New York: Campus, pp 193-238.

Glotz, P. (1984) *Die Arbeit der Zuspitzung: Über die Organisation einer regierungsfähigen Linken*, Berlin: Siedler.

Goodin, R.E. (1996) *Institutions and their design*, in R.E Goodin (ed) *The theory of institutional design*, Cambridge: Cambridge University Press, pp 1-53.

Gough, I. (1994) *Meanstesting in the Western world*, Richard Titmuss Memorial Lecture, Hebrew University of Jerusalem, May.

Gough, I. (2000) 'From welfare to workfare: social integration or forced labour?' Paper presented at the conference 'Policies and instruments against poverty in the European Union', Algarve, 2 February.

Gough, I., Bradshaw, J., Ditch, J., Eardley, T. and Whiteford, P. (1997) 'Social assistance in OECD countries', *Journal of European Social Policy*, vol 7, no 1, pp 17-43.

Gribaudi, A. (1993) 'Familismo e famiglia a Napoli e nel Mezzogiorno', *Meridiana*, no 17, pp 91-108.

Grover, C. and Stewart, J. (1999) 'Market workfare: social security, social regulation and competitiveness in the 1990s', *Journal of Social Policy*, vol 28, no 1, pp 73-96.

Guibentif, P. and Bouget, D. (1997) *Minimal income policies in the European Union*, Lisboa: União das Mutualidades Portuguesas.

Gullestad, M. and Segalen, M. (eds) (1997) *Family and kinship in Europe*, London: Pinter.

Gustafsson, B. and Lindblom, M. (1993) 'Poverty lines and poverty in seven European countries, Australia, Canada and the USA', *Journal of European Social Policy*, no 3, pp 21-38.

Gustafsson, B. and Voges, W. (1998) 'Contrasting welfare dynamics: Germany and Sweden', in L. Leisering and R. Walker, *The dynamics of modern society: Poverty, policy and welfare*, Bristol: The Policy Press, pp 243-64.

Gustafsson, L., Hydén, L.C. and Salonen, T. (1993) 'Decision-making on social assistance in major cities in Sweden', *Scandinavian Journal of Social Welfare*, no 2, pp 197-203.

Haataja, A. (1999) 'Unemployment, employment and poverty', in *European Societie*, vol I, no 2, pp 169-96.

Hanesch, W. (1999) 'The debate on reforms of social assistance in Western Europe', in European Foundation for the Improvement of Living and Working Conditions, *Linking welfare to work*, Luxembourg: OOPEC, pp 71-86.

Hanesch, W., Krause, P. and Bäcker, G. (eds) (2000) *Armut und Ungleichheit in Deutschland*, Hamburg: Rowohlt Taschenbuch Verlag.

Hantrais, L. and Letablier, M.T. (1996) *Families and family policies in Europe*, London and New York, NY: Longman.

Häußermann, H. and Kazepov, Y. (1996) 'Urban poverty in Germany: a comparative analysis of the profile of the poor in Stuttgart and Berlin', in E. Mingione (ed) *Urban poverty and the underclass*, Oxford: Blackwell, pp 343-69.

Healey, P. (1998) 'Institutionalist theory, social exclusion and governance', in A. Madanipour, G. Cars and J. Allen (eds) *Social exclusion in European cities: Processes, experiences and responses*, London: Jessica Kingsley Publishers, pp 53-73.

Heikkila, M. (1999) 'A brief introduction to the topic', in European Foundation for the Improvement of Living and Working Conditions, *Linking welfare to work*, Luxembourg: OOPEC, pp 5-12.

Hobson, B. (1989) 'No exit no voice: women's economic dependency and the welfare state', *Acta Sociologica*, no 33, pp 235-50.

Holland, P.W. (1986) 'Statistics and causal inference', *Journal of the American Statistical Association*, no 81, pp 243-60.

Hvinden, B. (1999) 'Activation: a Nordic perspective', in European Foundation for the Improvement of Living and Working Conditions, *Linking welfare to work*, Luxembourg: OOPEC, pp 27-42.

IARD (1998) *Essere giovani nel 2000*, Bologna: Il Mulino.

Istituto Tagliacarne (1998) 'Il reddito prodotto dalle 103 provincie nel quinquennio 1991-1995', unpublished report.

Jarvis, S. and Jenkins, S.P. (1997) 'Low income dynamics in 1990s in Britain', *Fiscal Studies*, vol 18, no 2, pp 123-42.

Jarvis, S. and Jenkins, S.P. (1998) 'Income and poverty dynamics in Great Britain', in L. Leisering and R. Walker (eds) *The dynamics of modern society: Policy, poverty and welfare*, Bristol: The Policy Press, pp 145-60.

Jeppsson Grassman, E. (1999) *Secteur associatif et protection sociale: situation en Suède et comparaison avec la France*, in MIRE *Comparer les systèmes de protection sociale en Europe*, vol 2, Berlin Conference, Paris: MIRE.

Jessop, B. (1993) 'Towards a Schumpeterian workfare state? Preliminary remarks on post-Fordist political economy', *Studies in Political Economy*, no 40, pp 7-39.

Jordan, B. (1996) *A theory of poverty and social exclusion*, Cambridge: Polity Press.

Joshi, H. (1989) 'The cash opportunity costs of childbearing: an approach to estimation using British data', *Population Studies*, no 6.

Katz, M. (ed) (1993) *The 'underclass' debate*, Princeton, NJ: Princeton University Press.

Kazepov, Y. (1995) *I nuovi poveri in Lombardia: Sistemi di welfare e percorsi di impoverimento*, Quaderni Regionali di Ricerca, Regione Lombardi, Milan, N1.

Kazepov, Y. (1996) *Le politiche locali contro l'esclusione sociale*, Quaderni della Commissione Povertà, Roma: Istituto Poligrafico dello Stato.

Kazepov, Y. (1998a) 'Urban poverty and local policies against social exclusion in Italy: the north-south divide', in H.J. Andreß (ed) *Empirical research on poverty in a comparative perspective*, Aldershot: Ashgate Press, pp 391-422.

Kazepov, Y. (1998b) *Citizenship and poverty: The role of institutions in the structuring of social exclusion*, EUF no 98/1, EUI Working Papers, Fiesole: European University Institute.

Kazepov, Y. (1999) 'At the edge of longitudinal analysis: welfare institutions and social assistance dynamics', *Quality and Quantity*, no 33, pp 305-22.

Kilkey, M. and Bradshaw, J. (1999) 'Lone mothers, economic well-being and policies', in D. Sainsbury (ed) *Gender and welfare state regimes*, Oxford: Oxford University Press, pp 147-84.

Kohli, M. (1986) 'Gesellschaftszeit und Lebenzeit: Der Lebenslauf im Strukturwandel der Moderne', in J. Berger (ed) *Die Moderne. Kontinuitäten und Zäsuren*, Göttingen: Schwartz, pp 183-208.

Kohli, M. (1988) 'Normalbiographien und Individualität: Zur institutionellen Dynamic des gegewärtigen Lebenslaufregimes', in H.G. Brose and B. Hildebrand (eds) *Vom Ende des Individuums zur Individualität ohne Ende*, Opladen: Leske und Budrich, pp 33-54.

Krause, P. (1998) 'Low income dynamics in unified Germany', in L. Leisering and R. Walker (eds) *The dynamics of modern society: Poverty, policy and welfare*, Bristol: The Policy Press, pp 161-98.

Kvist, J. (1998) 'Complexities in assessing unemployment benefits and policies', *International Social Security Review*, vol 51, no 4, pp 33-55.

Kvist, J. and Torfing, J. (1996) *Changing welfare state models*, Working Paper 5, Copenaghen: Centre for Welfare State Research.

Lancaster, T. (1990) *The econometric analysis of transition data*, Cambridge: Cambridge University Press.

Laparra, M. and Aguilar Hendrickson, M. (1997) 'Social exclusion and minimum income programs in Spain', in MIRE *Comparer les systèmes de protection sociale en Europe*, vol 1, Oxford Conference, Paris: MIRE.

Larsen, J.E. (2000) 'Lone mothers: how do they work and care in different welfare state regimes?', in T. P. Boje and A. Leira (eds) *Gender, welfare state and the market*, London and New York, NY: Routledge, pp 206-25.

Le Galès, P. (1998) 'La nuova political economy delle città e delle regioni', *Stato e Mercato*, no 52, pp 53-91.

Leibfried, S. (1987) 'Projetktantrag Sozialhilfekarrieren – Wege aus der un durch die Sozialhilfe und ihre sozialstaatliche Rahmung', in W.R. Heinz (ed) *Statuspassagen und Risikolagen im Lebensverlauf. Institutionelle Steuerung und individuelle Handlungsstrategien*, Antrag auf Einrichtung eines Sonderforschungsbereiches an der Universität Bremen, Bremen: Universität Bremen.

Leibfried, S. (1992) 'Towards a European welfare state? On integrating poverty regimes into the European Community', in Z. Ferge and J. Eivind Kolbert (eds) *Social policy in a changing Europe*, Boulder, CO: Westview Press, pp 245-79.

Leibfried, S. (1993) 'Towards a European welfare state?', in C. Jones (ed) *New perspectives on the welfare state in Europe*, London: Routledge, pp 135-56.

Leibfried, S., Leisering, L., Buhr, P., Ludwig, M., MädiJe, E., Olk, T., Voges, W. and Zwick, M. (1995) *Zeit der Armut. Lebensläufe im Sozialstaat*, Frankfurt am Main: Suhrkamp.

Leisering, L. and Leibfried, S. (1999) *Time and poverty in western welfare states*, Cambridge: Cambridge University Press.

Leisering, L. and Walker, R. (eds) (1998a) *The dynamics of modern society: Poverty, policy and welfare*, Bristol: The Policy Press.

Leisering, L. and Walker, R. (1998b), 'Making the future: from dynamics to policy agendas', in L. Leisering and R. Walker (eds) *The dynamics of modern society: Poverty, policy and welfare*, Bristol: The Policy Press, pp 265-85.

Leisering, L. and Zwick, M. (1990) 'Heterogenisierung der Armut? Alte und neue Perspektiven zum Strukturwandel der Armutsbevölkerung der Sozialhilfeklientel in der Bundesrepublik Deutschland', *Zeitschrift für Sozialreform*, no 36, pp 715-45.

Lewis, J. (1997a) 'Gender and welfare regimes: further thoughts', *Social Politics*, vol IV, no 2, pp 160-77.

Lewis, J. (ed) (1997b) *Lone mothers in European welfare regimes*, London: Jessica Kingsley.

Lewis, J. (ed) (1998) *Gender, social care and welfare state restructuring in Europe*, London: Ashgate.

Lødemel, I. and Trickey, H. (eds) (2000) *An offer you can't refuse: Workfare in international perspective*, Bristol: The Policy Press.

Ludwig, M. (1996) *Armutskarrieren. Zwischen Abstieg und Aufstieg im Sozialstaat*, Opladen: Westdeutscher Verlag.

Madanipour, A., Cars, G. and Allen, J. (eds) (1998) *Social exclusion in European cities: Processes, experiences and responses*, London: Jessica Kingsley.

Mahé, T. (1999) *Le RMI à l'échelle locale, une comparaison Rennes/Saint Etienne*, mémoire de DEA, Paris: IEP.

Manz, G. (1992) *Armut in der 'DDR Bevölkerung. Lebensstandard und Konsumtionsniveau vor und nach der Wende*, Augsburg: Maro Verlag.

Marradi, A. (1996) 'Una lunga ricerca sui valori e alcuni suoi strumenti', in A. Marradi and G.P. Prandsstraller (eds) *L'etica dei ceti emergenti*, Milano: Franco Angeli, pp 20-43.

Marsiglio, W. (1995) *Fatherhood: Contemporary theory, research and social policy*, Thousand Oaks, CA: Sage Publications.

Martin, C. (1997) *L'après divorce. Lien familial et vulnérabilité*, Rennes: PUR.

Martinotti, G. (ed) (1982) *La città difficile*, Milano: Franco Angeli.

Martinotti, G. (1993) *Metropoli. La nuova morfologia sociale della città*, Bologna: Il Mulino.

Massey, D. and Denton, N.A. (1993) *Segregation and the making of the underclass*, Cambridge, MA: Harvard University Press.

Mayer, K.U. and Blossfeld, H.P. (1990) 'Die gesellschaftliche Konstruktion sozialer Ungleichheit im Lebenslauf', in P.A Berger and S. Hradil (eds) *Lebenslagen, Lebensläufe, Lebensstile*, Göttingen: Schwartz, pp 297-318.

Mayer, K.U. and Müller, W. (1986) 'The state and the structure of the life course', in A.B. Sørensen, F.E. Weinert and L.R Sherrod (eds) *Human development: Interdisciplinary perspectives*, Hillsdale, NJ: Erlbaum, pp 217-45.

Mayer, K.U. and Scöpflin, U. (1989) 'The state and the life course', *Annual Review of Sociology*, no 15, pp 187-209.

McFate, K., Lawson, R. and Wilson, W.J. (eds) (1995) *Poverty, inequality and the future of social policy*, New York, NY: Russel Sage Foundation.

McLanahan, S., Casper, L.M. and Soronsen, A. (1992) *Women's role and women's poverty in eight industrialized countries*, Luxembourg Income Study Working Paper Series, Working Paper 77, Luxembourg: Ceps/Instead.

Merrien, F.X. (1997) *L'État-providence*, Paris: Que-sais-je? PUF.

Micheli, G. (1996) 'Downdrift: provoking agents and sympton-formation factors in the process of impoverishment', in E. Mingione (ed) *Urban poverty and the underclass*, Oxford: Blackwell, pp 41-63.

Micheli, G. (1997) 'Spezzare il retaggio, forse assecondarlo: intrecci tra dinamiche di povertà e modelli familiari', *Polis*, vol XI, pp 277-98.

Milano, S. (1995) *Le revenu minimum garanti dans la CEE*, Paris: PUF.

Millar, J. (2000) 'Changing obligations and expectations: lone parenthood and social policy', in T. P. Boje and A. Leira (eds) *Gender, welfare state and the market*, London and New York, NY: Routledge, pp 226-41.

Mingione, E. (ed) (1996) *Urban poverty and the underclass*, Oxford: Blackwell.

Mingione, E. (1997) *Sociologia della vita economica*, Roma: NIS La Nuova Italia Scientifica.

Mingione, E. (ed) (1999) *Le sfide dell'esclusione: metodi, luoghi, soggetti*, Bologna: Il Mulino.

MIRE (Mission Recherche) (1995) *Comparer les systèmes de protection sociale en Europe*, vol 1, Oxford Conference, Paris: MIRE.

MIRE (1996) *Comparer les systèmes de protection sociale en Europe*, vol 2, Berlin Conference, Paris: MIRE.

MIRE (1997) *Comparing social welfare systems in Southern Europe*, vol 3, Florence Conference, Paris: MIRE.

MIRE (1999) *Comparer les systèmes de protection sociale en Europe du Nord et en France*, vol 4, tome 2, Rencontres de Copenhague, Paris: MIRE.

MISSOC (1996) *Social protection in the member states of the community*, Brussels: Commission of the European Communities.

Moffit, R. (1992) 'Incentive effects of the US social assistance system: a review', *Journal of Economic Literature*, no 71, pp 498-573.

Muller, P. and Surel, Y. (1998) *L'analyse des politiques publiques*, Paris: Montchrestien.

Murray, C. (1984) *Losing ground*, New York, NY: Basic Books.

Mutti, A. (1998) *Capitale sociale e sviluppo. La fiducia come risorsa*, Bologna: Il Mulino.

Naldini, M. (2001) *Social policy and the institutional definition of family models: The Italian and Spanish cases in historical and comparative perspective*, London: Frank Cass.

Negri, N. (1982) 'I nuovi torinesi: immigrazione, mobilità e struttura sociale', in G. Martinotti (ed) *La città difficile*, Milan: Franco Angeli, pp 51-179.

Negri, N. and Saraceno, C. (1996) *Le politiche contro la povertà in Italia*, Bologna: Il Mulino.

Negri, N. and Saraceno, C. (1999) *Il Welfare municipale torinese*, Torino: Dipartimento di Scienze Sociali, Università di Torino.

Negri, N. and Saraceno, C. (2000) 'Povertà, disoccupazione ed esclusione sociale', *Stato e Mercato*, no 59, Agosto, pp 175-210.

Oberti, M. (1998) *Trajectoires des allocataires du rmi: analyse comparée de trois villes – Dreux, Rennes, Saint Etienne*, Paris: Observatoire Sociologique du Changement.

O'Connor, J.S., Orloff, A.S. and Shaver, S. (1999) *States, markets, families*, Cambridge: Cambridge University Press.

OECD (Organisation for Economic Co-operation and Development) (1990) 'Lone parent families: the economic challenge', *Social Policies Studies*, no 8, Paris: OECD.

OECD (1998a) *Employment outlook*, Paris: OECD.

OECD (1998b) *The battle against social exclusion*, vol 1-2, Paris: OECD.

OECD (1999) *Benefit systems and work incentives*, Paris: OECD.

Okin, S. (1989) *Justice and the family*, New York, NY: Basic Books.

Olk, T. and Rentzsch, D. (1997) 'Armutsverläufe – erste Ergebnisse einer Kohortenanalyse Hallenser Sozialhilfeemplfänger(innen)', in I. Becker and R. Hauser (eds) *Einkommensverteilung und Armut. Deutschland auf dem Weg zur Vierfünftel-Gesellschaft?*, Frankfurt am Main: Campus Verlag, pp 161-85.

Onofri, M., Bimbi, F., Bosi, P., Ferrera, M., Geroldi, G., Paci, M., Saraceno, C. and Zamagni, S. (1997) *Relazione finale della Commissione per l'analisi delle compatibilità Macroeconomiche della Spesa Sociale-Presidenza del Consiglio dei Ministri*, no 28, February, Rome: Poligrafico dello stato.

Orloff, A. (1993) 'Gender and the social rights of citizenship', *American Sociological Review*, no 58, pp 303-28.

Paci, M. (1989) *Pubblico e privato nei moderni sistemi di Welfare*, Napoli: Liguori editore.

Paugam, S. (1993), *La société française et ses pauvres. L'éxperience de revenu minimum d'insertion*, Paris: PUF (2nd edn 1995).

Paugam, S. (ed) (1996) *L'exclusion. L'état des savoirs*, Paris: la Decouverte.

Paugam, S. (1997a) *Integration, précarité et risque d'exclusion des salariées*, Fondation Nationale des Sciences Politiques, CNRS, Observatoire sociologique du changement, December.

Paugam, S. (1997b) *La disqualification sociale* (5th edn), Paris: PUF.

Paugam, S. (1998a) *Les revenus minimum en Europe*, Paris: la Documentation française.

Paugam, S. (1998b) 'Les types de pauvreté en Europe', *Génèse*, no 31, juin, pp 142-59.

Paugam, S. (ed) (1999) *L'Europe face a la pauvreté: les expériences nationales de revenu minimum*, Paris: La Documentation Française.

Peck, J. (1998) 'Workfare, a geopolitical etymology', *Environment and Planning D: Society and Space*, no 16, pp 133-60.

Pedersen, L., Weise, H., Jacobs, S. and White, M. (2000) 'Lone mothers' poverty and employment', in D. Gallie and S. Paugam (eds) *Welfare regimes and the experience of unemployment in Europe*, Oxford: Oxford University Press, pp 175-200.

Piachaud, D. and Sutherland, H. (2000) *How effective is the British government's attempt to reduce child poverty?*, CASE Paper No 38, London: London School of Economics.

Piore, M.J. (1979) *Birds of passage: Migrant labour and industrial societies*, Cambridge, MA: Cambridge University Press.

Priller, E. (1994) 'Unemployment-induced poverty: social change and the risk of impoverishment in the new Federal States', *Employment Observatory: East Germany*, vol VIII, no 12, pp 3-6.

Putnam, D. (1993) *Making society work*, Princeton, NJ: Princeton University Press.

Reyneri, E. (1996) *Sociologia del Mercato del Lavoro*, Bologna: Il Mulino.

Rimlinger, G. (1971) *Welfare and industrialization in Europe, America and Russia*, New York, NY: John Wiley and Sons.

Robbins, D. (1993) *Social Europe: Towards a Europe of solidarity*, Supplement no 4/93, Brussels: DG V.

Room, G. (1995) 'Poverty in Europe: competing paradigms of analysis', *Policy & Politics*, vol 23, no 2, pp 103-13.

Rosanvallon, P. (1981) *La crise de l'Etat-Providence*, Paris: Editions du Seuil.

Rossi, P.H. and Freeman, H.E. (1993) *Evaluation: A systematic approach*, Newbury Park: Sage Publications (5th edn).

Rowntree, B.S. (1901) *Poverty: A study of town life*, London: Thomas Nelson & Sons [now reissued by The Policy Press, 2000].

Sahgal, G. and Yuval Davis, N. (eds) (1992) *Refusing holy orders: Women and fundamentalism in Britain*, London: Virago.

Sahner, H. (1995) 'Leben in Halle. Ergebnisse einer Bürgerumfrage', in H.-H.Krüger, M. Kühnel and T. Sven (eds) *Transformationsprobleme in Ostdeutschland. Arbeit, Bildung, Sozialpolitik*, Leske-Budrich: Opladen, pp 127-45.

Sainsbury, D. (1996) *Gender, equality and welfare states*, Cambridge: Cambridge University Press.

Saraceno, C. (1991) 'Dalla istituzionalizzazione alla de-istituzionalizzazione dei corsi di vita femminili e maschili?', *Stato e mercato*, no 3, Dicembre 1991, pp 431-50.

Saraceno, C. (1997) 'Family change, family policies and the restructuring of welfare', in OECD, *Family, market and community*, Social Policy Studies, no 21, Paris: OECD, pp 81-100.

Saraceno, C. (1998a) *Mutamenti della famiglia e politiche sociali*, Bologna: Il Mulino.

Saraceno, C. (ed) (1998b) *ESOPO: Evaluation of social policies at the local urban level: Income support for the able bodied*, Final report submitted to the Commission, Directorate General XII, TSER Programme, First Call, Contract RB-SOE2-CT-95-3001.

Saraceno, C. (2000) 'Italian families under economic stress: the impact of social policies', *Labour*, March, pp 161-83.

Sassen, S. (1991) *The global city: New York, London, Tokyo*, Princeton, NJ: Princeton University Press.

Sassen, S. (1994) *Cities in a world economy*, Thousand Oaks, CA: Pine Forge Press

Sassen, S. (1996) 'Service employment regimes and the new inequality', in E. Mingione (ed) *Urban poverty and the underclass: A reader*, Oxford: Blackwell, pp 105-38.

Schulte, K., Stoek, H. and Voges, W. (1999) *Sozialverläufe im lokalen Kontext. Strukturelle und institutionelle Rahmenbedingungen in Bremen und Halle/Saale*, Arbeitspapier no 16/99, Bremen: ZeS.

Schultheis, F. (1996a) 'La famille, une catégorie du droit social?: Une comparison franco-allemande', in MIRE *Comparer les systèmes de protection sociale en Europe*, vol 2, Berlin Conference, pp 203-34.

Schultheis, F. (1996b) 'L'État et la société civile face à la pauvreté en Allemagne', in S. Paugam (ed) *L'exclusion: l'état des savoirs*, Paris: La Découverte, pp 428-37.

Schultheis, F. and Bubeck, B. (1995) 'Problemi teorici e metodologici nella comparazione interculturale del fenomeno delle povertà estreme', in P. Guidicini, G. Pieretti and M. Bergamaschi, *Povertà urbana estreme in Europa*, Milano: Franco Angeli, pp 123-60.

Seltzer, J.A. (1994) 'Consequences of marital dissolution for children', *Annual Review of Sociology*, vol XX, pp 235-66.

Sen, K.A. (1981) *Poverty and famine*, Oxford: Clarendon Press.

Sen, K.A. (1985a) *Commodities and capabilities*, Amsterdam: North Holland.

Sen, K.A. (1985b) 'Well-being, agency and freedom: the Dewey Lectures 1984', *Journal of Philosophy*, vol 82, no 4, pp 169-221.

Sen, K.A. (1992) *Inequality re-examined*, Oxford: Clarendon Press.

Sen, K.A. (1995) 'The political economy of targeting', in D. van der Walle and K. Nead (eds) *Public spending and the poor: Theory and evidence*, Baltimore, MD: World Bank and John Hopkins University Press, pp 11-24.

Sgritta, G. (1993) 'Povertà e diseguaglianza economica in Italia: forme, luoghi ed età', *Tutela*, no 2/3, pp 30-45.

Shaw, A., Walker, R., Ashworth, K., Jenkins, S. and Middleton, S. (1996) *Moving off income support: Barriers and bridges*, Department of Social Security Research Report No 53, London: The Stationery Office.

Silva, M. et al (1989) *Pobreza urbana em Portugal*, Lisboa: Caritas.

Simmel, G. (1908a) 'Der Arme', in G. Simmnel, *Soziologie, Über die Formen der Vergesellschaftung*, Berlin: Dunker & Humblod, pp 345-74.

Simmel, G. (1908b) *Soziologie*, Berlin: Dunker & Humblot.

Standing, G. (1990) 'The road to workfare – alternative to welfare or threat to occupation', *International Labour Review*, vol 129, no 6, pp 677-91.

Sunesson, S., Blomberg, S., Edelbak, P.G., Harrysson, L., Magnusson, J., Meewisse, A., Petersson, J. and Salonen, T. (1998) 'The flight from universalism', *European Journal of Social Work*, vol 1, no 1, pp 19-30.

Taylor Gooby, P. (1991) 'Welfare state regimes and welfare citizenship', *Journal of European Social Policy*, vol 1, no 2, pp 93-105.

Therbon, G. (1986) *Why some people are more unemployed than others*, London: Verso.

Théret, B. (1996) 'De la comparabilité des systèmes nationaux de protection sociale dans les sociétés salariales: essai d'analyse structurale', in MIRE, *Comparer les systèmes de protection sociale en Europe*, vol 2, Berlin Conference, Paris: MIRE, pp 439-603.

Titmuss, R. (1974) *Social policy: An introduction*, London: Allen and Unwin.

Townsend, P. (1979) *Poverty in the United Kingdom*, Harmondsworth: Penguin.

Uusitalo, H. (1984) 'Comparative research on the determinants of the welfare state: the state of the art', *European Journal of Political Research*, no 12, pp 20-56.

Vogel, J. (1997) *Living conditions and inequality in the European Union*, Eurostat Working Papers, *Populations and Social Conditions,* E/1997-3.

Voges, W. and Kazepov, Y. (eds) (1998) *Armut in Europa*, Wiesbaden: Chmielorz Verlag.

Walker, R. (1998) 'Rethinking poverty in a dynamic perspective', in H.J. Andreß (ed) (1998) *Empirical poverty research in comparative perspective*, Aldershot: Ashgate, pp 29-49.

Walker, R. and Ashworth, K. (1994) *Poverty dynamics: Issues and examples*, Aldershot: Avebury.

Walker, R. and Ashworth, K. (1998) 'Welfare benefits and recession in Great Britain', in L. Leisering and R. Walker (eds) *The dynamics of modern society: Poverty, policy and welfare*, Bristol: The Policy Press, pp 200-42.

Walker, R. and Shaw, A. (1998) 'Escaping from social assistance in Great Britain', in L. Leisering and R. Walker (eds) *The dynamics of modern society: Poverty, policy and welfare*, Bristol: The Policy Press, pp 199-242.

Weil, P. (1991) *La France et ses étrangers*, Paris: Calman-Levy.

Weitzman, L.J. (1985) *The divorce revolution: The unexpected social and economic consequences for women and children in America*, New York, NY: The Free Press.

Wilson, W.J. (1987) *The truly disadvantaged: The inner city, the underclass and public policy*, Chicago, IL: University of Chicago Press.

Wilson, W.J. (1993) *The ghetto underclass*, London: Sage Publications.

Wilson, W.J. (1996) *When work disappears: The world of the new urban poor*, New York, NY: Alfred A. Knopf.

Yuval Davis, N. (1996) 'Women, citizenship and difference', Background paper for the Conference on 'Women and citizenship', London: University of Greenwich, 16-18 July.

Zoyem, J.P. (1998) 'Le contrats d'insertion du RMI. Des effets contrastés sur la sortie du RMI', *Insee Premiere*, no 679, Octobre.

Appendix

Institutional frameworks of income support policies in 13 European cities

Italy

Characteristics/ cities	Milan	Turin	Cosenza
Name of the measure	Minimo Vitale (MV) and Minimo Alimentare (MA).		Assistenza Economica.
Legal basis	Regional law LR 1/86 and local deliberations.	Regional law LR 20/82 and LR 62/95 and local deliberations.	Regional law LR 5/87 and local deliberations.
Clear right or discretionary measure?	It is implemented with varying levels of discretion in Milan (medium) and Cosenza (high). In Turin the discretionary power is low, even though, from a legal point of view, the measure is not a right.		
Enforcement of entitlements and negotiation with social workers?	No enforcement, important role of individual negotiations.	No enforcement, relatively important role of individual negotiations.	No enforcement, important role of individual negotiations.
Agencies responsible for administering the measure at the local level	Municipality, which organises social services around specific categories: families with minors (SSMI); adults (UAD); older people (CADA and INPS).	Municipality (the social services are run by area social units, which are responsible for providing services in the various city districts).	Municipality and the Province, in relation to the target population. The social services are organised on a categorical base.
Financing	Regional (in Turin national) and municipal budget autonomously administered by the city.		
Target population	The measures are categorical, addressed to the household and means-tested on the basis of household income.		
Age limits	Adults without minors (aged 18-60) are taken care of by the Ufficio Adulti in Difficoltà (UAD). All minors or households with minors are taken care of by SSMI (jointly managed with the Province). Older claimants are taken care of by CADA and INPS.	According to the measure: MV (older, physically and mentally disabled people); MA (able-bodied adults); MIP (families with minors or households at risk of marginality).	Municipality: aimed at the family, minors (under the age of 18) cannot apply directly. Province: children of lone mothers and separated couples. The measure is limited to the first child aged up to two years in the case of lone mothers; to all minors in the case of separated couples.
Income thresholds below which entitlement is granted. Does the income threshold vary in particular cases?	Corresponds to the theoretical monthly amount paid in case of '0' income. The threshold varies according to the target population. In Turin it varies in relation to an upper limit (1997 = Ecu520), which applies to households consisting of three members or more and represents the threshold below which the entitlement is granted.		Municipality: Lira 9,500,000 (Ecu4,958) per year for a one-person household. Province: No income thresholds.

continued

Italy (contd)

Characteristics/ cities	Milan	Turin	Cosenza
Who checks the income threshold?	Social workers (and also public officials in Turin).		
Monthly amount of basic measure for an individual	MV: Lira 685,000 (Ecu358)* depends on the target population. MA: Lira 520,000 (Ecu271).	MV: Lira 685,000 (Ecu358)* depends on the target population. MA: Lira 363,000 (Ecu189).	*Municipality:* Lira 300,000 a year for a household up to two persons. *Province:* Lira 549,000 (Ecu287) for a lone mother.
Basic amount increased to take account of other costs (housing, heating costs, special needs, lone parenthood)	Housing costs are considered in the determination of the MV threshold. The consideration of other costs is at the discretion of the social worker.	Housing and heating costs are considered only in the determination of the MV thresholds. The possibility of supplementing the MA is provided only for electricity and gas expenses at the discretion of the social worker.	*Municipality:* Housing costs and special needs are considered, however, only in determining the access and not to increase the amount to be paid. *Province:* no additional provision.
Waiting time between request and first payment	40-60 days.	30 days.	nr
Duration of entitlement	Depends on the target population. For adults usually 3 to 6 months a year. Families with minors about 6 months within one year.	Depends on the target population and the related measure. MIP for one year. After this period they can receive MA as long as their need persists.	*Municipality:* no limit repeating the application every year. *Province:* 12/18 months, depending on the specific situation.
Criteria for keeping entitlement (besides income criteria)?	Yes (qualified need and willingness to work).	Formally no criteria, (de facto willingness to work, to follow training courses, and so on).	No.
Is there a monitoring system of income support?	Yes, on paper, but not very efficient.	Yes, centralised, automated, but not published.	No monitoring system.

nr = not relevant. *Corresponds to the Minimum Contributory State Pension (INPS).
1 Ecu = 1,916 Lira

France

Characteristics/ cities	Saint Etienne	Rennes
Name of the measure	RMI (Revenue Minimum d'Insertion).	
Legal basis	National law No. 88-1088, enforced in 01/12/1988. The law was modified through Law No. 92-722 on 29/07/1992.	
Clear right or discretionary measure?	Clear right.	
Enforcement of entitlements and negotiation with social workers?	Any individual who is in a condition of need has the right to a decent means of survival from the State. Individuals who believe their rights are not acknowledged may make an appeal to the Commission Départementale d'Aide Sociale (CDAS), which is a specialised administrative jurisdiction, and then, if necessary to the Conseil d'Etat, which is the court of appeal in administrative matters. Negotiations play a role only for the integration activities.	
Agencies responsible for administering the measure at the local level	Three different agencies play a role and help the applicants in administrative matters and are one of the key elements in the social integration policy: CCAS (Centres Communaux ou Intercommunaux d'Action Sociale), SSD (Service Social Départementale), local associations agreed by the State-agent (Préfet). A person in need can go to any one of them. The CAF (Caisse d'Allocations Familiales) is responsible for the payments of the allowance. The CLI (Commissione Local d'Insertion) supervises the integration activities.	
Financing	The minimum income is paid by the CAF, which is a national administration with local branches and is financed by the State, so the municipality has nothing to do with the income part. The département and the municipality can give exceptional aid. The integration programmes are financed by the State and by the département, which can delegate the administration of the budget to the municipalities. This is the case in Rennes, but not in Saint Etienne, where until recently each level of government acted on its own.	
Target population	It is a universal measure (with some exceptions) aimed at all persons not covered by other different category-based measures.	
Age limits	Any person over 25 years of age or below if they have children.	
Income thresholds below which entitlement is granted. Does income threshold vary in particular cases?	The income threshold is applied to everyone; no special categories exist. The benefit varies only according to the size of the household.	
Who checks the income threshold?	Checked by the paying authority (CAF) through the initial RMI application, then through a notification of financial resources to the CAF every three months by the recipient.	
Monthly amount of basic measure for an individual	FF 2,405 (Ecu370).	

continued

France (contd)

Characteristics/ cities	Saint Etienne	Rennes
Basic amount increased to take account other costs (housing and heating costs, special needs, lone parenthood)	Threshold corresponds to the monthly amount paid in case of '0' income. The basic amount is diminished by a fixed quota (12% for singles and 16% for couples), if the beneficiary is sheltered or has their own lodging.	
Waiting time between request and first payment	About 41 days on average.	
Duration of entitlement	As long as the condition of need persists and the income of the individual/ household is below the threshold.	
Criteria for keeping entitlement (besides income criteria)	RMI beneficiaries are supposed to sign an insertion contract (*Contrat d'Insertion*) in which they commit themselves to trying to improve their situation at the social or professional level. If they do not sign this contract or if they do not respect its contents, the payment of the benefit may be suspended or they may lose their entitlement.	
Is there a monitoring system of income support?	CAF (*Caisse d'Allocation Familiales*) publishes data about payments; SESI (*Service of Statistics, Studies and Information System*) publishes data about the insertion contracts.	

Note: Ecu 1 = FF 6.5.

Germany

Characteristics/ cities	Bremen	Halle
Name of the measure	Sozialhilfe, including HLU (Hilfe zum Lebensunterhalt, which is the basic measure), HbL (Hilfe in besonderen Lagen), which includes accompanying measures.	
Legal basis	Legal basis refers to the Bundessozialhilfegesetz (BSHG), a federal law approved in 1961 and implemented in 1962. The system was extended with some minor limitations to the former East Germany Länder in 1991.	
Clear right or discretionary measure?	Clear right with smaller local variations; some additional measures (ad hoc benefits, adequate rent, obligation to work) are more discretionary.	
Enforcement of entitlements and negotiation with social workers?	Everybody has a legal right to claim for it before a court; negotiations can play a role as far as the accompanying measures are concerned (see above).	
Agencies responsible for administering the measure at the local level	The municipality in which the individual is currently living.	
Financing	Social assistance is funded by the municipality (ad hoc budget).	
Target population	The measure is universalistic and addressed to the individual. However, the household's income is considered in determining the threshold of the condition of need, in particular in the case of cohabiting relatives/adults[1].	
Age limits	No age limits. Children can claim HLU, however, normally this has to be done by their parents. Children above 15 years can claim HLU on their own.	
Income thresholds below which entitlement is granted.	Threshold corresponds to the monthly amount paid in case of '0' income (benefit and housing costs).	
Does income threshold vary in particular cases?	Yes: varies according to the structure of the household (size and age) and housing costs.	
Who checks the income threshold?	The administrative officers.	
Monthly amount of basic measure for an individual	Bremen: DM 539 (Ecu274)[2] Halle: DM 519 (Ecu263) (standard rates, valid since July 1997). To this amount the cost of housing has to be added.	

continued

Germany (contd)

Characteristics/ cities	Bremen	Halle
Basic amount increased to take account of:		
- housing costs	Yes (100% up to a given maximum threshold);	
- heating costs	Yes (100% up to a given maximum threshold);	
- special needs (invalidity, etc)	Yes (in case of invalidity, old age, pregnancy, disability, illness);	
- lone parenthood	Yes (additional single benefits on demand).	
Waiting time between request and first payment	If necessary available immediately.	
Duration of entitlement	As long as the condition of need persists and the income of the individual/ household is below the threshold.	
Criteria for keeping entitlement (besides income criteria)	Obligation to work for able-bodied (registration at the State Unemployment Office and acceptance of work or training that is offered). Exceptions are made for example, for single parents with a child under the age of one year and for persons who are sick, disabled, near to the retirement age or have severe social or mental problems.	
Is there a monitoring system of income support?	Monitoring system of social assistance at the national as well as the local level, automated. Statistics are published regularly by the Federal Statistical Office.	

[1] Non-cohabiting kin are not considered *obliged kin* (legally expected to provide support) in Bremen, but are so in Halle and in most cities in Germany. However, in Halle the thresholds above which *obliged kin* are expected to provide support are quite high.

[2] Ecu1 = DM 1.97.

Portugal[a]

Characteristics/cities	Lisbon	Porto
Name of the measure	Subsídio Mensal; Normas de Atribuição de Subsídios Mensais e Eventuais (1996).	Prestações Pecuniárias de Acção Social (Pecuniary Allowances of Social Action).
Legal basis	Law 3228/91, 26 August 1991, approves internal regulation of Santa Casa da Misericórdia de Lisboa (SCML) under the tutelage of the State.	n.a.
Clear right or discretionary measure?	Discretionary measure: entitlement depends on subjective evaluation of need and on the financial resources of the services.	
Enforcement of entitlements and negotiation with social workers?	No enforcement and weak role of negotiations.	
Agencies responsible for administering the measure at the local level	Catholic private non-profit institution that replaces the Social Assistance Centre in this city (SCML).	Regional Department of Social Assistance Centre.
Financing	Financial sources of SCML.	National Budget.
Target population	The measure is 'universalistic' and aimed at the family.	
Age limits	No age limit.	
Income thresholds below which the entitlement is granted. Does the threshold vary in particular cases?	No income threshold – subjective evaluation of need by the social worker. In Lisbon, SCML defined a household income threshold (= 80% of the National Minimum Wage = Ecu220); however, this is totally disregarded due to the institution's financial constraints.	
Who checks the income threshold?	The social worker.	
Monthly amount of basic measure for an individual	Benefits granted are far below the threshold identified above and, moreover, insufficient to complement household income towards this level. There is no precise definition of the monthly amount. On average, it ranges from 25 to 100 Euros for the household. There is no clear relation between the amount and the number of persons. A single person may receive Ecu100.	
Basic amount increased to take account of other costs (housing, heating costs, special needs, lone parenthood)	Rent is taken into consideration in the definition of the threshold. Other expenses might be considered at the discretion of the social worker.	
Waiting time between request and first payment	60-90 days.	
Duration of entitlement	No maximum duration.	
Criteria for keeping entitlement (besides income criteria)?	At the discretion of the social worker, but restricted by financial budget.	
Is there a monitoring system of income support?	No.	

Notes: The description of these measures is valid until June 1997. Since July 1997, the new scheme of Guaranteed Minimum Income (see: Portugal [b]) entered its phase of experimentation and it is possible to be under the two measures. It is expected that the two old schemes will adjust to the new one.

Portugal[b]

Characteristics/cities	Lisbon	Porto
Name of the measure	*Rendimento Mínimo Garantido.*	
Legal basis	Legal basis, refers to the National Law no. 19-A/96.	
Clear right or discretionary measure?	Clear right.	
Enforcement of entitlements and negotiation with social workers?	Everybody has a legal right to claim for it. Relatively weak negotiations with the social worker.	
Agencies responsible for administering the measure at the local level	At the national level: National Commission of Minimum Income. At the regional level: Regional Social Security Centre. At the local level: Accompaniment Local Commission.	
Financing	National Budget, following the principles of the financing of the non-contributory social security scheme.	
Target population	The measure is universalistic and targeted to the individuals and their households.	
Age limits	Individuals with or above 18 years of age are entitled to the benefit; individuals below 18 have access only if they have economically dependent minors.	
Income thresholds below which the entitlement is granted. Does the threshold vary in particular cases?	Threshold should correspond to the monthly amount paid in case of '0' income. Income threshold is indexed to the amount legally fixed for social pensions of the non-contributory scheme of social security. The threshold varies according to the composition of the household.	
Who checks the income threshold?	Income threshold is checked by the Regional Social Security Centre through the beneficiary number that allows the assessment of the household's income.	
Monthly amount of basic measure for an individual	PTE 21,000/month = Ecu105/month (1997).	
Basic amount increased to take account of other costs (housing, heating costs, special needs, lone parenthood)	The basic amount is increased to take account of housing costs.	
Waiting time between request and first payment	About 30 days.	
Duration of entitlement	12 months renewable if conditions of need persist.	
Criteria for keeping entitlement (besides income criteria)?	The individual has to accept the insertion measures proposed.	
Is there a monitoring system of income support?	No.	

Note: Ecu1 = PTE 200.

Spain

Characteristics/ cities	Barcelona	Vitoria
Name of the measure	PIRMI = *Programa Interdepartamental de Rentas Mínimas de Insercion.* Includes: RMI (*Renta Minima d'Inserciò*), as well as emergency and accompanying measures.	The *Plan Integral de Lucha contra la Pobreza* includes: IMI = *Ingreso Minimo de Inserción.* There are also *Ayudas de Emergencia Social* (AES) and other accompanying measures.
Legal basis	PIRMI was set up by the decree 228/95 (11 August 1995). The new law that regulates the PIRMI is the Catalonian Law 10/1997 (3 July 1997), which abolished all previous regulations.	The IMI was set up by Law 2/90 in the autonomous Basque country (following the guidelines of two previous decrees of 1989).
Clear right or discretionary measure?	It is a clear right, however, only at a regional level, which is its level of implementation.	
Opportunity for individuals to enforce entitlement legally or negotiations between individuals and social workers?	If the application for social assistance is rejected, the applicant has the right to appeal to a court, however, it seldom happens. There is no legal possibility of negotiation, but in practice the administration of the means-test can be regarded as a negotiation, as the recipients' cultural competence and ability to present needs and motives may influence the decision. This is particularly true for emergency measures. In Barcelona, the social worker has the discretionary power to limit the amount of the benefit.	
Agencies responsible for administering the measure at the local level	Social services of primary care in the municipality, the local council and social initiative organisations. All these agencies fill in the forms and submit them to the Interdepartamental Commission of the Generalitat de Catalunya and its committees.	The City Council is responsible for receiving the applications and arranging procedures of implementation. Applications are submitted to the County Council.
Financing	PIRMI is funded by the Interdepartmental Commission and the Departments of Labour (RMI) and Social Welfare of the Catalan Government. The Local Council is only responsible for urgent expenses (for example, care).	The Basque government finances the benefits, through a demand-oriented budget.
Target population	The measure is universalistic and addressed to all households without sufficient resources to satisfy basic needs (with an income below the given threshold). In Barcelona this happens through an *individually* designed *Re-insertion Plan.*	
Age limits	Anyone between 25 and 65 years old can apply for PIRMI or IMI. Those under the age of 25 are under the care of their family. People below 25 years of age can apply if they have minors or people with disabilities in their charge.	

continued

Spain (contd)

Characteristics/ cities	Barcelona	Vitoria
Income thresholds below which entitlement is granted.	Threshold corresponds to the monthly amount paid in case of '0' income.	
Does income threshold vary in particular cases?	Yes: according to the structure of the household (size and age). In Barcelona the amount of the RMI is determined by the Minimum Interprofessional Salary, in Vitoria by the Basque government on an annual basis.	
Who checks the income threshold?	The social workers of the municipality and the officials of the PIRMI's department.	The social workers of the municipality. The County officials usually accept their assessment.
Monthly amount of basic measure for an individual	RMI can vary between Ptas 10,250 (Ecu38) and Ptas 77,900 (Ecu464)[1].	IMI is about Ptas 39,102 (Ecu233).
Basic amount increased to take account of other costs (housing, heating, special needs, lone parenthood)	No additional amount, but, at the beginning of the measure, the social worker could give the household money to pay debts (rent, electricity, water, and so on) incurred up to that moment.	Yes, for housing, illness and other expenses, (100% up to a given maximum threshold which cannot exceed 170% of IMI).
Waiting time between the request and first payment?	30-60 days. In Barcelona urgent payments can be made immediately by the municipality.	
Duration of entitlement	As long as the condition of need persists and the income of the individual/ household is below the threshold. In Barcelona the Interdepartemental Commission revises the payments yearly. In Vitoria the City Council does the same.	
Criteria for keeping entitlement (besides income criteria)?	Obligation to sign and to follow the PIR (*Pla Individual de Reinserció*); obligation to work, residency.	Obligation to work, residency.
Is there a monitoring system of income support?	No. Statistics are not published regularly and information on claimants are in their individual files.	

[1] Ecu1 = Ptas 168.

Sweden

Characteristics/Cities	Gothenburg	Helsingborg
Name of the measure	*Socialbidrag.*	
Legal basis	The legal basis refers to the *Socialtjänstlagen*, a law approved in 1980.	
Clear right or discretionary measure?	Clear right, even if the implementation of the law is affected by municipal regulations and guidelines depending upon the discretion of the social worker and the practices established in the local work group.	
Opportunity for the individuals to enforce entitlement legally or negotiations between individuals and social workers?	If the application for social assistance is rejected, the applicant has the right to appeal to a court. A judgement of the Supreme Administrative Court establishes a precedence, and thus limits municipal discretion. There is no legal possibility of negotiation, but in practice the administration of the means-test can be regarded as a negotiation where recipients' cultural competence and ability to present needs and motives may influence the decision.	
Agencies responsible for administering the measure at the local level	The municipality in which the individual is currently living.	
Financing	Social assistance is funded by the municipality (ad hoc budget).	
Target population	The measure is universalistic and addressed to all individuals without sufficient resources to satisfy basic needs (with an income below the given threshold).	
Age limits	No age limits. All persons above the age of 18 can apply autonomously. Exceptions can be made for persons below 18 years of age if the parental home is regarded as inadequate.	
Income thresholds below which the entitlement is granted.	The threshold[1] corresponds to the monthly amount paid in case of '0' income (benefit and housing costs up to a reasonable maximum amount).	
Does the threshold vary in particular cases?	Yes: according to the structure of the household (size and age) and housing costs.	
Who checks the income threshold?	A municipal board is legally responsible, but in practice the work is performed by social workers.	
Monthly amount of basic measure for an individual	For basic costs of living SKR 2,978 (Ecu337[2]) in Gothenburg and SKR 3,395 (Ecu384) in Helsingborg. Additionally the actual cost of rent is compensated.	
Basic amount increased to take account of:		
- housing costs	Yes (100% up to a given maximum threshold);	
- heating costs	Yes (100% up to a given maximum threshold);	
- special needs (disability, etc)	Yes (but disability is covered by a scheme other than social assistance);	
- lone parenthood	No (only through equivalence scales in the determination of the income threshold).	

continued

Sweden (contd)

Characteristics/Cities	Gothenburg	Helsingborg
Waiting time between request and first payment?	Usually between two and four weeks. Longer waiting times exist, but are regarded as inappropriate. There is a possibility of emergency assistance in large municipalities administered by a special unit.	
Duration of entitlement	As long as the condition of need persists and the income of the individual or the household is below the threshold.	
Criteria for keeping entitlement (besides income criteria)?	Obligation to work for able-bodied (registration at the State Unemployment Office and acceptance of work or training that is offered). Exceptions are made for single parents with a child under the age of one year and for persons who are sick, disabled, near to the retirement age or have severe social or mental problems.	
Is there a monitoring system of income support?	There are several levels of monitoring. The municipality has to deliver micro-data on social assistance to Statistics Sweden; Gothenburg and Helsingborg produce municipal statistics regularly.	

[1] According to a judgement by the Supreme Administrative Court, municipalities have to follow the thresholds set by the National Board of Health and Welfare. However, many municipalities have lower thresholds. The municipality cannot be sanctioned for this but the individual recipient can appeal to an Administrative Court and get the correct amount retroactively. During the 1990s, Gothenburg had lower thresholds. From 1 January 1998 amounts have been unified for the whole of Sweden.

[2] Ecu1 = SKR 8.82. In Helsingborg some extra money for transportation and other expenses is also included.

Index

Page references for figures and tables are in *italics*; those for notes are followed by n